HOMECOMING

HOMECOMING

BY **Jiro Osaragi**

TRANSLATED FROM THE JAPANESE

by BREWSTER HORWITZ

WITH AN INTRODUCTION BY

HAROLD STRAUSS

GREENWOOD PRESS, PUBLISHERS
WESTPORT, CONNECTICUT

0813 h

Library of Congress Cataloging in Publication Data

Osaragi, Jirō, pseud.
 Homecoming.

 Translation of Kikyō.
 Reprint of the 1955 ed. published by Knopf, New York.
 I. Title.
 ₍PZ3.O8O7Ho6₎ ₍PL835.S3₎   895.6'3'4   76-54833
 ISBN 0-8371-9369-9

Originally published in Japan as KIKYO

Originally published in 1968 by Alfred A. Knopf, Inc., New York

Reprinted with the permission of Alfred A. Knopf, Inc.

Reprinted in 1977 by Greenwood Press, Inc.

Library of Congress Catalog Card Number 76-54833

ISBN 0-8371-9369-9

Printed in the United States of America

INTRODUCTION

Hitherto we have been barred from the rich world of Japan's best modern literature. No contemporary novel has been translated into English since the war. Before the war a few, very few, translations appeared here by the merest chance—for instance, in the case of Yusuke Tsurumi's sentimental novel *The Mother*, the chance that the author knew English and made his own translation in 1932. When Charles A. Beard was invited to write an introduction to *The Mother*, he tried to beg off on the ground that it should be written by a man of letters, but he was won over by the argument that few such men had ever visited Japan or studied any phase of its civilization. Mr. Tsurumi, in his preface, said that "Very few people in the West know that Japan is now passing through her golden age of literature and art." Those Americans who were interested in the island empire regarded it as a rather large curio shop taken over by soldiers.

Who else at that time would have been foolhardy enough to undertake the singularly difficult task of translating Japanese novels—a task infinitely more difficult than translating the literature of the Europeans, with whom we share a common culture? The few pioneers such as Arthur Waley were scholars who devoted themselves to the Japanese classics.

Japan's traditional painting and even her theater were more accessible, and, as all her arts nourish one another, long ago hinted at the surprises and delights to be found in her novels. Would they not too capture the delicate, tranquil, often melancholy vein of the charcoal-ink paintings? Would they not fix the severe and accurate detail for a moment against the drift of time and space, like an old pine tree sharply painted against a vanishing landscape of winter hills, suggesting the Oriental sense of the brevity of life and the impermanence of earthly things?

The taste for Japanese paintings is a cultivated taste, and no doubt a taste for Japanese novels also must be cultivated. The differences from ours are not obtrusive, and one can easily overlook them; but the reader who watches out for certain traits will have the greater pleasure. The first five chapters of *Homecoming* are set in wartime Singapore, and are quite cosmopolitan in tone. Many of the more typical characteristics of the Japanese novel do not begin to appear until later chapters. In fact, the gradual change in tone and technique from modern and cosmopolitan to traditional is not without significance.

In Japan art is a consolation, preoccupied with the joy of the senses; but this joy is known to be fleeting, and therefore the Japanese have retained the implications of an old Buddhist word for it, "the floating world," implications of both pleasure and regret. Howard Hibbett notes that the Chinese have used the word in the same way, as in the line by the T'ang poet Li Shang-yin: "In this floating world there are many meetings and partings." One of Japan's greatest novelists, Saikaku, who was seldom dispirited, gave the word the same sense in the first of his erotic stories: "In this floating world where today we are still alive, how difficult to know whether we will tomorrow walk a lonely rocky beach, to end as sea-wrack on it!"

In *Homecoming* there are many glimpses of this floating world, and many meetings and partings. An example, considered outstanding by the Japanese, is the first half of Chapter Thirteen, in which Kyogo Moriya, the central character, having journeyed through devastated Japan to the unbombed ancient beauties of Kyoto, does little but sit quietly on the balcony of his inn. Kyogo has lived abroad for a very long time, so that he sees Japan almost with the eyes of a foreigner. Therefore Osaragi can observe with a detachment that makes *Homecoming* so perfect a bridge between Japan and America that "it was because they were so poor that the Japanese had discovered a world of beauty unknown to Western æsthetics, and called it by names suggesting melancholy and unfulfillment. . . . Kyogo had become too much of a foreigner to appreciate the old teahouses. The pure moss gardens of the Western Fragrant Shrine and the rock gardens of the Temple of Dragon's Peace interested him because of their different beauty; but here too he saw the taste of a people who had learned to bear the meagerness of their lives by cultivating a fondness for simple things."

Thus in a few lines Osaragi leads one into the floating world in terms comprehensible to the foreigner, and then writes an exquisite "floating scene." At such moments the action of a novel (or of a film or a play) will be suspended while Japanese sensibility turns instinctively to the symbols of nature. This is often mistaken for sentimentality by those who ignore the meaning of the symbols, and one of the translator's most challenging tasks is to provide graceful and unobtrusive hints. Brewster Horwitz, while working on certain of these scenes consisting of description and reflection, wrote me that they are the sort that Japanese motion-picture cameramen transpose into long landscape shots without action, and that most American editors would be tempted to cut them out; but that to do so would be to strike at the spirit of the novel. They stand.

These passages are subjective. But the content of the Japanese imagination is much more sensory than ours, so that where our subjective writing may be cloying or oppressive or self-pitying, Japanese subjective writing uses concrete symbols to evoke mood and atmosphere, and is intensely vivid and perceptive, much like French Impressionist painting.

The Japanese dislike strong resolutions. Sensitive to the drift and impermanence of things, they think such endings are artificial. Instead of using a distinctly tragic or a distinctly happy ending, they prefer to suggest that life goes on, according to one's character and one's fate. If one were to question a Japanese novelist about one of his endings, he would answer: "Why should I tell you? If you do not already know, I must have failed to draw my characters strongly." So sharp characterization becomes one of the supreme tests of a Japanese novel, and here of course we are on common ground. One of the attractions of *Homecoming* is its gallery of magnificent contemporary portraits. There is Kyogo, whose exile and Europeanization have made him yearn for old-fashioned ways. There is Professor Oki, a triumphant portrait of an opportunistic and hypocritical bureaucrat shaped by war and its aftermath. There are Saeko, the adventuress, and her husband, the ineffectual younger son of an aristocratic family, and Otane, his passive mistress, the prototype of the geisha. In Admiral Ushigi we find a remarkable probing of the attitude of former officers toward new times in Japan. And one must not overlook the students, even though they are minor characters—Toshi, the slick undergraduate who has cut himself off from all traditional ethical restraints and justifies his "democratic" egotism with glib argument; and Yukichi, also an undergraduate, but the repository of Japan's hope.

I have said that there are many meetings and partings in *Homecoming*. Often these take the form of confrontation scenes of a peculiarly Japanese nature. Contrary to Western belief, the Japanese are not fatalists, except insofar as character is fate; they are firm believers in moral character and strength of spirit. Therefore they are extremely fond of confrontation scenes which become a test of will. Two such scenes in *Homecoming* are excellent examples: the scene between Kyogo and Professor Oki; and the final climactic scene between Kyogo and Saeko, who has been corrupted by greed.

Finally a word must be said about the use of coincidence. In Japanese novels it is not a lame device for propping a shaky plot. Its origin lies in the tradition of the Kabuki plays, which from time to time assemble the chief personages onstage not at all to further the plot, but to deepen the characterizations by panoramic contrasts with ironic overtones. In *Homecoming* there is not the slightest *narrative* necessity for assembling several characters in the same car of a suburban train; but it is a rewarding scene nonetheless, with considerable irony.

Osaragi wrote *Homecoming* without the slightest notion that it would be published outside Japan. Obviously he wrote it without any of the self-consciousness, without any of the benevolent pretense, that so often overcome Japanese when they address foreigners. It reveals postwar Japanese feelings and characteristics with great honesty. James Michener was kind enough to read the translation and, as the author of a notable novel about Japan, *Sayonara*, was generous enough to write: "*Homecoming* conveys exactly many curious states of mind of the Japanese that no occidental writer could hope to catch. . . . The ending is difficult and yet in a strange way very Japanese. . . . It is good that we shall have a novel about Japan written from a purely internal point of view."

Osaragi himself had a moment of doubt about being read in English. "As I wrote this novel in the disordered time after the war, I am uneasy as to how it will be received by European and American readers. I think it lays bare the inner feelings of the Japanese, but it may be too outspoken about such things, and foreign readers may think it ludicrous. Our social order is different, and the way of thinking of our people is remote to foreigners. But I shall be overjoyed if from time to time, even if only to a small extent, Americans will understand the constrained existence of the Japanese in their narrow world, and how the Japanese think and feel."

I first met Osaragi in 1946, when he welcomed me in a Western-style living-room piled high with books, prints, and paintings rescued from who knows what ruins. In a little island of space at the center we looked at some colored reproductions of old Noh play masks so perfect that all their stylized, fragile beauty was preserved. After this excursion into an ancient art esoteric even to most Japanese, the conversation shifted to contemporary French literature, in which I found this gentle, sensitive, cosmopolitan man equally at home.

When I returned to Kamakura, where he lives, in 1952, it was raining heavily and the main street, which was being rebuilt, was a sea of mud. The first landmark I remembered was the public bath that marks the turn up Osaragi's lane. Two hundred yards up the lane I came to a high yellow wall with a large thatch-roofed gate, into which was set a small wicket gate about four feet high, with a nine-inch threshold. It was not easy to step through, and perhaps, like the miniature entrances to teahouses, these ancient wickets were designed to compel warriors to unbuckle their long swords before entering. The garden was narrow, luxurious, and full of slender, shivering young bamboo trees; but it was raining too hard to see much of it. A servant directed me from the main entrance around the outside walls to the semidetached teahouse. I was served tea and left alone a little while to compose myself after my journey. Custom required me not to rise when Osaragi finally came, in full kimono, a dress that dignifies any man.

Osaragi, now fifty-six, had been in the vanguard of change in his youth. His outlook is broader than that of most older writers, for he majored in political science and French law and literature at Tokyo Imperial University. But, he said, that was a long time ago, and unlike the contemporary imitators, he did not try to write "French novels." He used nothing from France he could not digest. "It is dangerous to ape style," he said. "Nor can a way of thinking be imported intact. But it can be useful to study foreign literature if you absorb its ideas. Even then, over the long run, one should accept only those ideas that really fit into Japanese culture. In Japan there is no abstract philosophy or religious dogma. We are unable to acquire thought as such." And he went on to speak of a life guided by feelings as characteristically Japanese. "But all the young people today are in too much of a hurry either to write well or to read well."

For three years, at the insistence of his father, who was a shipping-company official troubled by government red tape and wanted someone on his side in the bureaucratic nest, Osaragi worked in the Treaty Bureau of the Foreign Office. Officials were not allowed to publish anything under their own names; so when, in 1924, he could no longer repress the urge to write, he had to find a pen name. As he lives near the Great Buddha of Kamakura, he chose Osaragi, which is a variant reading of the characters for Great Buddha; and as a first name, Jiro, meaning "second son" or "next to."

His fine library is still located in the house in which we were; but because he has acquired eighteen cats and innumerable relatives, he has bought another large house near by.

Because of the eighteen cats, Osaragi serves no food in the old house. We went a short way through the rain to the new one, a superb example of Japanese elegance. The large living-room, bare except for a beautiful low table, a brazier, and a charcoal-ink painting of a duck with a flower arrangement below it, faces a garden containing a sweeping lawn, a huge old pine tree, a stone lantern, and many broadleaf evergreens, of which one kind, *sazanka*, was still in full white flower in late November.

We talked on and on for hours. That morning I had bought my ticket home, and perhaps I already felt the sadness of departure. Or perhaps it was the charm and sensitivity of Osaragi himself, and his extraordinary ability to capture essential human feelings even in casual conversation. At any rate, I felt very sorry to leave.

I cannot end this Introduction without a word about the translator, the late Brewster Horwitz. I first met him when he was a clerk in the office of the Japanese Consul General in New York, and he stamped my passport. It was only months later that I learned from other sources that he was one of the most brilliant products of the Army language training program, which in itself was an accidental by-product of war, and that he had an M.A. from New York University in classical and Oriental linguistics. And later still I learned that he had the kind of extraordinary genius for translation which appears only a few times in a generation, and which can cope not merely with the conversion of words from one language to another, but with essential overtones and implications. His unhappy death just after he completed the translation of *Homecoming* leaves a gap that will not easily be filled.

Harold Strauss

New York City
September 1954

THE PRINCIPAL CHARACTERS

Kyogo Moriya, a former Japanese naval officer exiled because of a scandal.

Setsuko Oki, his former wife, an old-fashioned woman who remarried when Moriya was presumed dead.

Tetsuzo Oki, her second husband, a famous but opportunistic university professor.

Tomoko Moriya, the twenty-two-year-old daughter of Kyogo and Setsuko, a modern, idealistic girl.

Saeko Takano, a restless, unconventional woman uprooted by the war, now a cabaret-operator and black-marketeer.

Nobu Takano, her estranged husband, the ineffectual son of an aristocratic family.

Otane, his mistress, a former geisha.

Kohei Onozaki, a painter who makes a living as a night-club entertainer.

Captain, later Admiral, *Toshisada Ushigi*, a classmate and friend of Moriya, old-fashioned and inflexible.

Toshiki (Toshi) Okamura, a postwar undergraduate, too young to have fought, who dabbles in the black market and in American habits.

Yukichi Okabe, a more mature undergraduate, a veteran of some stability and character.

HOMECOMING

THE PEACOCK

"What do you think of it?" the painter turned and asked his companion. "Oh—I think it's a beautiful sight," she answered.

A strong squall had passed over Malacca an hour before and washed the dull red tiles and white walls and tropical trees of the town into fresh and dazzling colors. An almost overwhelming sunlight poured through a break in the clouds over the city, but the sea along its border was still overcast and looked painted a muddy gray. It was clearing as they watched, however, and they saw it become tinged with blue. But a gloomy blue that blended with the black palm groves covering the long stretch of the cape in the background, and set off the radiant light that flooded the town and pushed out a little farther over the ocean every few minutes.

"We came just at the right time," the painter said as he turned to look up a gentle slope at the ruins of an old Christian cathedral. Only its four great walls were standing. He started toward it.

On the hill-slope a Malay was cutting grass with sweeps of his long-handled scythe. He stopped when he saw them and straightened up to get a good look at Saeko Takano's kimono—it amazed him, apparently. Even a Japanese would have stared a bit, here in the South, at this summer costume straight out of his homeland. In Tokyo itself before the war, no ordinary woman would have appeared so smartly and so conspicuously dressed except at a hotel or the theater.

Saeko Takano had worn only Western dresses in Japan, but when she came to Singapore, where Japanese wore Western clothes even if they never had before, she brought a wardrobe of summer kimonos and obi sashes with her. Outdoors, she dressed in remarkably quiet, almost matronly taste, but in her own establishment she would show herself nonchalantly to her guests in a crepe bath-kimono with a pattern of the boldest dye.

"You've startled him."

"Pardon me?"

"The Malay over there, I mean. He's gaping at you."

"He thinks I'm a monster, no doubt," she laughed, and there was only a soft luster on the white skin of her face. The polish of her manner told of no ordinary past.

"Oh, no. A beautiful woman looks beautiful in any country, no matter how different the customs."

"That's just your flattery, Mr. Onozaki."

"Not at all."

They looked up at a huge Chinese Bunga tree covered with large white flowers, heavily fragrant after the rain.

Not only the flowers were fragrant—every tree and blade of grass had its odor, and the earth too.

Inside the ruined church, there were only the bare sky where the roof had been, and the rich foliage trailing from the shrubs that had pushed through the gaps in the walls. They caught sight of the blue sea through the broken windows.

"There's nothing left of it, is there?"

"It's very old. The Portuguese built it, and the Dutch destroyed it when they attacked. That was in sixteen hundred something, they say—about three hundred years ago."

Set in the stone floor of the empty chancel was a flat tombstone with a Latin inscription. It marked the spot where the body of Francis Xavier, who had gone to

Japan as a Christian missionary in the days of Nobunaga, had been buried for a time. Several other tombstones of the same shape were still there, with carvings of ships, and crests, and inscriptions; but they had been stood up in a line against the wall, as though no one knew any longer where they should be placed. Some of them were carved, strangely for tombstones, with skull and crossbones.

But Saeko looked around as though she wasn't too interested in all this. The floor of the nave and transept was also covered with grass. The only sound was the singing of the little birds hidden in the foliage of the trees outside.

"This is all there is to it," he said.

"Still, it's a nice place."

"Once when I came, there were bats flying around in here—maybe because it was in the morning."

His head was full of history.

"First, there was a native kingdom here. The Portuguese came, conquered it, and built a fortress, and then the Dutch came and occupied it. After that, the English got in. And now the Japanese have come. . . . I wonder what country will come next. And it's such a tiny little place."

"There's some beautiful scenery outside, Mr. Onozaki. Wouldn't you like to sketch some of it?"

"I'd hate to keep you waiting."

"That's all right. I'll have Abdullah drive me into town to do some sightseeing, and come back to pick you up whenever you like."

"Thanks, but I don't think you'll even be able to do any shopping. There's probably nothing left in the town."

"There's no danger for a woman alone, is there?"

"No. It's a quiet place, and the people are nice. I go alone anywhere in town without having to worry.

6

You know it's an old place with a history. It's different from those new developments around Singapore with their swarms of uncivilized people. And it's very small. If you drove through it in an automobile looking for someone you knew was out on the streets, you'd be sure to come across him somewhere within twenty minutes—it's that tiny."

The chauffeur had gone over to the Malayan mower, and the two of them were sprawled on the grass, deep in conversation.

" 'Dullah!" Saeko called him in her clear voice. He got up with a little bow, and sprinted back to the car. A few minutes later Onozaki watched the gleaming enameled back of the automobile glide down the slope and disappear into the green shade of the trees ahead.

"She's going shopping," the painter told himself—Saeko Takano was that sort of woman. The colorful Dufyesque landscape of Malacca with its row of palm trees fringing the ocean like black fireworks held no interest for her, nor did the tomb of a Christian priest who had been in Japan three centuries before. More earthly instincts animated Saeko.

Saeko was thirty or thereabouts and had come to Singapore under the Navy's special protection to run her exclusive restaurant. Onozaki didn't know how that had come about, but he did know that remarkably worldly tastes underlay her quiet aristocratic appearance, and he wasn't especially surprised.

Onozaki was an impressive-looking man with boxer's shoulders, but he was nearing fifty and his hair was mostly white. All the other civilian information personnel were young men and treated him as an outsider, but he was too mature to let that irritate him unduly.

To tell the truth, Kohei Onozaki didn't think himself

a painter. He had gone to France in his youth, full of
enthusiasm, to study painting, but after a month of vis-
its to the Paris art museums he had stopped working
and renounced his ambition. He was rather clear-headed
for a painter. When he stood before works of the great
artists of the past and present, the limits of his talent
became clear to him and he was convinced that it would
be useless to study. He had gone gradually downhill
after that, becoming a sort of sharper, a guide to Japanese students in Paris, and then a backstage doorman
at a music hall. Even after he got back to Japan he didn't
do any painting, but dabbled in art criticism and art-
dealing and did some work for the modern theater.
When the war came, he saw that he couldn't make a
living if he stayed in Japan, so he became a painter again
and maneuvered himself into a civilian job with the
Army overseas. It was a bogus livelihood, just as in Paris.
It was easy enough to fool the soldiers with made-to-order
sketches—they didn't know anything about painting anyway. But as he stayed on here in the South he began to
feel that he really wanted to paint, for its own sake. He
was more surprised than anyone else when he became
aware of it. It wasn't only because he had nothing else
to do. His passion had returned, and that made him
happy.

Sometimes he was ordered out to dangerous places
near the front lines. It didn't worry him, but perhaps
this vague possibility of dying had made him feel he
wanted to accomplish something while he was alive.

He had become fond of Malacca on his earlier trips
there. The complex colors, the quiet surroundings, the
quality of the past that seemed to have seeped even into
the soil and the trees, appealed to his literary tastes and
let him forget the war for a while.

Onozaki walked around among the trees on the hill for a time before he picked his spot and opened his paint box.

In town, Saeko Takano ordered Abdullah to stop the car in front of an Indian jeweler's shop she had caught sight of. The street was an important one but narrow and dirty, and the shop itself was small. The one glass case contained nothing but a miserable display of earrings. The Indian chewed betel nut, and his blood-red spit was all over the bare earthen floor. It made Saeko sick to step into it.

The Indian was dressed in linen and had a tremendous beard. He got up from his chair to greet her.

"No diamonds?" she asked, in fluent Malay.

He shook his turbaned head from side to side. "I have none." He smiled so that the whites of his eyes stood out on the peculiarly Indian lead color of his face.

Saeko understood he was concealing something. "There's nothing to fear. You must have some hidden."

"Only rubies."

"Well, let me see some."

The midday light was strong outside, so that the shop was dim, but it was nevertheless stifling for Saeko, who had been riding with the wind on her face. As she took a Japanese fan from her obi, she looked out onto the street. Not a single Japanese walked by as she watched. Only some Malay women and Chinese men. The shops across the way looked deserted. They were dirty and their doors were shut. None of them had anything left to sell. Over their roofs rose a church-like building with two identical towers. It was painted a dark green, and together with the green trees made a dry, depressing sight. Saeko didn't realize that it was the cathedral with the monument to Xavier.

She looked at a few rubies without saying anything and bought one of them at the Indian's asking-price. She paid him in military scrip and insisted: "You must have diamonds."

She had bought the ruby in order to pursue the point. As she had expected, his attitude began to change.

"The Japanese Army requisitioned all the diamonds. They're all gone."

"Yes, but you must have one or two left. Even in Singapore, at the Chinese shops, they'll always bring some from the back of the shop to show you."

"If I did have any, they'd be very high."

"Show me."

His arrogant, strongly bearded face finally showed signs of weakening. The diamond he brought was only about three carats. When she picked it up in her elegant fingers its prismatic light glanced over her skin.

"I'd like something larger."

A beggar caught sight of Saeko and stood in the entrance of the shop. He was an Indian, as emaciated as a man could be. His ribs stuck out and his shins were like two sticks. Abdullah saw him and cursed him out, and then, as his mistress ordered, gave him some change and chased him away.

Malacca was certainly a compact little town. Five minutes' drive along the main business avenue and you were in the suburbs. Houses became scarce and you began to see cocoa groves and farm fields. When the first high-floored Malay dwellings came into sight, Malacca was suddenly over.

"Chinatown," Saeko directed Abdullah. With the British gone, the Chinese had all the goods and all the wealth of the South in their hands.

The Malacca River flowed between rows of houses like

a canal, its water stagnant and polluted. There was a bridge across it, and Chinatown was on the other side, stretching far along the seacoast. Only the streets near the bridge were covered with shops. Beyond them came quiet residential blocks lined with the mansions and estates of wealthy people who had retired here from Singapore. The gate doors of these residences were shut tight, even now in the daytime, and hardly anyone was on the streets. The houses were all built alike. They had curved tile roofs and white front walls with gateways in them, and in every gateway the thick panels of the closed doors were of painted wood. Over every gate was a big lacquered plaque with a Chinese couplet on it: "May the Lord of Heaven bless this household, and the five joys visit it"—or the like. The characters were carved into the wood and filled in with green or vermilion paint. These gates never were opened unless a visitor stood outside and called for admittance. And the voices of the people who lived inside never reached the street. Life was sealed away here, and it was very silent in the scorching sunlight. Saeko felt she was passing a row of empty houses as she rode down these alien streets.

Saeko had bought three diamonds at the Indian's. She was sure there would be other stores of the same kind here and she was looking for them from the car window. There was nothing to see but the unbroken row of houses that stood like fortresses along the quiet blocks. She was disappointed. She had heard that Malacca was full of retired millionaires and had expected to find plenty of jewel shops.

"Let's go back." Saeko had remembered the painter at work on the hill.

They turned round and drove back. Near the bridge, ahead of them, a car was standing in the middle of the road. Almost all the local automobiles had been requi-

sitioned and were being used by important people in the
Japanese military agencies, so Saeko looked to see who
the passengers were. The car was a new Cadillac.

They'd had a blowout and the driver was changing
the tire. The passengers had got out to stand in the
shade of the trees along the road. There were a young
Navy officer in summer uniform and a middle-aged gentleman in civvies with a helmet on his head. They
watched Saeko's car expectantly as it drew near.

"Stop, 'Dullah!" Saeko ordered.

Their sudden halt raised a cloud of dust, and the man
in mufti put his hand to his helmet and turned his face
away to avoid it. He was Captain Ushigi, a staff officer
at the Seletar Naval Station. Saeko had seen him before
only as a customer, and had found him reserved and
unsociable, as though always trying to preserve his dignity as a senior staff officer.

"A blowout?"

The Captain fixed her with that severe wooden-eyed
look of his. "What are you doing here?"

She felt the nastiness of the question. "I'd never seen
Malacca, so I asked a painter friend in the information
group to show me around."

"Sightseeing?"

"Yes. . . . Well, hello." Saeko smiled and greeted the
young lieutenant who was there as the Captain's
adjutant. He was a Tokyo graduate, and a friend
of hers.

"It doesn't seem quite the time for sightseeing, but
you say you're with someone?"

"Yes. He's working now."

The Captain stood like a stick, as always. "Are you
going back to Singapore today?" He used the Japanese
name of the city, as the regulations prescribed.

"Yes, I've my restaurant to take care of. But what

about your car? Is it all right? If you're on urgent business, please take ours."

"No. It's not that important. But I don't want you going back at night. It's a dangerous trip for a single car. You'd better leave early, or wait for us somewhere and we'll go back together. In daytime it doesn't matter, but we've had reports lately of strange things happening at night around Johore."

"You mean something mysterious?" Saeko put on a look of innocent terror. She was successful.

"Not ghosts exactly." He laughed for the first time. "Guerrillas appear, for one thing, and so do tigers—that district is famous for them."

"Oh, I'm not afraid of tigers. I've grown used to them from seeing everybody's trophies. You may not know it, Captain Ushigi, but Lieutenant Imanishi here is a very famous tiger-hunter."

The young Lieutenant blushed. "Please, ma'am!"

Captain Ushigi smiled too, but it was a distant smile, as though some other idea had seized his mind. "You mustn't make so light of danger. Really, you'd better drive back with us. It's dangerous for a single car. Better than that, why don't you come with us right now? Then you could show that genuine Japanese costume to the man we're going to see. What about it?"

"Where are you going?"

"I must caution you strictly before I tell you." His manner was military again, as though he were rendering an official decision. "You must keep what happens today absolutely secret. It's a private matter of my own, but you mustn't breathe a word to anyone about where you go or whom you see."

THE MAN WITHOUT A NAME

Ushigi was a changed man in mufti and not surrounded by subordinates. He was being much less formal in his conversation than Saeko had ever heard him before.

"Where was that painter of yours going to meet you? It's not nice, leaving him alone like this, but we'll have to make him wait about an hour."

"He won't mind. Once he starts sketching, he can stay by himself a whole day. Just let me go and tell him before we start."

"No, we'll send the adjutant later. He'll be able to find him if you tell us where he is. There aren't enough Japanese in Malacca for him to make a mistake."

With that the Captain grew silent. His face was shadowed by the rim of his helmet. It was a calm, expressionless sort of silence that could go on forever.

"Where are we going?"

The Captain looked back at her with his wooden stare. His answer had nothing to do with her question. "He probably hasn't seen a woman in Japanese dress for ten years. But we have something serious to talk about, so I'll have to ask you not to come in till we're finished."

"He's in the Navy, too?"

"No, he isn't."

The reply was in the austere manner again. It left Saeko with nothing to say.

The tire was finally fixed. They got back into their cars, and the Captain's automobile led the way over the road by which Saeko had just come. A hot wind came in through the windows.

Soon they were on Heeren Street, according to the English lettering on the metal sign. It was that same district of Chinese mansions sealed in by their white walls, with all the painted doors shut fast in the long row of gates. The Captain's car slowed down noticeably and Saeko knew they were near their destination. The adjutant was their guide, and he was leaning out the window, examining each of the gates as they moved slowly by. Suddenly the cars came to a halt.

The adjutant stepped out, casting a black shadow on the sunlit street. Abdullah opened Saeko's door too, but as she was about to get out, the young Lieutenant walked straight over to her.

"Would you mind sitting here for a little while?"

The Captain didn't get out either. Saeko could see the back of his white suit through the rear window of the car ahead. The Lieutenant walked up two stone steps and rang the bell near a little opening beside the gate. He made a fine figure as he stood there waiting, his finger on the bell.

In the sun the street glittered, deserted and absolutely still. Saeko glanced over the Lieutenant's head at the creepers growing over the gate and the red flowers they sent down the wall. She heard a motorcycle approaching from the distance. When it came nearer, she saw that there was a Japanese soldier on it, wearing an M.P. arm band. He seemed puzzled by these cars parked in front of a Chinese house, and looked them over curiously as he rode slowly past.

All the street-fronts of the Chinese mansions in Malacca were exactly alike, and when one went inside, one found that all the houses were laid out in very much the same form.

They were deep, narrow buildings. If its gate faced

Heeren Street, the house stretched right back to the ocean at the rear. For the plots were slender strips of land and the houses covered them entirely.

There would be a tiny garden just inside the gate, from which one entered directly into the front guest hall. Here there would be an ebony table on the stone floor against the far wall, and chairs set out in front of it. On the right and left of the wall, doors would open into the room behind, and when one crossed the threshold, one found oneself in a room just like the first. On the right and left of the facing wall would be doors that led into still another room behind. Some of these rooms had Chinese verses hung on the wall opposite the door one first entered, and some were arranged like temples, with little Buddhist altars.

But one of these rooms would be sure to have rows of framed portraits displayed on its walls. These were the successive heads of the household, each with his wife, starting from the founder: the history of the house. The older portraits, from the days before the camera, would be color paintings of old men in Manchu period costume, with dragons embroidered on their robes and peacock feathers in their hats; and next to them their *t'ai t'ai*, all with bound feet, but each with a different hair style. The people in the earliest photographs wore simplified Chinese clothing adapted to the Southern climate; but one or two generations later the men were wearing Western suits buttoned high at the neck, like Sun Yat-sen in his pictures, and their wives had cotton-print sarongs falling from their waists, in Malay style, and over them thin jackets closed in front like a pajama top. By the next generation the men were in ordinary Western clothes. But even in the latest pictures the women would still be dressed in Malay style or else in modern Chinese fashions imported from Canton. The whole history of the family since it left China stared gravely down upon the visitor.

The rooms would be decorated with artificial tray-gardens and potted oleanders from China, but also with marble maidens and horses and dogs by Western sculptors; and color prints of hunting scenes and horse races would hang on the walls next to scrolls of ancient calligraphy. The young master would have brought these statues and pictures back with him, together with an ornamental table clock and other souvenirs of England, after his graduation from Oxford or Cambridge. A new page in the family history.

The young master would speak English fluently, with a genuine Oxford accent.

Behind this long series of salons would come the kitchen, a kind of inner courtyard, unroofed, with an earthen floor, a stone well, and an oven. A flight of stairs led from it to the family bedrooms and sitting-rooms on the second floor. The kitchen yard was shaded from the sun by the big trees that grew there and by the eaves projecting from the roof on one side, so that cool shadows played on the surface of the water in the row of water jars.

A servant had brought in Captain Ushigi's card, and handed it to the young master of the house just as he was coming down the flight of stairs into the courtyard.

The young master was a plump man, dressed quite elegantly in a gray lounge suit. His shiny hair was brushed down with precision.

"A Japanese?" he asked the servant sharply, and without another word went down to the kitchen and walked over its earthen floor toward the rear.

There was a detached building there, closing in the courtyard from the rear. It had been a warehouse in the old days, when the junks had been brought right up to

shore and unloaded behind the house. The shoals had
not reached so far out then, and Malacca had been a
flourishing trade port. But Singapore had the trade now,
and the Chinese houses in Malacca had become quiet
residences and places of retirement. The warehouse was
no longer in use, and part of the roof had caved in.

Mr. Yeh, the young master, went to the door and
called out: "Sir!"

He could see the ocean through the windows. The
place felt empty. But a voice answered from the farthest
room.

Mr. Yeh walked back to that room and through the
door. A man stood at the entrance to a veranda that
faced the ocean. He had just gotten up from a cane
chair behind him, scraping it against the porch floor as he
rose.

"You have a visitor. A Japanese Navy officer." Mr. Yeh
spoke in English. He looked at the card in his hand, but
couldn't make it out too well. He was Chinese, of course,
but didn't know many characters, and, anyway, this was
a Japanese name.

The other man said nothing, but walked over to him.
He was wearing a long pale-blue Chinese robe. He was
unusually robust for a South Asia Chinese, light-complex-
ioned and full-faced. A prosperous-looking man with a
gentle manner.

He took the card and looked at it. The blood rushed
to his face. For all his youthful appearance, he was about
fifty, but his skin was crimson as a child's. The blush
became him.

"Don't worry," he said in fluent English, "it's an old
friend of mine. He probably saw a letter I wrote recently,
and decided to come and see me. Is he alone?"

The still-worried expression on Yeh's face revealed that
he didn't know.

"Would he have brought anyone? I want to see only this man. Would you tell him that, Yeh? If there are other people with him, let them wait outside. Show him in here, please. It will be all right. But only him."

"Yes. All right."

Yeh went away, and the other man looked at the Japanese card again. Some violent emotion distorted his usually placid features. To control his excitement, he went over to the window and gazed out on the ocean, brightly sunlit as far as he could see.

At high tide the surf came to just below the stone steps that were part of the foundation of the building, but the tide was out now, and ugly mud flats bordered the shore. The giant trees that grew in the kitchen courtyard stretched their thick branches over the roof of the old warehouse and covered the window with a luxuriant screen of large tropical leaves. The sea looked dark green between the leaves, even in the sunshine. The room was cool but dim, and furnished only with a simple Chinese bed, one trunk, and a few Western books.

Moriya heard the regular cadence of Captain Ushigi's footsteps approaching across the kitchen yard. They entered the building, marched down the wooden floor of the corridor, and stopped at the entrance to his room. He turned around from the ocean and met Ushigi's steady gaze.

"Moriya, it's you; you're still alive!"

Moriya smiled and stared back for a moment without answering. "You?" he whispered. There was a great loneliness in his voice. "It's been a long time since anyone called me Moriya. How many years, I wonder? But you didn't forget my name, did you?—you've come."

"Your letter was a surprise. But it took me awhile to place your name exactly—seeing it written out in Roman letters. K-y-o-g-o M-o-r-i-y-a—who *is* that, I wondered."

"You're looking wonderful. But, Ushigi—you're a captain already!"

"So it seems." Ushigi laughed. "But tell me, how do you come to be here?"

"When a man has no definite citizenship, like me, you shouldn't be surprised no matter where you find him. But even I was surprised this time. I'd just sailed from Sumatra and found the war on when I got to Singapore. The *Prince of Wales* was just leaving port, and my ship passed it coming in, but I didn't realize the war had started. I went ashore and was caught in Singapore. Japanese bombers were flying overhead. They were Navy planes, weren't they? What a strange feeling."

"Yes, Moriya." The Captain nodded gravely. "You might have been in one of them."

"That didn't occur to me. It was my life I was worried about. I might have been killed in the bombing—by the Imperial Navy. Fate likes ironic conclusions—that's all I could think about."

"What did you come to Singapore for?"

"To get a ship back to Europe. You see how successful I was." There was a wry smile on his boyish face. "And then the landing party attacked Singapore. There were Japanese soldiers in the streets and I couldn't help seeing them—for all my resolve not to have anything to do with Japanese again as long as I lived. If they were professional soldiers, I'd just look away and walk past. But the kids, they looked as innocent and helpless as children—it really hurt to see them. I didn't want to go back to Japan and it was as if I'd been put back there against my will—worse, maybe."

"Did you talk to any of them?"

"Yes, I did—but not as Kyogo Moriya; only as a foreigner who could speak Japanese. And they're not like the Japanese you meet in Europe—they don't cross-examine you about your private affairs. . . . I heard some very tragic things. This is a terrible war Japan's started. Don't you think so, Ushigi?"

The mention of that subject, even by an old friend, froze the Captain's face into grim lines. He didn't say a word. A military man acted as he was ordered to act, and his silence protested that Moriya should know that.

"If I were still in Europe, I might be more indifferent to the fate of Japan. But, quite by accident, I find myself in Singapore, where I can't go out without running into Japanese soldiers and sometimes talking with them. That makes things different. A bitter business, Ushigi. You're going to lose this war. Don't you see that?"

Captain Ushigi smiled a hard smile. "I can't say anything about that. Let's not talk about it, if you don't mind."

"Of course, I'm sorry—I've been very rude. Worse than rude, I suppose—I'm not a Japanese any longer."

"Moriya, haven't you ever thought of going back into the Navy? You'd have somewhere to die at least. I have a feeling there are ways of managing it. That's why I came today."

"I take it you mean that as a kindness. But if I may ask a question, is the Imperial Navy so far gone that it would take back an embezzler of government funds, a man who absconded abroad?"

"Even you can't say things like that, Moriya." The Captain was angry, his face flushed. But he regained his self-control immediately. "I've heard something about what happened. You're not so bad as you make yourself out. Knowing the kind of person you are, I suspect you took the blame on yourself for something that wasn't entirely your fault. Isn't that how it was, Moriya?"

"Do you mean to pity me?" Moriya spoke quietly. "It's

quite unnecessary. More than ten years abroad and one loses that sort of sentimentality. I'm like a Jew. To tell the truth, I haven't been able to get my bearings in speaking to you, Ushigi. We're talking at cross-purposes, and that makes it rather difficult. I have to make a tremendous effort and think back before I can get you in focus, and then, of course, I see that it's just that you haven't changed. You've developed in one straight line from the old days. And so what you say makes sense from your perfectly military point of view. First of all, you intend to die in this war sooner or later. And not because you think you're sacrificing yourself for victory. You're no fool. You know what's going on. In absolute certainty of defeat—"

"Stop it!" The Captain's tone held a sharp rebuke. He rose from his chair. "I'm going to show you a beautiful woman in Japanese clothes. I didn't come to talk about this."

Moriya looked at him as though he'd said something startling. "You mean you want me to go somewhere with you?"

"No. I wanted to show you a beautiful Japanese woman, so I picked one up on the way over."

"So you're with a woman. All right, but let's leave that till later. I want to talk to you about something first. I had a reason for taking the risk of writing that letter. I'd heard some time ago you were a staff officer here, but never thought of asking to see you. But now there's something I'd like you to do for me. The people who are taking care of me here have a house in Singapore. The Navy wants it for something or other, and has issued a requisition order for it. My host's mother is living there, an old woman and too sick to be moved without danger to her life. If the Navy wants to set up a restaurant or something there, the family's ready to offer another house instead so that the old woman won't have to be moved. But if you absolutely must have that house, couldn't you send a car to move the patient? You know the Chinese can't even use their automobiles freely."

"Is that what it's all about? Surely they could have handled that themselves without bringing you into it."

"No, they couldn't. Some of these supply officers are regular tyrants. They won't even listen to an appeal from a Chinese."

"I'll take care of it. Where is the house in Singapore?"

"Here, I've written down the address for you. I'm eternally grateful to you for this. I've caused these people a tremendous amount of trouble, a foreigner in their house, and it's been painful not to be able to do anything for them in return. So it means a great deal to me to get you to do this for them. It's a Chinese family and the worry about their old mother has made every one of them sick with grief. You'll really do this for me?"

"Certainly I'll do it. The Imperial Navy shouldn't have to do anything so contemptible anyway."

"Thank you. I'm really sorry to have put you to all this trouble, though. You're a busy man, and you've taken the time to come all the way out here yourself. I won't forget your kindness."

Ushigi was beginning to be oppressed by the gloominess of the room, with its tree-shaded window. "Is that all you wanted to talk about? . . . Tell me, Moriya, have you been here all through the war?"

"No, I moved here a little while ago. Before that, I was in the Singapore house we've been talking about."

"Didn't the M.P.'s bother you?"

"I have a Chinese passport. If it were known I'd come from Europe, there'd be trouble, I suppose, but my host and the others who know about me haven't said a word.

Chinese secrecy. It's kept me safe. But what about the
woman with you? Is it all right for me to see her?"

"She won't talk. Just be careful what you say when
you meet her and you needn't worry. Nobody knows who
Kyogo Moriya is."

"That's true too. I died some time ago, didn't I?"
Moriya said softly with a smile. "If I go back to Japan,
I suppose I'll find my grave there."

It was cool in the guest hall, for it was stone-floored
and far from the light outside. Coffee and cake had been
served, and slices of papaya with silver spoons. Captain
Ushigi had relaxed into an unusually jovial mood. He
didn't introduce Moriya to Saeko by name, or tell her
anything about him. To Moriya he said: "Saeko Takano.
She runs a bar in Singapore."

" 'Bar' sounds awful," she protested to the Captain,
and turned to Moriya. "I'd be honored to have you visit
my place."

She saw that this man in Chinese clothes was a Japanese. He was probably on some special mission, she
thought. That was why he was living here in a Chinese
house, and why she wasn't being told his name.

"I'd really like to. . . . It's a long time since I've seen
anyone in a kimono," Kyogo said quietly. "Once, in a little museum in a German country town, I saw some
Utamaro prints on exhibition. It was a wonderful surprise. . . . Japanese clothes are really beautiful—on a
Japanese."

"Are you on your way back from Europe?"

"No." He caught Ushigi's look. "I'm pretty well rooted
in Europe. It's a beautiful place. The Parisian women, for
instance, certainly know how to dress themselves. And
some of them are really beautiful. But—when you've been
there a long time, their demonstrativeness begins to get

on your nerves. Japanese feel the same way, I think. When you get to my age, even the most beautiful foreign woman becomes cloying somehow, almost oppressive."

"But Japan is changing too," the Captain said. "When a woman like this has the courage to come flying all the way down here, it's a new age."

"Japan's going to change even more now," Saeko answered.

"The war, you mean," Kyogo said. "Yes, war has a tremendous influence on the way people live. Whether you win or lose. I suspect that Japanese women are going to abandon the kimono for good, after this."

Saeko laughed. "Oh, I don't think so. Good things have a way of lasting forever."

"I'm not so sure. That may be so with the Chinese, but the Japanese are easily influenced. Too easily, you might say. They're a very changeable people."

"No, that's not so. Especially now, since the war began. I think everyone's become conscious of the old things, the good things in Japanese culture."

"You can't be sure there won't be a reaction away from that later on. The effect of a war is very powerful, in whatever direction it happens to work. I'm surprised that the men who fight the wars aren't conscious of that, Ushigi, or at any rate don't seem to care about it."

Captain Ushigi didn't answer. Kyogo ignored his silence and said emphatically: "It means total ruin. There'll be nothing left whole."

Captain Ushigi looked at his watch. "I'm sorry, but it's two o'clock already. We'll have to be leaving."

"You don't have to go so soon, surely."

"Yes, we do. We've decided to go back while it's still light."

He signaled with his eyes to Saeko and Lieutenant

Imanishi. They said good-by and went out to the front garden, leaving him alone with Moriya.

"That matter you asked me about—don't worry, I'll take care of it." His eyes were on Moriya's. "I would like to hear more about yourself."

"No, put your mind at ease on my account. I don't want to trouble you."

As he stood up to go, the Captain spoke in a low voice. "I'm getting a ship, Moriya, very soon."

Moriya's whole body tensed at that. "You're leaving Singapore?"

"Yes—so I doubt I'll be able to see you again. But I want you to take care of yourself. Be well."

Kyogo looked depressed for the first time. His hand-shake was heartfelt. "I should be saying that to you. 'Good fortune in battle'—is that the expression?—I pray that you'll have it."

Ushigi's face was blank. "There's not much chance that I'll ever see Japan again. But you may go back there, I think, sooner or later."

"Me! What are you saying?"

"Nothing." Ushigi smiled. "I won't say anything. But it may turn out that way. That's just an idea of mine. As far as I'm concerned, with my son dead already, I can perform my duty without any regrets."

"Your son! Where, how?"

"Midway. He was twenty-three. . . . Pardon me, I must go." He walked out in military posture.

Moriya overtook him rapidly. "Ushigi!"

The Captain turned around and looked at him.

"I'm sorry now for the stupid way I acted when I was young. But you, you mustn't die in this idiotic war. Stay alive somehow, and go back. Stay alive to help end the war more quickly. In your position—"

"It's too late. Too late."

His tone was final. He turned his back and got into the car. Their eyes locked again for a few seconds until the car slid away smoothly.

"Adjutant!" The Captain called to Lieutenant Imanishi up front. "Let's drive around to the M.P.'s. It's not necessary, I suppose, but I want you to make sure there'll be no trouble. A sergeant motored past before and saw us. They're all such fools—they make every little thing their business."

❀ ᔕᔕᔕ III ᔕᔕᔕ ❀

TENTACLES

Every city in Malaya had its amusement center. They called them "parks." Chinese theaters, classical and modern, Malayan playhouses, movies, and dance halls clustered inside an enclosure, and you had to buy a ticket to get in. The townspeople would go there after the heat of the day to cool off and amuse themselves.

When you stepped inside the park in Singapore you were greeted by a gay confusion of sounds and a startling daylight brilliance—startling because there was a grave shortage of electric bulbs in Singapore. But the war seemed not to have touched the park.

It was called "The Great World" and, of course, was the largest in Malaya.

When Saeko Takano, dressed as stylishly as ever, stepped out of her cab and walked into the park, her white socks catching people's eyes as they appeared and disappeared under the hem of her skirt in the darkness, she wasn't thinking of going to the movies or of meeting someone at the dance hall.

She was thinking of the little booths where luxuries that had vanished from the rest of Singapore were on proud display and you could buy French perfume and powders, or American soap, without any trouble. Earlier, Saeko had bought Coty cosmetics in these shops, but lately she'd been interested only in the remaining bottles of Bayer medicines from Germany.

Germany had just been defeated after several years of isolation, so it wasn't likely that any new shipments of Bayer's were coming in. But Saeko would place an order for them, and return to the shop a few days later; and when the proprietor saw her coming he would put the bottle of pills out on the glass display shelf without saying anything. It was one of the mysteries of Chinatown, and so was the way Saeko never failed to get diamonds when she wanted them, even though the Army had requisitioned them all and there were none to be found. She knew what channels to go through, and price was no object with her.

Saeko had a rather unusual use for these medicines, and it had to do with the diamonds. She would hide the diamonds she had collected in the pills or powders, refill the bottle, and seal it up again very carefully so that it looked like a perfectly ordinary bottle of medicine. Then she would give it to one of the Navy officers or information people she could trust when he was leaving for Japan.

"My sister uses them regularly, but she can't get them in Japan now. She can't do without them, so I'd be awfully grateful if you'd send this bottle to her when you get back. Registered parcel post will do perfectly well."

The young man would be only too happy to play knight errant to such a beautiful woman. "Delighted, ma'am."

Military people didn't have to go through customs, and, anyway, they could hide a bottle of medicine in their pockets quite easily.

Saeko was preparing for the future. She had decided that Japan was going to lose the war. Her ears picked up information that most people never knew anything about. She never showed her knowledge, but went on ushering the guests in and out of her restaurant with the same everlasting charm. What might happen to other people left Saeko absolutely unmoved.

The central walk of the park was covered with visitors. But it started to rain suddenly and the violent downpour scattered them like a troubled swarm of newborn spiders. They rushed for shelter under the eaves of the shops and into the theaters.

It was one of those brief tropical storms, but so violent while the rain fell that it drowned out the music and the singing of the Chinese theater. Pools of water formed instantaneously on the ground and reflected the garish light of the neon signs in crazy images between the bursts of spray that danced up from their surfaces under the thick strokes of the continuing rain.

Saeko went into the tea shop attached to the dance hall, took a table, and calmly watched the storm. A distinguished, somewhat Chinese-looking man in a Sun Yatsen suit came in and took off his soaking helmet. Saeko made an unconscious little exclamation and rose to greet him with a smile. It was the man Captain Ushigi had taken her to meet at the Chinese home in Malacca.

"Ah! You!" he said. "Are you alone?"

"You're all soaked."

"It came down all of a sudden. You can't tell at night —the sky's dark anyway. Did you come to dance?"

"No—just waiting for it to let up, like you. Are you staying in Singapore now?"

"Uh—awhile . . ." He avoided answering. "Is it all right if I join you?"

He was incredibly polite for a sailor. Her face bloomed into a smile. "Please do. I'm alone too."

"It'll be thirty minutes before we can leave. Do they serve beer? What would you like?"

"I'll have beer also, if they serve it."

"Surely. Pardon me a minute."

He turned, called the waiter, and gave their order in rapid English. There was some white in his hair, but he

was a handsome man, and there was something refined
about his gestures and facial movements.

"What's become of Ushigi?" he asked.

"Why, haven't you heard?"

"He's gone?" His stare seemed to penetrate and sur-
round her at the same time. "Well, has he? Has he
gone?" The question had a strangely heavy ring and he
answered it himself suddenly with an angry emphasis
that startled Saeko. "He's gone to kill himself. . . . But
they're all headed for death in this cruel business. Those
who go out to meet it are better off than those who stay
behind and wait for it. And their wives—I know how
they must feel."

Saeko added a shade of reproachfulness to her deliberately tender gaze. But she wasn't the woman to touch
on dangerous topics herself. "What about the war? What
do you think will happen?" was all she said.

Moriya smiled enigmatically and flicked the ash from
his cigarette onto the ash tray. "Don't you know more
about that than I do?"

Saeko's surprise was a work of art. "I! How would I
know anything?"

"I think you do." There was something military in the
look that flashed like a comet across Kyogo's tranquil
face and then disappeared. "People like you have a mysterious instinct for smelling out the things that the Army
and Navy try to hide. It's only the general public that
doesn't know what's going on, and only the Japanese
public at that. Of course, the soldiers have this naïve belief in a Japanese victory—it's been pounded into their
heads."

"I believe we're going to win too."

"So you say."

That hit her like a slap. "What a nasty thing to say!"

"By no means. I didn't mean it in a bad sense at all.

For example, the Chinese know already that Japan's going to lose the war. Look at the way prices have been going up lately. They reflect the war situation as accurately as a barometer. I live with the Chinese myself, but I don't know how they smell these things out. The M.P.'s have taken all the short-wave radios, so they can't very well be hearing the broadcasts from Chungking or London. But they still know everything that happens. . . . And every piece of news shows up immediately in that day's prices. The more lies Japanese Imperial Headquarters tells, the faster prices go up. A bowl of noodles used to be six cents and it's sixty yen already."

He fixed his eyes on Saeko's face suddenly. "Diamonds must have gone up too. How much does one carat cost these days?"

The rain sounded as violent as ever. Saeko was careful to smile easily. "I wouldn't know."

He was silent for a minute. "You say you don't know?"

"No. How much is it?"

"You don't have to keep it secret from me. Just this morning, I understand, you picked up quite a number of diamonds at Leangshaw's shop. Isn't that so?"

Saeko was startled enough to change color this time, but Moriya stared out the window as though that had nothing to do with him. The rain was coming down like a waterfall, reflecting the colors of the neon signs. Luxury stores and pool parlors and game arcades crowded together along the other side of the walk, and in front of them a solid row of Malayans was waiting for the rain to stop. Some of them were squatting down, looking like bundles with their sarongs lifted up from the bottom and thrown loosely over their heads.

Saeko couldn't think of anything to say. She was frightened by the way Kyogo had said just so much and then had fallen silent again. She crooked her arm and ran

her hand along her hair and looked up at him in a yield-
ing movement that she knew would appeal to any man.
He looked utterly unmoved, however.

"You know everything, don't you?"

"Not I. My Chinese friends know everything. I just
listen to what they say and find out about things."

"They exaggerate a bit."

Kyogo relapsed into silence. It was as though a wall
had risen before his eyes. There was a quietness about
this man that revealed some inner discipline, something
that wasn't at all like military training. It was in the way
he talked, not so simply as Captain Ushigi, in a gentle
tone, full of hidden subtleties.

"They really do know everything, my Chinese friends.
Not only what's going on here in Singapore; if something happens in Taipeh or Saigon, they're sure to know
it. And not only the big things—for example when they
tell me that the Japanese Army has suffered a disastrous
defeat on the front line at Imphal, they also describe
how the commanding general is living on a cool estate
in the rear where there are pines and cherry trees, and
how he's had a Japanese room, complete with tile roof
and mats on the floor, built in under the ceiling of the
grand hall of the Western villa."

"But some of their stories must be pure rumor."

"You mean about your diamonds?"

She laughed. "Don't worry about them so much. You
know, women are fond of jewels."

He only grunted.

"Well, you say I believe Japan's going to lose the war,
but can you say we're going to win? You're the type that
looks ahead."

Kyogo turned his profile to Saeko again and stared
outside.

The squall was finally dying down. The racket of gongs

and strings from the theater was growing steadily louder as the rain abated, and black shadows stretched from the crowd onto the walk in the glare of the shop lights.

Kyogo turned to her suddenly. "Would you like to dance?"

Saeko was still uneasy, but she smiled as if rescued by his invitation, and accepted. Kyogo seemed to have forgotten all about their conversation. The politeness with which he let her walk before him into the dance hall suggested that nothing in his manner all evening could have been at all discomforting for her.

The band in the dance hall was playing a tango. There were no other Japanese there, only young Chinese men with the hostesses. As they stepped down onto the floor, Saeko attracted immediate attention.

The attention spread through the hall as she followed Kyogo's lead in the tango. Saeko herself didn't notice it at first. She concentrated on following her partner's lead for a while, amazed at his skill. "How light you are!" The words slipped from her mouth. Kyogo must be nearly fifty, but the unexpected grace and speed in the flowing movement of his body exhilarated her. She caught on to his Parisian tango finally, and they breathed together. She could relax now, and said: "You must find me awkward."

"Not in the least."

"But you surprise me. After all, for a Navy man—"

It wasn't Saeko's heart or head that was surprised. It was her body. Even as they talked it was being swept along by the easy, pleasant motion. The anxiety that her partner had made her feel was still rooted in her mind, but as she became aware that everybody was looking at them she couldn't resist the pleasure of slipping obliviously into the linear and precise yet ever flowing movement that united their two bodies.

"This is delightful," she said.

"I learned to dance in Europe. I suppose I'm out of date by now."

"Not at all. That's the place to learn. The musicians are looking at you."

"It's you they're looking at," he said rather curtly, and then startled her by whispering in her ear: "You'd better get to work on someone and get yourself back to Japan as soon as you can. Make up any reason. The longer you stay, the more unpleasant things will be."

"Are you staying here?"

"No. I don't want to stay a day after the war ends. I'll probably go back to Europe."

Saeko looked at him, surprised. "Not Japan?"

"Probably not—almost certainly not. I can't, really."

"I'm jealous—your going to Europe."

"You really feel jealous?" he asked quietly. "I'm not happy or unhappy about it. Things have just worked out that way. There's no reason for you to envy me."

"It's your job?"

His smile said no.

The band stopped, but, in answer to the applause, swung right into the next number. It was a lively fox trot, but Kyogo started dancing a slow tempo, deliberately out of step. Saeko gave way once more to the sensation of turning into water and flowing effortlessly, and she shut her eyes in the pleasure of the motion.

And she thought of Kyogo. What a strange man he was! A very different man, now that he was dancing with her, from when he had frightened her by talking about the diamonds and then turning away in sudden silence. And on his profile, as he looked out at the rain after speaking so cruelly, there had been a shadow, as it were, of loneliness. Perhaps it was only that he was so handsome, but that expression reminded her somehow of a statue she'd seen once—it had the same virile sadness.

She opened her eyes and smiled, gloriously drunk with the sensations of the moment. "Well, then, we must separate soon, and put half the world between us."

"That's how things are."

"You're mean."

"Why?"

"Why, you say! It makes me unhappy to think of it."

"How very Japanese! What is there between us?"

She looked at him resentfully. "How can you talk that way?"

"Because I'm such a blasé vagabond. . . . When you live away from Japan you lose your sentiments. Like being in a desert—that's it, an arid desert. And once you get used to it, you find that's the best way to live."

"Won't you tell me about yourself? But not here—in a quieter place. Why don't we go to my house?"

"It's a restaurant, isn't it? There'll be Navy people there. I—" He shook his head. "I don't mind enlisted men, but I don't want to see any professionals."

They went back to their table. The storm was over.

"Do let's go. I have a separate room, where the customers aren't let in." Saeko was fervent.

Kyogo laughed easily, his eyes flirtatious. "I don't want to. Even the smell of sailors makes me sick."

"But what about yourself?"

"I don't have that smell, surely. It's gone by now, I should think." His tone changed. "War is the greatest of crimes. Europe's going to be hell when I get back, but Japan will be even worse. You'd better make your mind up to it before you go. And why? Because of a war that needn't have happened. That's why it's so terrible. God, war's hell, even if you win it—any war!"

"You are a strange one."

"Loathsome, huh? Un-Japanese?"

"Quite. Do you have a family?"

That unhappy look flickered in his eyes again as he turned them away from her. He was slow to answer. "I had a family. A wife and a daughter."

"Really? Where are they?"

He answered calmly, heavily: "They are in Japan."

"So you live apart?"

"That's hardly strange nowadays. It's the war. Are you with your husband?"

"No." A smile of natural charm came to her face. "I'm single. There's just myself."

"Pardon me. . . . I heard a story about your being married. That was just for the Navy, then?"

"Just some nonsense."

"Well then, you're one of the lucky ones."

"You say you have a daughter. How old is she?"

"Twenty."

"What's her name?"

"Tomoko. Let's not talk about that any more now. I think we have other things to talk about."

"And don't you think we could talk about them more comfortably at my house?"

"No. Come with me where I'm going. Forgive me for saying it, but the whisky's better there than at your place. The rain seems to have stopped."

"Where is this place?"

"Just come along. You've made me remember my wife and daughter. You owe it to me to make me forget them again."

"You say some very strange things."

❀ ᑌᑌᑌ IV ᑌᑌᑌ ❀

DAWN

On Bean Curd Street (it was a strange name for Singapore, and Saeko didn't know why they'd named it that)
there was a Central Chinese restaurant called Apricot
Blossom Village, which catered especially to people from
the local Japanese firms. Saeko had been there a few
times. Musei Tokugawa, the popular journalist and com-
mentator, had eaten there and written an article about
it in a monthly magazine when he went back to Japan.
He said the cooking there was better than at any other
place he had eaten in on his trip. Someone had sent
copies of the article to the Apricot Blossom Village and
they had framed the clippings under glass and hung them
conspicuously on the wall in the dining-booths.

Saeko had always been driven there by someone, so
she didn't remember the route exactly, but she knew that
it was down in Chinatown, in a district crowded with
the most varied kinds of buildings, where old Chinese
whisky bottles were piled up in the street, and the children played in swarms like flies; where the houses
stretched up three and four stories and each floor tried
to outdo the others in the quantity of wash hung out
to dry. As their car rode down the wet streets that night,
Saeko realized that Kyogo was taking her to some place
near the Apricot Blossom Village. The block where they
got out of the car looked the same, and the smell was
unmistakable. It was very dark in the blackout and they
could make out only the vague whiteness of the pavement.

Kyogo knocked at a closed door; someone opened it

and they entered what looked like a general store. The polished wooden posts and shelves shone black. They went up two flights of wooden stairs and through an opening in a wall to the third floor of the next-door house. It was very dark, the air was stagnant, and people seemed to be lying on the floor around them as they picked their way across to yet another opening and walked through to the third story of yet another house.

Here they were in a place that resembled the second floor of a restaurant, divided into little rooms by corridors. The rooms were lit, and people were playing mahjongg, to judge by the click of the tiles.

Saeko and Kyogo went up another flight of stairs and into an illuminated hall furnished with sofas and tables, like a Western lobby. Here they were greeted by a waiter dressed in white.

While Kyogo talked to him in his easy English, Saeko looked into a room where she could see a great number of strangely silent men sitting around a large table. None of them said a word. An electric bulb hung low, shaded so as to light only the top of the table and the front of the people around it, leaving their backs in shadow. They sat stiff, staring at something until one of them called in a low voice, and then they started into motion, putting out their hands and drawing them back, empty or full of bills. Saeko's intuition had not misled her. The long table had a roulette wheel set in its middle, and its surface was divided into numbered squares.

"Come," Kyogo said, as he followed Saeko's gaze, and led her into another private room. "I'm something of an expert at roulette. That, at least, I learned in the right place. It gives me a lot of face around here, so you can feel perfectly safe. . . ."

A thick, heavy-hanging drape of velvety stuff hid the exact location of the window. The drape shut out the air also, so that the flowers in the little vase on the glass table smelled all the more strongly. They were white flowers, like gardenias, their odor sweet and overpowering. "That window can be seen from the ocean. If any light shines through, we'll be in trouble."

They poured their Martel brandy into glasses filled with cracked ice. Saeko was no weakling as a drinker, but she couldn't keep up with Kyogo.

"How quiet it is!" she said.

"Yes—like being in a box." He looked for a few moments at the seltzer bubbles rising in his lifted glass. "Indian fortune-tellers see destiny by gazing into crystal balls, they say. Do you feel it? At this very minute, as we sit here, somewhere out on that ocean a submarine is coming up for air, and somewhere else a naval engagement is going on, ships are sinking, and their sailors are being carried by the waves beyond all hope of rescue."

He looked sorrowful, and somewhat drunk.

"It won't do any good, our thinking about it."

"I agree. You're absolutely right. But what a world it is. . . . Every minute, every second that passes, someone is losing a son, someone else a young husband. Things as terrible as that are happening, but unless they touch us personally, we can be incredibly indifferent to them. No—I had no right to say that. I abandoned my wife and child long before there was any war."

"Tell me about it."

"No. That sort of thing becomes less and less important the longer a man lives. That's how human beings are. You feel yourself plummeting straight down, and in no time at all you land somewhere where you can feel at ease. It's simple. Only, when you have no ties, living becomes a hideous bore. You have nothing to hold on to. It's like not being able to get hold of a strap on a crowded trolley. A weak man finds that painful. Westerners take it more easily. You run into so many people like that in Europe. People living alone, and not bothered by it. You were just making conversation when you asked about my family, I suppose. You reminded me of my wife, I said, didn't I?"

"Yes, you did."

"It's only that you're a woman in Japanese clothes. Really—that's all there was to it. Honestly, though, something struck me when I saw you. Something that made my heart ache."

"I made you think of your wife? Thank you. I feel honored."

"That isn't it. I thought so too, but I was wrong. I've forgotten her completely. I try to remember what she looked like, and nothing comes. Just a shadow. It has no reality at all. To tell the truth, I believed somehow that couldn't happen. But the distance time has put between us is greater than I'd realized. I seem to remember, but I don't really remember anything. I see that now."

"Is that possible?"

"It's happened. And there's nothing tragic about it. It's not even sad. . . . It's just so—inevitable."

"How lonely you must be."

"No!" He smiled. "I thought you were too strong a person to feel that way about it. If you're saying that to console me, please stop. It serves no purpose. For one thing, I'm no longer capable of feeling lonely. I told you. As soon as the war's over, I'm going back to Europe."

Kyogo swallowed another glass of brandy, and then went on. "There's a legend in Europe: the Wandering Jew. It's been told for a very long time, since the Middle Ages. When Christ was being taken to Golgotha, there was a Jew among the onlookers who reviled him. He was punished—death was denied him, and he must wander over the earth forever. No millennium will bring him rest. That's the story, anyway. As I wandered all over Europe myself, unable to go back to Japan, I thought of that story, and the Jew seemed no stranger to me. Ahasuerus was his name. Never to be able to die would be terrible, I think. But my life has the usual limits, so I needn't worry. And there's plenty of roulette and baccarat in Europe to kill the time. I'm going back there."

Then he lifted his glass toward Saeko and smiled courteously. "What's the matter? You're not drinking at all."

"I don't know—I'm depressed."

"If you're depressed, that's all the more reason to drink."

"You're really going to Europe? Then I don't know whether I'll ever see you again."

"The world is made up of good-bys. Think of Ushigi. I wonder where he is right now—out there on the ocean."

Saeko shook her head vigorously. "I'm not thinking about Captain Ushigi. It's you I feel sorry for, somehow."

"That's absurd. Ushigi has gone to seek his death, and here I am quite alive. That makes me the fortunate one."

"But still, why aren't you going back to your wife in Japan?"

"Because I've been punished like the Wandering Jew. Europe is better for me. Not so narrow as Japan. People don't gossip about their neighbors. They aren't always finding fault. They just leave you alone."

"But that isn't what I meant."

Saeko sighed and suddenly picked up her glass, lifted her head, and drank it all down. Kyogo could follow the brandy, as she swallowed, down her lovely white neck.

"Since you're going to Europe, I want to make an occasion of it."

"What difference does my going to Europe make?"

"Why, I may never see you again. So—"

"So—?"

"It's because I've had a liking for you ever since I met you."

"The Navy may scold you for that."

"Let them scold me as much as they like."

Kyogo stood up. Saeko was trembling, suddenly, and no longer flirtatious. The skirt of her kimono was disarranged, and she straightened it automatically.

"Saeko!" His eyes were gleaming. "May I kiss you?"

A siren screamed outside with a long trailing sound. It was the real thing. The Chinese below became noisy suddenly. They could hear them running downstairs.

Saeko had looked back at Kyogo, and hung her head meekly. "Please!" she answered, with a break in her voice. Then her eyes grew gay again and words came easily. "Think of your wife, please."

There was an uproar in the street below, as though the people had rushed out of all the houses. Doors were slamming to, each louder than the next. All the lights in the room went out suddenly. The siren went on howling.

"Shall we leave?"

"No."

She seemed to shake her head, deep in Kyogo's embrace. The odor of her hair and sweating skin, mixed with the strong scent of the flowers on the table, turned the sudden darkness into an ocean. As Kyogo sank into it, he enjoyed the soft resistance of her moist, burning lips. There was the sound of teeth on teeth.

The car went through the gate, drove up the tree-lined drive, and stopped below the white-painted porch. It was a very elegant villa that had belonged to an

Englishman. The grass in the garden was very green and carefully trimmed, and wound around all sorts of tropical trees and flower beds.

Saeko rang the bell at the entrance. Lights went on inside at once and shone through the screen door, awakening the shrubs and trees near the entrance into color out of the darkness.

A Japanese girl in a simple dress and heavy make-up opened the door for her.

"Good evening, ma'am."

Saeko walked into the house without taking off her sandals. She looked back at the servant, who was shutting the door.

"I was caught by the air raid. I won't want anything else. Go to bed now."

She started toward the staircase to her bedroom on the second floor, but turned and went into the bar. This had been built into a corner of the hall on the right, which had been the reception room of the old villa. Saeko walked through the narrow door the bartender used, switched on the light on the counter, and opened the refrigerator.

She took out a chilled bottle of soda water, and, just as she was doing so, heard the creak of a chair somewhere in the unlighted hall. She peered into the darkness, puzzled and suspicious, and made out someone lying, cramped, on the chaise longue. He seemed to be looking at his wrist watch, arm up and elbow bent.

"Who's there?"

He sat up and looked toward her. His movements were still clumsy and drunken. "Uh-h—that you, ma'am?"

"Mr. Onozaki? . . . How extraordinary! Did you get drunk?"

"Ah, I must be a spectacle." He managed to keep himself upright on the sofa, but wasn't able to stand yet. "But, Mrs. Takano, where have you been? It must be morning already."

Saeko avoided the question. "Haven't the mosquitoes been at you, sleeping in here?"

"I came to say good-by, Mrs. Takano. I'm leaving for Burma tomorrow on the morning train."

"Nonsense! Going to Burma now?"

"No nonsense. Burma's the only part of the front I've never been to. And if we win at Imphal, we're marching into India next. I've made up my mind to go."

"Don't do it, it'll be too much for you, Mr. Onozaki. Why, you must be fifty already."

"Physically I'm as good as any younger man!"

He stood up at last and walked toward Saeko at the counter. His hair was tousled from his nap and whiter-looking than usual, his good-natured face still bleary with drink. "I'm going to India. I'm going there and I'll paint it."

"Will you join me in a drink? This is soda."

"Water for me."

"Not water, when you're leaving us. Take beer."

"All right. Water's improper? I never know about these things."

"Oh, Mr. Onozaki—" Then Saeko's face became serious. "Have you really decided to go? Aren't we going to lose at Imphal too?"

"Lose! We're winning! India's in sight already—they announced it."

"Really?"

"We're just across the border. I must go and see India."

"It's on the other front, out in the Pacific, that we're losing, then."

"No such thing. We're drawing the enemy to Japan to finish him off. That's our strategy. Imperial Headquarters

has announced it, and Imperial Headquarters doesn't lie.
I'm sure of that. The Japanese are such good citizens,
they just couldn't lie to them, not Grand Imperial Headquarters—it's impossible."

Saeko was silent.

"I'm so near India anyway, I've got to get a look at
it at least. So, it's good-by for a while."

"This morning's train?"

"Yes. I don't mind the train. Tried to get a plane
ticket, though. But I enjoy these slow trips with the
natives for company. For me, it's better—I can make
sketches all along the way. I've been in Paris and seen
civilized people till I couldn't look at any more. But the
natives here are different, there's something exciting in
their faces, something transparent, as though they were
gods or Buddhas. Maybe it's ignorance. They're really
good people, people you can love. Not like civilized
people—their faces aren't dirty and tired with knowledge. . . . That's how I feel, anyway. I've come across
such beautiful faces among them. But, forgive me, Mrs.
Takano. You want to get to bed, don't you? Let me sleep
here till morning, though. I'm tired too."

"It's none of my business, I suppose, Mr. Onozaki,
but did the military say it was all right for you to go to
Imphal?"

"Absolutely. Go right ahead, they said. I thought
there'd be trouble getting an Army O.K., but they were
delighted."

"Indeed? Well then, go ahead. I'll see you again tomorrow morning, but I must get to sleep now."

"Don't bother getting up on my account. I'm not going anywhere dangerous or anything."

"Let me find you a better place to sleep."

"Never mind. This is fine. I've been to the front lines,
and this is heaven by comparison."

Saeko watched him go back to the couch and sprawl out again. Then she turned off the light and went upstairs.

In her bedroom, she locked the door and switched off all the lights except the little lamp beside her bed.

Saeko was in the habit, since she had come South, of taking a cold bath every morning when she got up and every evening before she went to sleep. She was preparing for it now, and had just begun to untie her obi when she heard the muddy song of a night bird out in the garden thickets. Her arms and legs were deliciously fatigued and her body tingled. It was a lazy feeling. But she went on undressing and soon felt the tepid night air against her thinly covered skin, floating in from the garden through the screen door and carrying the scent of grass and flowers into the dimness of her room.

The first touch of the bath was icy cold. Saeko gritted her teeth and slapped the water with all her strength over her chest and shoulders. As always when she bathed, her mind emptied of everything but the pleasure of feeling her skin grow cool and tauten. She splashed the water all over the bathroom and smiled, without knowing it, the smile of a mischievous child.

She dried herself with a thick towel and rubbed in her lotion. Her skin woke up. She got into thin pajamas and lay down in bed, and noticed soon that she was lying in an unusual position. One isn't conscious of one's natural position in bed, but Saeko had so placed her arms tonight that they followed the contour of her body, so she knew.

She lay motionless, eyes closed. The netting moved with the night breeze. She could sense it. Faraway night jars and gecko lizards sang. Morning was near; somehow she knew it.

Without opening her eyes or changing her position,

she stretched her hand under the bed and took up a
black glass perfume bottle. It was a d'Orsay product.
They sold perfumes and lotions in these cosmetic bottles
of black glass cut into diamond crystals. And in this
bottle Saeko had hidden the real diamonds that she'd
bought, dozens of them.

She took out the stopper, tilted the bottle, and let
the diamonds flow down like glittering iridescent water
and pile up on her open palm. Some of them spilled
over onto the sheet and rolled down Saeko's side, under
the white skin of her uncovered breast. She picked them
up and, as she did so, felt a surge of hatred for the man
she'd just left, who knew so ominously much about her
diamonds. Her body was still penetrated by his touch.
She was still excited. She still craved him physically, and
hated him all the more. Her eyes were fixed on the colors
flashing from the prisms on her palm. She shook her
hand, and when the diamonds fell at different angles
their radiance varied as the sunlight varies through the
waves of air on a summer day. But this play of lights
didn't gladden Saeko as it did on most nights. There was
no consolation in it. There was only danger.

Saeko suddenly swept up the diamonds, put them
back in the bottle, went out through the mosquito netting, switched on her dressing-table light, and sat down
facing the triple mirror. Each of the glass panels reflected
a bit of the dawn outside. She took out a fountain pen
and started writing a letter. When she'd finished, she
put it in an envelope and wrote the address: "Headquarters of the Military Police, Japanese Army, Singapore; To whom it may concern."

V

THE STRANGER

The Malacca prison was a small building on the outskirts of the city. It stood on Banda Hila Street, in a neighborhood where only Indians lived. Three hundred yards away rose a hill from whose bald top the ruins of a Portuguese fortress looked down over the sea.

The entrance to the prison faced the street, its iron door shut, and a copper plaque was set high up in the wall beside it with an inscription that said the prison had been built in 1860, during the Governorship of Colonel Cavenagh.

On August 20, 1945, an automobile flying the blue-and-white flag of Nationalist China pulled up in front of the iron gate. A well-tailored man got out and rang the bell.

A panel was set in the solid iron door, and it could be opened from inside to permit the inspection of visitors.

The man from the car handed an English document through the window. It swung to again, and a few minutes later he heard the rattle of unlocking. The heavy iron door of a small gate beside the main one opened, and he was conducted inside.

He found himself in a tunnel-like passage, with the warden's room and the offices on the left and a blank wall on the right. Another locked iron door stood at the end of the passage and sealed it off from the cells that one could see through its row of iron bars.

The warden was part Dutch, part Malay. He read

through the document, nodded, greeted the visitor in Malay, and ordered a Eurasian jailer to open the iron grill. The cells started a few feet beyond and ranged down either side of a clearly lighted corridor. The jailer stopped at the entrance to Cell 16 and began to unlock it. This door was solid except for a grilled opening that reached up only a foot from the floor. The prisoner in the cell could see outside only by getting down on his hands and knees next to the door.

The visitor couldn't wait for the jailer to get the door open. "Sir!" he called. "It's Yeh. I've come to get you." His English was loud and clear.

"Mr. Yeh?" a voice asked softly from within.

The door opened on a long and narrow solitary cell, lit only by a blue patch of sky through the ventilation window on the inmost wall. Kyogo Moriya stood up from the wooden bench and looked fixedly at his young Chinese friend.

"You're free!" Yeh shouted. "You can leave this place." He couldn't quite bring himself to step inside the cell, but stretched out his hand from the corridor for Moriya to shake.

"So—" Kyogo nodded—"the war's over, then."

"Yes, it's over, Mr. Moriya."

"And you've come to get me. A Chinese so kind to me, and my own countrymen forgot all about me. The M.P.'s just left me here, it seems."

Yeh *was* very considerate for his age. He had even remembered to bring a light Chinese top-robe for Moriya to put on over his prison clothes so as not to attract attention on the street.

When they reached the center of town, Kyogo noticed the Chinese flags flying on the shops, and the Union Jack too on some of them. Otherwise Malacca looked very much the same. On Heeren Street the lacquered doors of the Chinese houses still were shut tight in the midday heat, and the gold and vermilion characters on the panels over the gates shone softly in the sunlight reflected from the surface of the road. And the bougainvillæa branches were still there, stretching their weight of red blossoms over the walls.

They walked through Yeh's gate and found the whole family waiting for them in the front room. The young mistress—Yeh's wife, who had gone to London with him—was there in a Cantonese dress that left her arms bare. She had her two children with her, and she smiled at her husband and Moriya as they came in. Their coming had been loudly announced through the house, and the old master, quite an elderly man, had hobbled out on his cane to meet them. He said his hello's to Moriya in Chinese.

The children did too, the seven-year-old boy and the girl, who was five. Moriya looked at them, and tears suddenly came to his eyes. He took their tiny hands in his, and felt their smoothness against his palms and wondered that there should be anything so soft in this world.

The boy's hair was neatly brushed, and he wore shorts in the Western style. The girl was dressed like a little Malay woman.

Yeh's eyes sparkled with excitement as he remembered. "Mr. Moriya, I've had a warm bath drawn for you. I know you prefer it to the Japanese arrangement."

Yeh and Moriya spoke in English, as they always did. Kyogo thanked him, then said suddenly, as though to himself: "So the war's over."

"Yes, everywhere in the world," Yeh laughed and answered with Western emphasis and even Western gestures.

"I'm glad of that," Kyogo said. His own words sounded

strangely empty to him, and he had to make an effort to get the right expression on his face. He had heard about Japan's surrender while still in prison, but he couldn't feel it yet. He was afraid that if he spoke about it, the words would just float away into thin air. "What's happened to the Japanese in town?"

"They collected them in one place. They're all right. There was no trouble." Yeh questioned his servant in lively Chinese. Then he turned back to Kyogo and went on. "He says the Japanese are being moved to Singapore, bit by bit. Nothing happened here. And they have enough food and everything."

The sun stood like a dazzling ball far out over the Malacca Straits and sent its light over the water. Beyond its radiance, the sea was a muddy blue, and heavy. The window of Kyogo's room was still screened by the branches that spread over the roof of the old warehouse from the kitchen courtyard. It was dim and cool in there. In the mornings he could make out the hazy shoreline of Sumatra across the straits, but by noon the sunlight obliterated it.

Kyogo sat in the wicker chair and gazed vacantly out at the ocean. That morning Yeh had told him he was going to Singapore and invited him along, but he had refused. He didn't want to go out. Not at all.

"Of course, you're tired."

He had shaken his head and looked rather morose. The servant had brought him a bottle of Suntory whisky—it must have belonged to a Japanese once, and he wondered how it had got here. And Kyogo asked him to bring newspapers, it didn't matter how old, as many as he could get together. Leyte, Iwo Jima, Okinawa . . .

The newspapers stopped suddenly before the end of the war. But Kyogo read the monotonous reports—each bombastic prediction of inevitable victory followed by the unperturbed acceptance of defeat—and through it all was able to make out fairly well the relentless march of reality. Those air raids on cities in Japan—always reported as relatively ineffective . . .

"I'm tired!" He shouted it out loud, sitting there alone.

There was something that excited him, and it wasn't in the newspapers. None of the vaguely written articles mentioned it. Something formless and indescribable, something beyond his imagination. Things had turned out as he had expected, surely, but when he tried to grasp exactly what had happened, he found himself out of his depth. Even his military experience couldn't help him here. The blank months he had spent looking at walls seemed to have taken effect all at once and left him a dull old man in a strange world.

Out in the ocean the ever moving water glistened. The light from its surface shone through the branches that hung down over the window, outlining every vein on every leaf. Crabs crawled in the mud shoals exposed by the ebbing tide.

"I'm really not a soldier any longer." That was Kyogo's deepest feeling. And he thought of his old comrades, suddenly, with a vast anger.

"That's it! It was a world where only rank and position counted. They made a man strong or weak. I was expelled from my position, so I became unmilitary. Naturally. What else could have happened?"

Maybe it was the sudden change in his life, but all he felt was a great fatigue. Every afternoon he developed a fairly high fever. He took advantage of it to shut himself in his room. But he had the newspapers delivered to him there, one in English and one in Chinese, the same newspapers that had been managed by Japanese a little while before. He read about the signing of the surrender aboard the *Missouri* and about General MacArthur's arrival in Japan. And he looked at the pictures.

While the fever was on him, Kyogo would lie motionless on his bed. Lizards crawled on the ceiling above his head. The ceiling was painted white, so the lizards made themselves white too. Protective coloration. They cried and made tiny noises. They were a family—parents and children. Sometimes the babies dropped onto the mosquito netting and scampered frantically for a while. They kept in the shade during the day, without moving. When the light went on, they would start marching toward it to catch some of the insects the brightness would attract. It was a regular schedule. When Kyogo noticed them, they would freeze in position, as if pasted on the ceiling, parents and children together, their white bodies in a row.

A face would come to Kyogo out of the past as he lay there in fever: the face of the M.P. who had examined him. It would come with a burst of pain. An unforgettable face, like a monster's in a dream. He was a young man, twenty-two or twenty-three and just out of school—a mere child to Kyogo—but drunk with his own power. A fleshy, insensitive face, the lashless eyes always bloodshot.

"You spy! You dirty traitor!" he would shout in Kyogo's face over and over again. And then he would lean over toward him, all sympathy and understanding, offer his cigarette case, beg him to take one, and even give him a light from his old-fashioned lighter with its long-trailing textile wick. Then he would make his proposition.

"You're a Japanese too, now, aren't you? We're making plans here at the military police to pick up all the pro-Allied elements in the Chinese community in a single raid. Won't you help us get the information we need?"

There was torture too. The M.P. would do it himself, smelling of whisky despite the regulations. And immediately afterward he would show Kyogo some sort of kindness, ask him whom he knew in the Navy, and start the routine about being Japanese. His voice would grow sorrowful. This was Japan's hour of crisis. His florid face would redden suddenly. And he could fix his pupils in an unblinking stare straight into his prisoner's eyes. Kyogo had once had that same military habit of looking at people fixedly. It returned to him now, and when the superior discipline of his years worked its effect on the immature M.P., he went mad, shrieked, and exploded. "You're Japanese! Japanese! Japanese!" He looked maniacal, capable of any violence. The ferocity of his appearance contrasted strangely with his youth.

The white backs and little hands and feet of the unmoving lizards on the ceiling soothed Kyogo's excitement now. "He was right, I am Japanese."

He was murmuring out loud, half delirious with his fever. Clearly, he was Japanese, but a different sort of Japanese, who hated the madness of the torturer.

It took more than a month for the fever to lighten. When he was well enough to go out walking, Kyogo was delighted by the day-long quietness of Heeren Street. Tranquil, elegant, and clean, the blocks stretched empty of everything but the lacquered doors in the white walls, on which the flowers of the creepers spread and the white oleander bloomed. He crossed the Malacca River and started up a hill toward some temple ruins, but remembered that the Japanese government had had its office there till recently, and lost his desire to go.

The Japanese had vanished from Malacca. There was no trace of them. In their place, the English were beginning to come back. Kyogo limited his rambles to Chinatown. It was still safer that way.

One evening he went to the amusement park, bought a ticket, and went in. He was struck by the Chinese of good family who had never shown themselves in town during the war, but who were here in the park now with their wives and children, chatting comfortably outdoors in the evening coolness or sitting in long rows in the theaters. And long-hidden luxury items crowded the shelves of the illuminated stores. Peace had come. Some of the townspeople looked back at Kyogo suspiciously when he walked by, but no one stopped and questioned him. A Chinese matron Kyogo knew by sight was there, watching her children on the merry-go-round. When she saw him, she stopped her fan and nodded a greeting. She was wearing a cool cotton print dress that left her arms bare.

He stopped at a gambling booth and caught sight of a young man who came to work on Yeh's estate. He was sitting there, intent on the game. Each of the players had a wooden board in front of him with a rough checker-board pattern on it, and a number painted in every square. A man in the middle was shaking a wooden box of the sort used in temples to cast lots, and reading in a loud voice the numbers on the chits that came out. There were girls in front of the players and their job was to put peanuts on the squares containing the numbers called. You won when your board was filled, and took all the money that the players had staked for that game.

The players sat next to one another quietly, their eyes on their boards. The girls who placed the peanuts also had to see that the guests played fair.

It took a while before all the squares on a board were covered. It was a slow game and gave the player no chance to make a choice. A purely passive game of luck.

Yeh's employee didn't win once. Kyogo smiled. The servant noticed him and smiled back ruefully. Kyogo watched the play attentively. In an hour or so, when a player got up and left, Kyogo called Yeh's servant over to the empty seat and gave him some money to play with.

He did more than give him money. He stayed with him, standing behind him and watching the board. His eyes shone with concentration.

The number-caller went on shaking his wooden box noisily and shouting the numbers that came out. In a while another player raised his hands and yelled. He had won.

Kyogo whispered confidently in the servant's ear: "It's all right. Go on playing."

Next game, the girl near them was kept busy putting peanuts on their board after every number was called.

Only one square was empty.

"We've made it," Kyogo said, softly but with complete assurance. The box shook, and the chit that came out bore exactly the number they needed.

The girl raised her hands to show that the game was over. A pile of bills was put in front of Yeh's servant—more than ten times what he had staked. Kyogo slapped him on the shoulder gaily.

"You'll win once more. Play till then. As soon as you've won, stop," he ordered.

The young man seemed hesitant, but obeyed. He lost three games. The fourth time, his board was filled again. He took his winnings and looked up at Kyogo, bewildered.

Kyogo refused to take a share of the money. And when the servant asked how he had known that he would win, he only laughed. As he walked away his eyes were drawn to the moon in the sky over the park lights, as large as a moon in a stage set. Its light was so strong that outside, beyond the illumination, the streets still had the whiteness of early evening. The palms rose to absurd heights between the houses, spreading their fronds in the sky like black shadowy bursts of fireworks.

Kyogo felt terribly alone. In Europe he had also had these sudden attacks of loneliness from time to time. There was a pattern to them. They came after he had been to a casino and won heavily, while he was on his way home. The gambling had excited him, it seemed, despite his efforts to stay calm, and then loneliness would creep up on him like a draft through a chink in the wall. Could this childish game of peanuts have had the same effect? By noon tomorrow the news of Kyogo's marvelous eyes, able to foresee the lucky square, would have spread like wildfire through the working class of Chinatown. But even that couldn't bring a smile to Kyogo's face.

He had started back to the Yeh house, but turned off now onto a road that led out to the suburbs. In Europe, when one of these fits of loneliness came on him, he would walk on and on, alone and silent, through block after block of unknown streets. He had found it the best and only cure. It wouldn't be bad to walk so tonight, he felt, along the road through the rubber plantations, under the brilliant moon. With his own shadow for companion, following on the moonlit ground.

It was a windless, quiet night. The native villages were flooded with moonlight against their background of palm groves and black forest. The road was a long streak of white in the darkness. A rubber grove would spread over several square kilometers, uphill and downhill and level as the ground rose and fell, clean and regular as a botanical garden. Nothing grew below the carefully tended trees; the grass and weeds were neatly cut away. The moonlight filtered through the branches and fell on the ground between the trees in uneven patches.

Somewhere far away a native was singing. A slow, monotonous song. As Kyogo listened, the voice fell silent, and the rustling of the leaves stole to his ears like a shadow creeping on the ground. Above the road only a long thin line of sky was visible between the tops of the trees on either side. Even in the moonlight the stars sparkled, tiny and innumerable, like grains of silver sand.

If he had had a motor bike, Kyogo would have liked to go riding on and on along this road, which ran straight ahead as far as he could see. But as it was, he decided to walk on to the top of the slope that rose before him and turn off there onto a path that would take him back to town.

As he started up the slope, he heard voices again, people talking, and apparently not very far away. Almost at the top, he looked ahead and saw four or five men sitting in a cluster on the grass beside the road. They were shaded from the moonlight by the trees behind them and he couldn't make them out. Probably it was one of the native home-guard units organized during the war. They had been trained with the Japanese commands, armed with man-high poles, and put on night sentry duty at the entrances to the suburbs.

In darkness and silence, the men watched Kyogo approaching. No one challenged him in the broken Japanese of the natives or got up to examine him.

When he got near enough to see them in the moonlight, Kyogo found that they were Japanese soldiers. And thirty or forty more of them were scattered in the rubber grove beside the road, lying like dead on the ground, sprawled on their blankets and knapsacks.

The face of the young M.P. who had tortured him floated into Kyogo's mind. In this out-of-the-way place the soldiers might attack him, for all he knew. He was anxious and on his guard as he came up to them, but they didn't stir, just squatted there without even saying a word. It was weird. There were five soldiers, but only one of them looked at Kyogo, vacantly, a thin smile on his face. The others turned their eyes away as he approached, and looked down at their feet or to the side.

The leaves murmured faintly in the dark wood. The soldiers had neither guns nor swords. Weaponless, they sat like coolies, with only their bundles piled beside them. They were wordless in the moonlight, almost unalive. They didn't glare. They avoided his eyes. They looked cruelly tired and unhappy.

The turn-off wasn't five yards ahead. Suddenly, with the suddenness of something flashing through the sky for an instant, the dull, heavy burst of an explosion sounded from behind him. A gust of wind blew toward him from between the trees. What was it?

One of the silent soldiers spoke. "Somebody's killed himself." He stood up and looked back into the grove. The others didn't move from their crouch, and none of the soldiers lying on the ground got up.

Like an assembly of mutes suddenly given speech, they started talking. But their talk was strangely subdued.

"It's him, I bet," one of them said.

"Yeah. Him," the one next to him answered. His hand moved on the ground as though he were plucking grass or picking up pebbles.

"He was done for anyway."

The talk stopped. Kyogo had halted to listen to them, and they were staring at him now. He walked on. The road was dark, shaded by the woods.

Someone called out in a soldier's voice. "Tamura's dead. Cut off his little finger in the morning and take it with you. You were his best friend."

Kyogo walked away quickly, and as softly as he could, with the forest on either side of him. Something dark and indescribable welled up in his breast. He felt his face grow stiff.

The soldiers in the forest, lying on their blankets against their knapsacks, were either fast asleep or had lost the energy to move. They lay there in the darkness, totally unconcerned. Some of them were leaning against the tree trunks, the moonlight in their faces. Some of them lay with their backs to him, clasping large bundles. One of their companions had just killed himself with a grenade. He had been sick, of course, but still—that not one of them could summon the energy to get up and look! So far gone. Kyogo smelled decaying flesh on the warm night air. And the stench came not only from the rent body of the suicide. It seemed to come from all of them—those live bodies lying there on the ground.

Now that business had revived, Yeh was driving to Kuala Lumpur to make contact with the Chinese associations there. He told Kyogo about it.

"Would you mind taking me along?" Kyogo suggested. "I'd like to get a look at things outside."

"Certainly. Why don't you go see the Batu caves? My business will only take an hour or so. The chauffeur can take you there and show you the place in that time. The area's safe, nothing to worry about."

Yeh's automobile was a Buick he had picked up in Singapore recently. Once out of town, they started along the road through the rubber plantations where Kyogo had walked the night before. Kyogo couldn't take his eyes from the window. But of course the soldiers were gone from the grove by now.

"Mr. Yeh, would you mind stopping over there a minute?"

61

"What is it?"

"Oh, nothing, just—"

Something white hanging on the trunk of a rubber tree caught Kyogo's eye while he was still in the car. He got out alone and went over to it. It was a dirty knapsack with a scrap of paper attached to it that must have been torn from a notebook.

Kyogo turned the paper over and found "Salt" written in pencil. The single Japanese character, written large, and next to it, in a running scrawl: "Not dirty." And the bag hung heavily, as though full of salt. This must be the work of the soldiers who had been here last night. And Kyogo knew that the bag and the salt must have belonged to the soldier who had killed himself.

Human leavings covered the roots of a near-by tree. Flies buzzed around them. A couple of plantation coolies came out from among the trees. They had noticed the car.

Kyogo raised a hand and called them over. He ordered them not to touch the knapsack. Just leave it as it was. Then he asked suddenly: "Didn't you find a Japanese soldier dead in the grove?"

"Yes, over there." They answered in Malayan, turning around, pointing out the direction.

"Has he been buried?"

"No." Their faces were expressionless.

Mr. Yeh was peering from the car window. He seemed tired of waiting.

Kyogo took out some bills hurriedly and handed them to the coolies. "Bury him, please. I'll come back tomorrow to see."

Yeh had been waiting to question him. "What's going on?"

"Nothing, really. I'm sorry I kept you. Let's go on."

The coolies had the honest look of workmen. They

weren't from families like Yeh's, wealthy for generations and always increasing their store. They had come to Malaya with nothing but their labor to sell. They had no capital yet. They did faithfully the work they were given to do.

Yeh put his Malay chauffeur in the assistant's seat and took the wheel himself. He drove at various speeds to see what his new car would do.

"It rides beautifully," he said, and Kyogo could see his satisfied grin in the rear-view mirror. "It used to belong to the Japanese naval station at Seletar. It's in perfect condition."

Kyogo nodded blankly, and stared out at the rubber trees flowing past at terrific speed to the right and the left. The road was perfect for speeding. It stretched ahead in one straight line, level and narrow.

And suddenly a swarm of men straggled toward them like a black flood over the road. Yeh slowed down, and at the same time the swarm made an opening for them. Two long rows of men in khaki shirts and pants soiled to the color of earth, each carrying a vast bundle on his back, moved swiftly but endlessly past them on either side. Each whiskered, dirty, sweaty face looked vacantly inside the car and vanished to the rear. The Chinese flag on the hood sped forward between the lines, fluttering its beautiful colors liquidly, excitingly.

Kyogo became aware that he was shutting his eyes, and deliberately steadied his gaze on the soldiers outside. There was no sign of anger or resistance on any of their faces. In answer to his stare they looked up in surprise or turned away embarrassed as they drew near the car, and then passed to the rear in the same silent pose. They had changed completely, these soldiers of Japan. They were disarmed, of course, had no flags, or guns, or swords. They tried to turn their eyes away, but Kyogo fixed them with his strong stare. His eyes had the hard glitter to which they had once been trained to respond.

The disarmed Japanese troops were being concentrated in Singapore. Those who had been stationed in the cities and towns all over Malaya had disappeared from the countryside almost immediately, but the troops from Burma were still coming. The railroads weren't working, so the men came on foot, following the tracks. You saw them occasionally traveling south along the highways. They were horribly wasted by defeat and hunger and fatigue. The sick died en route, one after another, for it was a terrible trip across the mountains. Only those who had managed to store some food made it back alive, almost swimming down roads that had become mud swamps in the rains. Abandoned Army horses wandered in the jungles. When they recognized Japanese soldiers, they showed themselves, in even more wretched plight than the men, and followed the columns, yearning for human attention. But the men had no strength left, not even enough to finish off the horses that were too sick to walk. Some of them staggered on behind the troops until they fell down dead on the road. Others were left tied to trees, and their shrill whinnying followed the men for miles. The soldiers who fell sick would leave their comrades, saying nothing, hide themselves in the jungle, and use the grenade each had been given when they set out. Early in the war they had advanced, flags flying, in motorized columns, some of them; now they came back in rags, agonizing on the highways.

Kyogo had chosen to see this today. He would not let himself turn his eyes from it.

These men had parents in Japan, and wives, and children, it occurred to Kyogo suddenly. The man who had killed himself last night, too—he'd had someone back home. The order and cleanliness and other virtues of the Army he had known in his time flashed through his mind, blown in on the breeze coming through the window. But the sight of the men in front of him chased those ideas away. They were like dirt one wouldn't touch with his finger.

An unhappy business. A fearfully unhappy business. That's all one could say about it. And Japan was far away. Yeh's servant had told him there was an examination center on the way into Singapore, with white tents and gray tents and black tents. The proved war criminals were detained in the black tents, the suspects in the gray. These men were walking there now. Some of them were grocers, some white-collar workers. They had been living peaceful little lives, hadn't wanted to go to war, most of them, but lashed by duty and anxious about what the neighbors would think and say, they had marched away from home in as manly a posture as they could muster. They had all wanted peace instead of war, every one of them. Until their country called them, they had lived quietly in their own little nests, and never dreamed of parting from their wives and children.

Far behind their comrades came the wounded, walking in a cluster. Many of them on crutches, moving forward as in some sort of dance. Kyogo struggled to suppress a sob.

One of the wounded looked up at the car and yelled something, then laughed with his mouth open. He was still a young man. This time Kyogo had to shut his eyes.

When he opened them again, the road was finally empty. Only the sun shone white upon it, and the palm trees hemmed it in monotonously on either side. An endless stream of Chinese settlements edged the road. There were Indian cows and little children playing. Green fruit showed on the papaya trees.

"Salt—not dirty."

Kyogo remembered the dirty knapsack hanging on the tree. It was a gift from the soldiers he had seen to those who would follow them along that sun-baked road and reach the grove exhausted. They had been utterly indifferent to the death of their comrade, but they could feel for the suffering of those who were still alive.

Yeh drove into Selembang, the seat of the state government. Hills of bananas were piled on the floors of the market buildings. A game was going on in the hockey field and spectators hedged it around. It was a beautiful sight, like a painting—players in their varicolored shirts and shorts running about over the bright green grass. A Phœnix tree spread its thick, leafy branches in front of the field.

Yeh had urged him to see the great cave of Batu, and it was well worth the trip. It was a large stalactite cave, but light and very wide, like the hall of some great temple; it didn't feel like a cave at all.

Stone steps led up the mountainside to it, hundreds of them, in almost unbroken ascent. You climbed and rested, climbed and rested, and when you finally reached the entrance, found it entirely different from what you had expected. The whole interior spread out before your eyes at the first glance, a strange, magnificent spectacle.

The cave sloped away from the entrance toward the valley floor, but its whole width was visible at once, thousands on thousands of square feet. Through natural gaps in the roof the sunshine poured straight in, and there were bright patches on the walls where light seeped through from outside, so that the cave was a medley of shadow and brightness. Innumerable stalactites hung from the high roof, like suspended lamps, and on the hilly floor thick spikes of stone sprouted in clusters like bamboo. The roof and the walls were gray, but streaked, wherever the rain had reached, with a gorgeous moss-green, very like the green in a three-tone T'ang painting.

It was three hundred feet to the roof. As you went down into the cave and looked up, you felt how small you were inside this fairy-tale palace of stone.

There was a path to walk on, sloping up and down like a road in a park. It passed the deepest, dimmest part of the cave, where the rock was hollowed out to form a niche, and candlesticks and incense bowls stood as if for worship. There was no sign of anyone about, but a perfectly ordinary clock hung on the stone wall beside the niche. The moving hands and tick-tock of the works gave the place a weird domesticity. Kyogo went all the way into the hollow and looked around. While he was there the clock struck three—bong, bong, bong—and Kyogo smiled at the dull, spaced sounds, and listened to them echo among the innumerable stalactites and die away against the high rock ceiling.

People had scrawled their names all over the walls, as far up as hands could reach—in Chinese characters and English letters—memorials of their visit.

Among them were many Japanese names, always with the name of the person's home town written beside it. Kyogo thought of the soldiers he had passed on the way here. And of others who had left their names here and then died in the long, cruel war. Their families would never know that they had come to this great cave and written on these walls.

Kyogo's eyes stopped suddenly on a particular name: "Saeko Takano."

The smile mounted slowly to his face. She had been even here. The names around hers were sailors', probably. And all of a sudden Kyogo was able to make up his mind. He had been playing with the idea of going back to Japan. Now he knew. He was going back.

He had promised to meet Yeh at an Indian restaurant, the Taj Mahal. As he walked upstairs he noticed an Indian employee in a corner of the lobby, pounding curry nuts into powder on a stone slab with a round stone. The dry, bitter, pungent odor hovered all around.

The dining-room was set up neatly in Western style. Yeh was sitting at one of the tables reading a local newspaper to pass the time. He was the only customer.

"I'm sorry I'm late."

"Oh, it's just a few minutes."

Yeh was his usual polite and quiet self. "Beer?" he asked Kyogo, and beckoned to the waiter. "How did you like the cave?"

"Wonderful."

Yeh's pure King's English always made Kyogo feel he was looking at a man without a country. On the wall, over Yeh's smartly clipped and tended hair, a framed photograph of the Taj Mahal reflected the light.

Kyogo told Yeh he intended to go back to Japan as soon as the way was clear.

Yeh shook his head in amazement. "Japan will be awful—unbearable."

"I agree. That's why I'm going back. I don't want to return to Europe any more, Yeh."

"This is incredible. Why?"

The inside of Kyogo's mouth caught fire from the curry he was eating. He sipped some beer, then answered Yeh softly. "It was when I saw those Japanese soldiers this morning, my countrymen, miserably defeated. . . . Suddenly I felt I wanted to go back."

"Incredible. What'll you do when you get there?"

"I don't know. As a matter of fact, there's nothing

I can do. I realize that, but still— I suppose it's because I was Japanese once. . . . I just have to go back, anyway."

"You?" Yeh kept shaking his head disapprovingly.

Kyogo changed his explanation. "I have a wife and child in Japan. I haven't seen them for years."

"Oh! In that case, it's all right." Yeh was finally convinced.

On the way back, Kyogo asked Yeh to do him a favor. He had an account at a London bank, and he wanted Yeh to convert it into dollars and get them to him in Japan somehow. Yeh promised to do it.

They had to pass the soldiers again. The rear of the beaten, bedraggled column was just in front of them. Black clouds overhead foretold a squall, and the trees below had awakened into vivid green.

❀ ᘐᘐᘐ VI ᘐᘐᘐ ❀

NIGHT BIRDS

The days were springlike, but in the evenings it became bitter cold again. When the painter stepped in off the sidewalk and slammed the door behind him, his breath was white in the dark interior.

As he walked upstairs the neon sign on the wall outside dyed the back of his old overcoat in garish tones and colored his white hair under the brim of his hat.

The elevator didn't work. He had to walk up the four flights. Malaria and malnutrition had brought him near death time and again on the Burma front, and the stairs were a little too much for what was left of him.

He walked up slowly, very slowly.

On the second and third floors were only business offices. It was dark and silent there at night. Only the staircase was lit. The noise of a jazz tune descended from the cabaret on the fourth floor.

The painter stopped on the third landing. A child, one of the vagabonds of postwar Tokyo, was sitting on the stairs, his arms around his knees, looking up at him.

"Hi." He looked down at him. "You'll get another scolding. Go home right now."

The child looked away as if he hadn't heard. "You can pass," his whole posture said, "even if I am sitting here. There's space enough beside me."

The painter was fond of children, all children. But he knew the perversity of this type of child which the war had brought into being.

"What's happened to your brush and polish?"
"Stolen."

"O.K." He changed his guitar case to the other arm and took some bills out of his pocket. "You'll turn into a beggar if you waste your time. Next time I see you, you'd better be hard at work with your brush and polish. I won't let you off so easily again. Understand?"

There was no market at all for Kohei Onozaki's paintings in Tokyo, even now, three years after the war. But he had learned to play the guitar as a hobby, and that was good for odd jobs. He had got used to that sort of work in his poor days in Paris. None of the jobs he got lasted very long. He worked at one place awhile and then moved on. Now he was at the cabaret that had just opened on the fourth floor. His experience had been of some use when they were talking about how to decorate the place. All the time he had wasted in cheap Paris cafés stood him in good stead now. He might spend his days painting in an unheated room, but at night he enjoyed a little respect, if nothing else.

The child got up slowly and went downstairs to the door. It opened at that moment and someone came in, blocking the exit.

It was a woman wearing a thick white overcoat, her lips distinctly outlined in rouge. She was so made up that the child took her for a foreigner. A young man came in after her and she turned around to hear what he was saying.

"We've got to walk up. The elevator doesn't work."

"What floor?" Saeko Takano asked him.

"Fourth."

Saeko shrugged her shoulders in a very foreign gesture of surprise. "And people actually come, when they have to walk up four flights of stairs?"

"Well, they make up for it. Wait till you see the elaborate show they put on, Aunt Saeko."

The young man's voice took on a wheedling tone when he called her "Aunt Saeko." He started up the stairs, holding out his hand attentively as if worried that Saeko might trip on her high heels.

"They say this is the most successful cabaret in town. They change the show frequently, and always have the biggest stars from the Asakusa amusement district on the program. They do it very well, and people love it."

"The city's packed with dance halls and cabarets now, isn't it? You see one wherever you go."

"Yes, the competition's fierce. But in the long run only the good ones will survive. This place is terrifically expensive, but Mr. Murata, the painter, says it's more like a real Montmartre cabaret than any other place in town."

Saeko looked out at the night through the window beside the stairs. The lights from the shacks among the ashes and the ruins spread out over the ground beneath the cold stars set in the winter sky. The windowpanes rattled in the wind.

"That child we saw downstairs must have been a war orphan."

Her escort hadn't noticed her glance down at the dark, cold scene outside. "Yes," he said, "they push themselves in everywhere."

Saeko went up a whole flight of stairs, passed in front of the elevator, and started up the next flight before she answered. And she spoke with all the authority and mockery that her age allowed.

"But Toshi, dear, you push yourself in everywhere too, now, don't you? Incidentally, has everywhere included school lately?"

"Well—yes. I go when there's a lecture I want to hear. But, Aunt Saeko, isn't that an awfully old-fashioned sort of question for you?"

The noise of the band blared into their faces. It made
Toshiki lively. Even the color of his skin lightened at the
sound. He was that sort. "I'd like to check my hat. A
minute, please."

A young waiter in white came forward to him. "Your
usual waitress? Which is she?"

Toshiki was unembarrassed. "Mitchan."

He took off his hat and overcoat. His well-tailored suit
and loud, red-striped necktie were as inappropriate for
an undergraduate as the practiced manner with which
he showed Saeko to her seat.

Saeko kept her overcoat on. There didn't seem to be
any heating and she was a little surprised at Toshiki's
courage. The walls were plastered with foreign tourist
posters and cabaret ads. She wondered where they had
come from until she got a good look and saw that they
were copies. The tables were set against the walls and
the middle of the floor was left empty for dancing. The
floor was bare concrete. Two or three couples were doing
a tango. Saeko drew the collar of her overcoat together,
covering her shoulders.

Mitchan came, smiled at Toshiki, then greeted Saeko.
She looked the older woman over, discreetly, but with
feminine minuteness. The glitter of admiration came
gradually to her eyes.

"Aunt Saeko, would you like to dance?"

Saeko refused, her lips twisting with laughter. "Not at
all."

She could see the bandstand on the other side of the
room through a thick screen of tobacco smoke and
drunken conversation.

The room was darkened suddenly, and three strong
lamps glared onto the center of the floor from different
points on the ceiling. A girl leaped into the light, naked

except for strips of cloth around her breasts and thighs, and started twisting her arms and legs and hips in a new dance number. She was young and bosomy, and her face was intensely gay. She danced toward the customers, coming straight up to the tables, and the lights followed her as she moved.

"She's Helen Mizumachi," Toshiki announced. "She's making a hit right now in an Asakusa revue."

Saeko didn't have anything against Helen Mizumachi or her number, but those bare feet dancing on the concrete floor annoyed her. She felt the grating and the chill against her own skin. But Helen's legs were certainly well-shaped, even if the soles of her feet were not, and exciting even to another woman.

"The regular customers are informed when Helen's going to appear. The occasionals don't know about it."

Saeko took a cigarette from her case and lifted it gracefully to her mouth. Toshiki was too intent on Helen Mizumachi's dance to mind his manners. He failed to reach for his lighter, so Saeko, smiling to herself, took her own from the handbag on her lap.

The dance ended and the lights came on again. The musicians stepped down from the bandstand and walked over to the guest tables to play request numbers. The customers handed over their money resignedly. They couldn't refuse these private performances.

Saeko's eyes wandered over the room, studying the guests. A voice beside the table startled her.

"May I play something for you, ma'am?"

She lifted her head and her eyes rounded in astonishment, fixed on the guitarist's boyish grin and the white hair that sat on top of his head like a white beret.

"May I play something for you, ma'am?" This time he bent his beautiful white head in a playful bow.

"Mr. Onozaki, you!"

His laughter was friendly. "Yes, me. I was sure I knew you from somewhere."

"What happened to you?"

"We were beaten."

He handed his guitar to the waitress standing near by and told her to put it away for him. "It's been a long time since we last saw each other. But, pardon me—" he nodded to Toshiki—"I hope I'm not being a nuisance."

"Don't be silly," Saeko shouted. "I'm glad you came back alive anyway. But I can't get over seeing you in a place like this. When did you get back to Japan?"

"Almost immediately after the surrender. I was a noncombatant, of course, and they repatriated me on the first ship back. But that trip from Burma to Singapore, Mrs. Takano—you know, we had to walk the whole way. I remember now, I came to your house the night before I left for Burma, didn't I?"

He was still standing, to observe the proper distance between customer and employee.

"Do sit down, Mr. Onozaki."

"Ah, thanks." He drew up a chair and went on. "It has been a long time, Mrs. Takano, but I felt sure it was you the moment I saw you. You have changed a lot, though. And your Western dress made me doubtful."

"Ah, I wonder what you really thought when you saw me. You say I've changed—I suppose you said to yourself: 'What an old hag she's turned into!' "

"Ridiculous! You've grown three or four years younger. Look at me. My hair's gone dead white. Burma was terrible. You remember, Mrs. Takano? That night, you told me not to go. They said we were going to win, so I went, and we lost. It was terrible."

"You said you were going so you could see India. Did you?"

"India? Not a chance! I was too busy running away from the enemy, with nothing to eat most of the time. But I did manage to get back alive. It seems unreal to me even now, you know, that I'm still alive."

Saeko remembered the proprieties and turned to Toshiki, who was sitting there watching them and not saying a word.

"Order some beer for Mr. Onozaki, Toshi, dear."

"Yes," the painter said with his usual naïveté, "do buy me a drink. Beer is so expensive these days I can only watch other people drinking. But—" his tone changed suddenly—"I *am* painting now, Mrs. Takano."

"Really!" Saeko had forgotten that he was a painter until he made the remark.

Now that he had mentioned his painting, Onozaki became enthusiastic. His childishness burst to the surface. He blushed and then, embarrassed at his blushing, laughed. "Through all that hell of the march back from Burma, what hurt most was the thought that I might die then, after I'd finally started to paint. Absurd, isn't it? It was all I could think about, and people dropping dead all around me. They'd issued each of us a hand grenade to kill ourselves with in case we had to. I had one too. When I started raving with malaria, I realized I might want to use it, so I threw it away. I mustn't have such a thing near me. I must get back to Japan alive and paint. That's what I kept telling myself when I was shaking with fever, and when I was sick with pain. Now that I'm back I still can't paint very well, but anyway that's what I kept repeating to myself, over and over. I concentrated on it, and it saved me from shaking hands with death."

"It sounds like a nightmare—the whole story."

"So it does. A horrible experience."

It was too much to talk about. Their eyes met and they smiled at each other.

The beer came and he emptied his glass at a gulp. In Singapore he used to boast that he could drink any sailor under the table.

"Well, the war's over and it's the age of the Onozakis now, isn't it?"

"Age of the Onozakis?"

"Yes, of art, of literature—"

"Drivel!" He opened his eyes wide and waved his hands. "A cultural nation? I despise people who go around mouthing that claptrap. Only politicians are irresponsible enough to talk that way. Anyway, the great master Kohei Onozaki can't feed himself by his painting. He isn't even recognized."

He saw the other musicians going back to the bandstand, and stood up with a little grunt. "Work. Work. Pardon me. If you're staying, I'll come back and talk to you again later."

And the white-haired painter turned his broad back to them and walked away. He joined the other players on the stand and picked up his guitar. The lamplight glared on his white suit. He didn't look gay at all, but very serious.

"An old acquaintance, Aunt Saeko?"

Saeko looked around at Toshiki's slender, prettyish face. He was laughing.

"But why does he say such things when he's just a band player?"

"What things?"

"Calling himself a painter! And why did he have to bring up the war—in a place like this?"

Saeko protested. "He's a good man, an earnest man. And he never was a soldier, really."

"I know, Aunt Saeko, but I hate people who insist on talking about the war at this late date."

Saeko realized suddenly that there was in this light-skinned student something of the demi-monde habitué one saw in the Kabuki plays about the old gay quarters. And the idea made her decide to do what she had been thinking of doing. She opened her pocketbook and took out a piece of paper and a lipstick to write with.

"This is clumsy," she said under her breath. "Toshi dear, lend me your fountain pen."

"What's up?"

"It's a secret."

Her left hand hooded the paper from Toshiki's eyes as her right raced down the page. "I'm sending a car for you later," she wrote. "Please come. I'm giving a party in your honor." And then she added a line in running characters: "I promise to get rid of my cool young man beforehand."

Laughing to herself, she folded the note in front of Toshiki's eyes and held it in her hand. "Let's go, Toshi. Get the bill."

"So early? There's more entertainment."

"That's all right. I've got the general idea already. I'll talk to you outside."

She was looking straight at the band. Toshiki stood up immediately. He looked unhappy about it, but did as he was told. When the bill was ready, Saeko paid as a matter of course, counting out the hundred-yen notes from her handbag.

She nodded a proper little farewell to the waitress and said: "I'll be right back."

Then she walked straight across the dance floor, avoiding the couples on it, to where Onozaki was sitting on the bandstand, playing his guitar. Her graceful, arrogant figure caught the eyes of everyone in the room, but Saeko was totally unconcerned. She handed her note to Onozaki mechanically and walked back to join Toshiki.

"All right. Let's go."

The streets had grown darker, so that the thin radiance of the scattered stars seemed brighter than when they had gone in.

Toshiki didn't wait for Saeko to start the conversation. "Are you going to meet that fellow somewhere, Aunt Saeko?"

"Yes, I am." The answer was clipped and clear. "I'm going to ask him about that cabaret, for one thing. I'd like to know all about it."

"Maybe you'd better let me listen in on that."

Saeko parried lightly. "I'd better not, I think."

"But Aunt—" His voice was gentle as a woman's, but swept down on Saeko like a bird of prey and fixed its talons in her. "If I listen in, I'll be able to judge whether or not he's telling the truth. I'm sure of that."

"It doesn't matter that much to me. I've got a pretty good idea already of what I want to know. There's a limit to that sort of thing, and these cabarets have just about reached it."

"You think so?"

"Looking at the customers there convinced me. Drinking and dancing like mad. There's something very unhealthy about it. The atmosphere is deceiving if you don't have any experience in these things. It was so obvious there, though, anyone could see it. Their guests are all postwar millionaires, but they haven't got any steady custom. They couldn't, running the place the way they do. It's a one-visit place, one high-stake hand between owner and customer. That's why they need dancing in the nude. And the cost of it keeps customers away. The best thing to do with that sort of place is to make a name for it as quickly as you can and then sell it. It's worthless once the novelty's worn off. You're not going to last long if you have to bring in new customers every day. If I were running a cabaret, I'd do it very differently. I'd run it so that the same customers would have to keep on coming back as long as their money lasted."

"Are you going to open one, Aunt Saeko?"

"I'm thinking of it, but it's a tough proposition. It's not my cue yet. I'll start when the others give up. Well, it's been a pleasant evening. Thanks."

But Toshiki didn't say good-night. He went on walking beside her. "Aunt, I understand there's some cocaine for sale."

"That's dangerous stuff, Toshiki. You have to be more careful with it than with the other things." Plainly, his question hadn't upset her. "But, if you're interested, I'll find out about it and let you know next time we meet. Which way are you going? Ginza?"

"I haven't decided. I thought I'd be with you."

The car that Saeko had sent for Onozaki drove across the Ginza into the Tsukiji entertainment district, then slowed down and drew up next to a thick concrete wall.

"We'll stop here. There might be trouble if we parked in front of the gate."

"Thanks."

Onozaki stepped out into total darkness. But he could tell that the building was a large teahouse or restaurant. The gate was shut, but the wooden door at the side opened easily when he pushed it. A stone pavement ran forward to a lamplit entrance. He walked in and smelled plum blossoms. White-flowered branches swept over a stone lantern. The night had turned piercing cold.

He stepped onto the pavement of the wide entrance-way and called out to announce himself.

"The others are waiting for you," a maid answered.

He sat down on the low bench of beautifully polished cypress to take off his shoes. His soles were cracked and he was ashamed.

"It's a cold night."

"Yes, indeed," the maid answered. "It turned chilly all of a sudden, didn't it?"

She was standing at the head of the front corridor. She bowed and showed him up the stairs. It was a large building, magnificently constructed of fine old timber, and had come unscathed through the bombings and the fires.

"This is the room." She slid the panel doors open and pointed inside.

"Ah, he's arrived," Saeko's voice came from the next room. The painter took off his coat before going in, and a young geisha, her hair done up in traditional style, came out to greet him.

The lights were blinding for a moment in the salon beyond the panel door. Saeko was waiting for him there with four more geisha, some old, some young. They sat up formally as he came in.

"How beautiful!" Onozaki exclaimed.

"I thought you'd like them. I got them together for your sake."

The oldest geisha bowed forward from her knees, her hands to the floor, and spoke with mock surprise. "But the gentleman came in the back door!"

"As though he were coming to his love. How nice!" Saeko answered as she waved Onozaki to the seat of honor. "But do say 'rear entrance,' at least. 'Back door' sounds a trifle—"

"Contemporary. Nowadays, for lover and patron alike, it's always the back door."

The painter sat down before the alcove post between

the flaming brazier and an arm-rest. His eyes were still
blinking in the light as he looked around at the women.

"Extraordinary!" The word came loud and heavy. "Japan is still Japan. This could happen only here."

"But I thought it was India you loved." Saeko was
gay. She laughed, shaking the overcoat that hung around
her shoulders. "I've changed to Western clothes since
I came back to Japan. That's why I had these ladies come
in traditional dress. I thought you'd like it."

"I didn't realize there were any geisha left in the ashes
of Tokyo."

"A few, barely surviving." The old geisha grinned.
"But this is the end. We're dying out now, and there's
nothing to be done about it. The wind's changed a little
lately, to be sure, and the mighty ones are graciously
preserving us for the use of foreign visitors. Like the
puppet theater and other ancient arts. And when the
foreign visitors have been entertained, we'll be shipped
off to the museum, I suppose. Well, we're still here, at
least, but who's to carry on when we're not? The young
girls prefer the cabarets and dance halls. It's so much
easier for them."

"And also they're living in an entirely different world."

"A world turned upside down, Mrs. Takano."

"Nevertheless, there'll always be geisha, I'm sure of
that."

"What about this new regulation that's coming out?
The Labor Standards Law, they call it."

"My, you're a scholar!"

The old woman slapped her chest and looked aside.
"It was easier to breathe in the shade. We were brought
up that way, for things were different then. Now we've
been dragged out into the full glare of day all at once
and everything's become horribly awkward. But it's the
times we live in. People have certainly become bold, I

must say, and use foreign words to excuse their boldness. 'Avec' dancing, 'kiss,' 'erotic!' 'Romance-seats' in
movie theaters! They certainly say what they mean, but
I get a headache every time I hear one of them. And
one hears so many. Pretty soon you won't be able to
get around in Japan if you talk Japanese."

"Oh, I don't think so," Saeko said. "But please take
something to drink. Mr. Onozaki came late, so we've got
to get him drunk quickly. Would you pretty young
ladies over there be kind enough to serve him?"

"What beautiful white hair you have, sir," one of the
geisha said to Onozaki.

"The war did that. Actually, I'm still a young man."

"Your life lies before you. You can accomplish what
you will."

"I mean to! I've gone to some trouble to stay alive."

"Mr. Onozaki," Saeko interrupted, "it just occurred
to me, there's something I want to ask you about."

"What is it?"

"A person named Kyogo Moriya. He was in the Navy
once, but that was a long, long time ago. I was thinking,
he must have been on the ship you came back on. Do
you remember him?"

"Moriya?"

"Your ship carried only non-combatants, didn't it? Of
course, he might have been left for later. But, you see,
this man had been living with the Chinese and the
M.P.'s arrested him on suspicion of being a spy. He
must have been released as soon as the war ended, and
as he's Japanese, I was thinking he must have been repatriated on the first ship, like you." Saeko drew a long
breath and went on. "Isn't there any way of finding out,
someone we could ask?"

As Saeko finished her sentence, the panel door slid
open and they saw the maid on her knees just beyond

the doorway. She bowed forward, touching her hands to the matting, and announced a new arrival. "Madam's nephew has just come and wishes to see madam. Shall I show him in?"

"My nephew!" Saeko looked at the maid. "Who is it? Did he give his name?"

"Toshiki, he said."

"Oh—" Saeko made a face. "Loathsome fellow. He must have called me 'aunt.' Did you tell him I was here?"

"Shall I send him away?"

"It doesn't matter. Show him in."

Saeko turned to Onozaki and explained. "It's the young man you met earlier this evening. He comes from a good family, and goes to college and all that, but he's as mild-mannered as a woman. There's something strange about the young people nowadays. He's awfully clever, though—not like a student at all. More like— what shall I say? A businessman, perhaps, but a real businessman wouldn't stand a chance against him. He can get anything for you, even when there isn't any. He's convenient, all right, but still—"

But Toshiki himself was just stepping into the room beyond the panel door. "Aunt, I hope I'm not putting you out."

"But you are. This is no place for students."

Saeko's smile was a trifle chilly, but Toshiki came in, unperturbed. His narrow face was totally placid. "I was sure you'd be here. I thought of it on the way home."

"Well, look at the pretty women and go away again, please." Saeko introduced him to the painter again. "Mr. Toshiki Okamura, the young man I was just telling you about. He's no relative of mine, but insists on calling me his aunt, God knows why."

"But Aunt Saeko—" Toshiki maintained his composure—"it's because you're so much older than I am."

A quiver of annoyance passed along Saeko's shoulders, but she smiled and went back to her conversation with the painter. "If you have no ideas on that matter I was talking about, I do know that this man has a family here in Japan. I wonder whether we could locate them. There is no Navy Ministry any more, and anyway he's been out of the Navy for years. How *do* I go about finding him? I've been thinking and thinking."

It had grown warmer in the room, and Saeko let her overcoat fall from her shoulders. It slipped off smoothly, revealing the lovely lines of her body. Onozaki thought of the skin sliding from a banana when you peel it. It was an exciting motion, even to his painter's eyes. A young geisha leaned forward and started folding the coat.

"Kyogo Moriya, you say." Onozaki was quite drunk by now, and Toshiki was sitting there cold sober. He hadn't liked this glib young man much to begin with. "Moriya . . . But why are you so eager to find him?" Then he burst out laughing, a little wildly. "I tell you what, Mrs. Takano. Give Toshiki here the job of finding him. He's your man for a search."

Toshiki seemed to sense no irony in Onozaki's recommendation. He spoke up quickly, glad of the opportunity. "What is it, Aunt Saeko?"

Saeko's eyes twinkled, but she didn't answer.

"What is it you're looking for?" Toshiki persisted.

"A man, not Coty powder."

"What man?"

"Twenty questions, eh?"

"I'll find him, if you tell me to." Toshiki's quick ears had picked up everything that had been said. "Kyogo Moriya, you said. An ex-Navy man. In that case, he must be listed in the Naval School register or as a member of the Navy Club. It's a simple problem of deduction. If you know where his family comes from, I can send an inquiry to the local government office to see if they have anything in the records. There are ever so many ways. There must be classmates who didn't die in the war. I could ask them too."

"But it isn't like the old days when everything was organized," Onozaki said. "No one's where he should be, and even the closest friends don't know what's become of each other." The painter was serious again. "The whole country's smashed up, completely. Just like the United Fleet. Everybody's moving around, hunting for a place to settle. Lots of people have even been burned out of their homes."

"That makes it all the easier to find things out, in my opinion. Just because things are topsy-turvy all of a sudden, everybody's sure to be talking about what his old friends are doing. It's easier to get information than it used to be. My cousin was in the Navy too."

Saeko broke in. "Rear-Admiral Toshisada Ushigi was a classmate of Moriya's. He's still alive, they say."

"You see, look at that!" A smile of self-satisfaction spread over Toshiki's white face. All the geisha were looking at him. "There are no mysteries. The world looks complicated, but it's really simple. I only have to trace a line from my cousin to Ushigi in order to find Moriya. You'll see."

Onozaki would gladly have seen the last of Toshiki, but they had to go in the same direction. After their good-nights to Saeko as she was driven off in her car, they walked to the station together.

The platform was still crowded despite the hour. Onozaki was very drunk, but pulled himself together as soon as he found people around him. It was a habit from his Paris days. Drunks lay sprawled face down on the benches and crouched at the foot of the posts, as if

they had tried to stand up against them but had col-
lapsed with the effort. The painter looked at them with
sympathy, but felt something dark and anxious in his
chest underneath his old overcoat. "Nobody gives a
damn any more," he thought.

Certainly nobody on the platform looked happy at
this hour of night—not even the sober ones. Many were
hatless and coatless in the cold wind. They didn't look
like people who had been out late enjoying themselves.
Vagabond children played in the waiting-room because
they had no place to go.

Toshiki spoke up beside him. "Tell me, old man, do
you know whether Mrs. Takano has bought that geisha
place?"

"No, I don't." Onozaki was irritated by the question
and lost control. He was almost shouting. "I don't
know about such things."

Toshiki didn't understand why Onozaki was annoyed.
He went on with the same impenetrable calm: "If I
know Aunt Saeko, she has something up her sleeve."

Onozaki realized that Toshiki was being childish. That
was all that stopped him from letting his anger explode
and yelling at Toshiki again. He was a night-club musi-
cian, playing for guests who were rather unpleasant
people but could throw hundred-yen notes around like
scraps of paper. And he was fifty years old. But he
dreamed of painting great pictures eventually, and that
dream made his night-time job endurable. Saeko Takano
seemed a stranger to him suddenly, a person from another world. He had been fond of her in Singapore, but
that was because she had been another civilian where
there were only soldiers and sailors to talk to.

"She devoured the Imperial Navy, that woman." His
thoughts burst out. "I don't know what she's planning

to gobble up now, but she's a monster, a soft-spoken, pretty-faced monster."

Toshiki's eyes showed no surprise as they surveyed the painter. And he spoke in his usual tone. "You're a bit old-fashioned too, aren't you, old man?"

"Old-fashioned?" But it wasn't that that broke Onozaki's self-control. He was enraged. "Stop calling me 'old man.' You don't know me that well. Don't do it again, ever."

Toshiki was taken aback, but his *sang-froid* was unruffled. Not that he felt he should forgive Onozaki because he was drunk. He had weighed the facts objectively and decided that he had nothing to gain by quarreling with him. The painter was much older than he was, but also much bigger.

"Why don't you offer your services to Aunt Saeko? I'm sure she'd help you."

"No, thanks." Onozaki's voice was unyielding. "I don't mind being poor." That ended their conversation.

The train came, and they got on and sat down next to each other. Toshiki closed his eyes and pretended to fall asleep. There was a group of young people at the end of the car, coming from a dance hall. One of the girls was singing a jazz number in a clear voice, and the others joined in for the refrain. One of the boys was dancing to the song, his arms around an imaginary partner. Onozaki glared at them for a while. Then his eyes, still glittering with the anger he had felt for their merry-making, shifted to the other passengers, over bodies wasted with overwork and hunger, and faces shut in sleep, and vacant, staring eyes. Not only their faces looked fatigued. Their very clothes were tired.

Onozaki started the conversation this time. "Listen! Do you know what I'm going to do? I'm going to put

the misery of men on canvas. I'm going to paint the tired
people and the pain they have in living."

Toshiki opened his eyes. Onozaki's face had changed.
There was a deep gentleness about it now.

"Of course, my paintings aren't pretty; they're not
for the elegant drawing-rooms of the rich. They won't
sell. I knew that before I started."

Toshiki couldn't think of anything to say to that.

"I've been in the South and seen the wretchedness of
the natives there. And the sufferings of our soldiers, I've
seen that too, every bit of it. I can't paint that yet, remembering hurts too much, but I will in time, I'll paint
my heart out, getting it down for everyone to see. Then
there are the war orphans. And the *lumpen* of Tokyo.
And the dischargees. And long ago I saw how people
lived in the slums of Paris. I don't think anyone else has
seen so much of human misery all over the world as I
have. That's why I paint. Some of my paintings will
capture such pain as only I could put on canvas. I'm
sure of that. The people in this car, I'm going to paint
them too. My painting isn't good yet, but it will be, and
when it is, I'm going to paint the filth of the world, paint
it out completely, and make people see it. That's what
I'm going to do."

Just as he finished, his eyes found a beautiful face
among the passengers. A gentleman in a well-tailored
overcoat, sitting motionless as though posing for a
sketch, his eyes nailed in a rigid stare.

❀ ᘛᘚ VII ᘛᘚ ❀

REUNION

Onozaki tried not to stare at the man with the beautiful face, but after a momentary glance at the other passengers his eyes turned back of their own accord to his profile, which he examined with the deep, steady look of a painter. He had seen that face somewhere before, Onozaki felt—the mask of severity and, underneath, the strange loneliness it failed to hide. He had seen that face, certainly, but he couldn't remember where or when. Or maybe he was confusing him with someone he had seen in Paris. The neat, stylish clothes, so conspicuous in the railway car, might account for the mistake. The quiet grayish tones of the suit and overcoat were very much in the French taste. The French never dressed themselves in the bright colors with which Americans like to dazzle their beholders. They liked dark, tranquil tones, and didn't worry about their clothes being old-fashioned.

The man was dressed that way, and the hat that shaded his face was a dark-brown Borsolino with a faded ribbon. But the quality of his clothing was plainly the best. The middle-aged naval officer sitting next to him made a perfect contrast in his unmended, shabby-colored overcoat.

Onozaki looked at the man's face and knew that he wanted to paint it. The strength and tautness there attracted him. The nose was perfect, and the eyes shone in a strong, unwavering stare. But the lines that formed the face were gentle. The strength came from within.

Onozaki thought of the four guardian gods in the ordination hall of the Great Eastern Temple at Nara. Gracious forms, but they gave an impression of power, a power the sculptor had driven inside the statues. They were very different from the guardians of the Kamakura period, whose rage was expressed in strong external lines, or statues like the famous Unkei, rigid with bone and sinew in powerful relief. These were softly, gently strong.

The train pulled to a stop. It was Shinjuku, Onozaki's station. He came to himself suddenly, stood up, and was at the door before he remembered Toshiki. He turned to shout a good-by over his shoulder, and stepped down onto the platform. The automatic door rumbled shut behind him. The train started forward again.

Toshiki was going on to Nakano. He relaxed now that he was alone, and thought of Onozaki with contempt. A strange old bird, and such crazy ideas. He should know better at his age. But he was just a cabaret guitarist. Whatever painting he did, he did with his mouth. Toshiki had no doubt of that.

Kyogo Moriya sat immobile, his arms folded before him, in exactly the posture the painter had observed. And his eyes never moved from the face of a young man sitting obliquely in front of him. Surely this was a former Army officer. Everything about him bespoke the fact. The uniform with the buttons changed, the Army briefcase under his arm, the boots he was wearing. He was only twenty-six or twenty-seven, but the fleshy face was blatantly arrogant. Its owner cared only for himself, that was plain, and had no particle of understanding for others.

This young, expressionless, unfeeling face had pursued Kyogo even in his dreams. The young man had got on the train at Ricefield Bridge and sat down opposite

him, and as soon as Kyogo saw that face he had begun
to stare as if to make sure that it was real.

Their eyes had met; the young man had realized that
Kyogo was staring at him and had tried to stare back
challengingly, but only for a moment. Then he had
lost his courage and looked aside to escape Kyogo's eyes.
He was uneasy. He didn't know what to do with his
hands. Kyogo could see that his adversary hadn't forgotten either. He could tell by that first searching glance,
and then by the evasion of his eyes. He had looked more
childish when they had met in Malacca. There was a
touch of slyness in the face now. Life and people had
made their mark. But this was the man. Even the mole
was there.

This was the man who had interrogated him at the
M.P. Headquarters, who had posted relays of guards
around him to keep him standing at attention for
twenty-four hours at a stretch without closing his eyes,
and had kept on asking him the same questions over and
over again, deliberately, to wear him out, and prodded
him with his stick whenever he felt like it, and beaten
him. This was the man who had tortured him until he
fainted, then tortured him again, and again. When Kyogo had denied that he had anything to confess, this
man had only called him a traitor and continued to
question him mercilessly.

And there was one thing that made Kyogo grind his
teeth whenever he remembered it. The pain had become
unbearable once and he had pleaded: "I'm old enough
to be your father." But that had only made the M.P.
angrier. The memory came to Kyogo now, and his
whole body felt afire inside his overcoat. This was the
man!

He had wanted to forget this man, and here he was
suddenly, in front of his eyes. Right here in Japan, on this

urban railway, in this car, pretending not to recognize him. Looking aside as though he didn't care, displaying the mole beneath his ear. Kyogo saw those stout military boots; he saw the khaki-colored uniform; and at the sight of them his anger burst uncontrollably into flame.

Of course the man was only a child to Kyogo, a child with an unspeakably sullen face, looking sideways as though he had forgotten everything that had happened. A proud, blank face. As though he was deliberately reminding Kyogo of his cruelty to unhappy people in the past, of how he had looked as he trapped them with his questions. It wasn't the face of a man. It was like a lump of flesh that could feel no pain. Kyogo had resolved not to take his eyes off him. Hence the intense stare and unmoving posture that had interested Onozaki. The young man was looking at the students, who were still singing jazz songs and fooling around. But he realized soon that Kyogo was still staring at him, so he shut his eyes and pretended to be asleep.

His face was uncannily childish with his eyes closed. When they reached East Nakano he opened his eyes as if startled by the sound of the door opening, stood up, and walked out heavily. Kyogo got up too and followed him. He turned back once and looked at Kyogo, then walked past the ticket booth and out of the station. They went on along the road, which ran through a group of shacks at first and then through ruins left by the fires. The crowd of passengers that had poured out of the station with them was splitting up and vanishing in different directions farther and farther behind them as they walked ahead. When Kyogo caught up with the young man, the late moon was just rising over the black hill beyond the charred expanse.

He walked beside him and looked him in the face. "Hey, you! You haven't forgotten me?"

The other straightened the briefcase under his arm and turned to look at Kyogo, but went on walking. "Who are you, sir?"

"You don't remember?" Kyogo smiled. "All right, then, I'll make you remember."

"What's this?" The other's voice rose. "Aren't you being a little impolite, taking me unawares like this?"

"That's right, completely mannerless. There's more than one way to skin a cat." Kyogo's tone was crisp and definite. "If you're living with your parents, let's go to your home and talk in front of them. Or if you don't want it that way, let's find a place among these ruins where we won't be disturbed and talk it out there. Take your choice, which do you prefer?"

Kyogo spoke with an insistent strength of will that finally left his opponent shaken. But his own face remained perfectly composed. That was clear even in the darkness.

The young man tried intimidation. He bellowed in his soldier's tone: "You mean you want to fight?"

"That's right."

"I don't want to fight an old man like you."

"Thanks, but you need feel no compunction. I may look oldish to you, but I've gone all over the world with no country to protect me. A man in that position has only his own strength to rely on against danger. I've trained myself accordingly, and I'm still alive. So you can fight me without troubling your conscience. Or would you rather take me to your parents?"

"I only have my mother." There was an appeal in the loudness. His morale was breaking. "My father's dead."

Kyogo's voice was quiet. "I see; then let's settle it between us."

"Haven't you made a mistake?" the former M.P. asked.

Kyogo stood still. "Trying to get out of it, you coward? Let's hear no more of that. To tell you the truth, though, I was surprised myself—that you should be the first person I met on my return to Japan! The person I least wanted to see.

"I'm tough myself," Kyogo continued, "I've been abroad for a long time and lived on meat. That may have something to do with it. But I think it's because I've been alone so much among foreigners. But still, I'm not like you, not sly and cruel. Above all, I don't rely on others for my strength. I don't turn into a weakling and a coward when I'm not sitting in a position of authority. What I've decided I must do, I do by my own self. I know you were an M.P. and had to question me. But that doesn't excuse you. I couldn't fight back, and you tortured me for no reason but your own sadistic pleasure."

"It was war. I didn't like doing those things—I was under government orders. Everything I did—"

"That's not so. You went beyond your orders, didn't you? That part of the responsibility is yours. You must bear the consequences."

"I was wrong."

"Yes, you certainly were. As you admit it, assume your responsibility like a man. I'm not telling you not to resist. I warn you that you'd better. . . . What about this spot? There's nobody around."

The other didn't answer.

"I was in the service myself once, and I hate to see soldiers turn into whimpering, groveling cowards as soon as they lose their swords and epaulets. Fight like a man."

The other held himself rigid as a stick.

"Come on, why don't you?"

"I won't resist."

"Because you think you can't win? Somebody's got to smash in that thick, unfeeling face of yours so you can begin to understand the pain that others feel." Kyogo was speaking slowly, emphasizing every word. "You've got to learn what pain is, bodily pain that makes men shriek out against their will, and cry and whine like animals. Maybe then you'll see it isn't nice. Maybe then you'll understand you must never treat another human being the way you treated me. I'm an old man, but we're going to fight on equal terms and I'm going to pound that lesson into you. Here's a clear spot. It'll do."

He grabbed the young man's arm in a vise-like grip and dragged him into the clearing. "If you're afraid to fight because I used to be an officer, you're even more contemptible than I thought. It's just man to man. Act like one!"

"Let's go to the police and talk it over there."

Kyogo was unbuttoning his overcoat. "So young and so helpless when you have nothing to lean on but yourself? You're the kind that has no qualm about treating other men like animals once you get a little authority."

The wind was cold, but Kyogo went on undressing. He took off his jacket and started loosening his necktie. The other could see every slow, deliberate movement of his hands in the moonlight.

Suddenly he knelt down and bowed forward, his hands to the ground. "I have done wrong, forgive me." And he touched his forehead to the earth.

Kyogo looked down at him. "Stop that, it's disgusting. Like a ham actor in a country play. I hate melodrama. . . . These lukewarm compromises before things go too far may be very Japanese, but I don't like them. When I've decided to do something, I've got to do it all the way. If I don't, I have a bad taste in my mouth and can't sleep. You've done me an injury. Stop that vile play-acting and stand up."

A brick or stone cut through the wind and grazed Kyogo's ear. He grunted as he dodged it, and at almost the same moment sprang on his opponent, who had stood up and was turning around to run away. Kyogo's first blow landed on his chin and laid him out full length on the ground.

"That's not all," Kyogo said. "I'm waiting for you, so get up when you feel better. Forgive me if I repeat myself, but I have no mercy. There's all the time in the world, so I think we'll fight this out to the bitter end."

He took out a cigarette and put it in his mouth. He lit it, cupping the flame of the lighter with his palm against the chill wind. He waited, stiff and upright. The other should have been able to stand by now, but he stayed where he was. Kyogo relaxed and enjoyed his cigarette. The tobacco smoke trailed away as he exhaled in the brightness of the moon.

"Hey," he called. His eyes were steady on his fallen enemy, but his easier tone indicated his readiness for the truce. "You found out about me from a letter someone sent you, didn't you? Hm? And the letter was in Japanese, in a woman's writing, wasn't it?"

There was no answer yet.

"I know all about it." Kyogo's voice was very calm.

❀ ᛒᛒᛒ VIII ᛒᛒᛒ ❀

CHERRY BLOSSOM TIME

As the train pulled out of Ofune station, Toshiki closed the new issue of the *World* that he'd been looking at, rolled it up, and held it in his hand. He certainly had no desire to read the articles in this very intellectual magazine and he wouldn't understand them if he did. But he clung to a vague infatuation with scholarly and difficult writings, and always had a book about his person. Its function was purely ornamental, like those impractical handbags women sometimes carry. For Toshiki had pushed his studies into the background of his life, where they served as décor for the very realistic outlook he had formulated so minutely. The postwar world, he had convinced himself, must be measured by practical standards. Tuition and living expenses had skyrocketed in the inflation, and even serious students were being forced out into the streets to get odd jobs to support themselves. Toshiki was confident that he could achieve the same effect, much more efficiently, by relying on his cleverness, of which he was not a little proud. And that cleverness would gain him entree to the world of affairs, he believed, on much better terms than serious study, provided that he managed to pass his exams and win the status a degree confers. Toshiki was a half-finished man of the world, and his schooling was little more than a formality. He didn't think life a vale of tears, as young men his age so frequently do, or grope for God or ideals or noble aspirations in its chaos. Toshiki was sure that he could take care of himself, and that was enough to let him live without unhappiness.

Outside the window, the scenery was gentle and spring-like, even this early in the year, under a dull, clouded sky. Hills rushed toward the train. Red and white flowers still covered the plum trees in the farm gardens, but they were past their prime. A long row of quiet villas, hedged with shrubs, gave way suddenly to the bright blossoming of cherry trees that swam past one after another and seemed to brush against the windows.

"It *is* warm, isn't it? The cherries are in bloom already."

The men who stood in front of Toshiki were talking, hanging on to the straps over their heads as they bent down to look out the low windows.

"They came out suddenly enough."

"Yes, it must have been the rain last night that did it."

The train slowed down, and the North Kamakura station came into sight.

Toshiki got up and walked to the door. He looked up again at the spreading, flowered branches of the cherry trees as he stepped out. Only a few people got off with him. They waited for the train to start again and pull out of the station, then crossed the tracks and poured out the exit. They disappeared almost immediately. For the giant cedars in front of the Temple of Perfect Awakening swept down overhead to cut off the sunlight and enfold them in deep shadow.

At the station Toshiki asked for the nearest police booth. It was right out front, they told him.

"Mr. Ushigi? That Navy fellow?" The middle-aged policeman came out of the booth and told Toshiki how to get there, pointing out the direction.

A farmwife from the neighborhood passed by, pushing a wheelbarrow, and called out in greeting to the policeman. "The flowers are beautiful, aren't they?"

"Yes, indeed, the weather's wonderful. I get sleepy, though, in all this sunshine."

A kite sang somewhere. Inside the booth, the clock ticked out the seconds.

"Admiral Ushigi is still living here. He hasn't been able to get a place in the country." His expression, as he looked at Toshiki, was rather strange. "I'm sure he's in."

Toshiki walked away with a sense of perfect satisfaction. He had been able to find out where Ushigi lived without any effort. The house was in the Kamakura Hills, but he hadn't known whether or not Ushigi was living there now.

He crossed the tracks again and walked past the Temple of Perfect Awakening toward the city. Pedestrians and oxcarts were passing over a crossing in the distance. The track ran straight ahead, lined with trees. The hills were just behind it, edged by a narrow plain covered with houses. These were private homes, each with its hedge or simple bamboo fence around it and a little flower or vegetable garden inside and the mountain cliffs behind it. The golden balls and plum trees and camellias were in bloom and the earth smelled fresh after the rain. A pleasant change for a man from Tokyo.

But Toshiki was hardly aware of it. His head was full of Saeko. For Toshiki wanted his "aunt" to fall in love with him. She was richer than Croesus, and her wealth would be very useful to him in his career. But it wasn't only that. He liked her. She was entirely different from the innumerable young women he knew. There was her physical beauty, with its perfect symmetry. Then, she had none of that silly, sultry crudeness the girls had taken to since the war. There was nothing superfluous about her. Her flawless polish made his heart dance when he thought of her, even at a distance. And her age only meant that she had reached the summit of a woman's beauty. Nevertheless, Toshiki would make no advances to an older woman. He waited passively for Saeko to give her love to him. The truth was that she treated him rather coldly at times, but that only made her more attractive to him.

He turned off into a lane, as the policeman had directed, and followed its complex, hedge-lined windings until he caught sight of a new sign with the single name "Ushigi" written on it. He stopped in front of the old wooden gate and looked over the shrubs at the little house roofed with crude zinc sheeting. There was a vegetable garden inside the gate, and behind that a latticed door served as entrance to the house.

Toshiki walked toward the house and saw a tall, bald man standing in the passageway beyond the entrance and looking at him.

He had no jacket on, only a lined under-robe of cheap silk. He had been sitting cross-legged on the back porch, but had gotten up to see who was there when he heard the gate opening. Toshisada Ushigi couldn't remember ever having seen this young man before.

"Is this the residence of His Excellency Admiral Ushigi?"

"I'm Ushigi," Toshisada answered in his straightforward way, then smiled. "But excellencies and admirals don't exist in Japan any longer. Better watch your words."

They were talking across a bamboo fence. Ushigi made no motion toward the entrance, but stood in the position he had taken when disturbed. His old, gentle face had nothing of the sailor in it, but he was of another generation and Toshiki foresaw no pleasure in their conversation.

"There's a little matter I've come to ask you about. Are you acquainted with a certain Kyogo Moriya? He was a classmate of yours."

"I know him. He's coming here today. Sent me a telegram to say so. I've been waiting for him."

This information took Toshiki by surprise. "He's back
in Japan?"

"Apparently. His telegram says he's coming here. If
you have some business with Moriya, you can wait for
him. It's about time for him to be here."

"No, thanks." Toshiki was flustered. "I'm just making inquiries for someone else. My seeing him wouldn't
do any good. This person asked me to come here and
find out whether Moriya was back in Japan, and if
so, where he was living. That's all I know about the matter."

"I haven't seen him yet myself. I didn't even know
he had returned to Japan until I saw that telegram yesterday." Ushigi spoke quietly, gazing out at the vegetable garden. A sudden silence punctuated his last sentence before he went on. "To tell the truth, I don't
want any visitors. But he didn't wait for an invitation,
just sent his telegram to announce himself, and here I
am waiting for him. Haven't even been able to go out
today. If you have a message for him, write it on one
of your cards and leave it here. I'll give it to him."

Toshiki felt the abrupt change of tone, but didn't understand it. The invitation to wait for Moriya, and then
the suggestion that he leave a card and go.

Ushigi stood stiff and silent. Toshiki's eyes caught a
bottle behind an open panel of the paper-screen wall.
It was a half-gallon jug, wrapped in a cloth so that he
couldn't tell whether it was full or empty, and all ready
to be picked up and carried outside. There was nothing
else to be seen in the room, and the spring afternoon
sunshine poured unhindered into the empty house.

"This is my name, sir." Toshiki handed the Admiral
a card. "I should be very grateful if you'd have Mr.

Moriya send me his address. Or, if you like, I'll call again."

"That won't be necessary. Moriya will probably let you know."

Saeko had told Toshiki not to mention her name in talking with Ushigi, so the news of Moriya's arrival shortened his stay.

Outside the gate, he turned back to look at the red rust of the zinc-sheeted roof again. "So that's how a sunken admiral lives." The thought passed through his conceited young brain and changed into a sense of his own superiority. Toshiki had all the cruelty of his unripe youth.

An idea struck him suddenly, and he turned around, walked back to Ushigi's gate, opened it, and went inside.

Ushigi had sat down on the wooden block before the door, bathed in the sunlight. His eyes were still fixed on the vegetable garden. He looked up at the intruder suspiciously.

"Pardon me." There was a note of inquiry in Toshiki's peculiarly tranquil tone. "Are you by any chance interested in renting one of the rooms in your house to a student?"

Ushigi laughed, once he had recovered from his bewilderment, and looked into Toshiki's young face. "No, I'm not."

"If you should change your mind, would you be kind enough to let me know? It's rather difficult now, you know. There just aren't any rooms to study in."

Ushigi seemed to take that at its face value. "Indeed? Is that how things are?" His eyes sank a little. "Yes, I suppose that's true, with all those houses destroyed in the fires. It's too bad. If I ever do want to let a room, I'll let you know. I've been thinking of moving to the country myself."

"If you do, I'd be awfully grateful to be informed. Here, let me leave another card with you."

"No, that's all right. I don't need it. I'll copy the address from the one you left for Moriya." And his look at Toshiki had all the depth and gentleness of an old man's eyes. "Pardon me, but how old are you?"

"Twenty-one."

"My son's age when he died. I had a feeling—no, I *knew* that's how old you were."

Toshiki walked out the gate and shut it behind him. Ushigi sat motionless on the block, staring at the vegetable garden, a desolate patch of ground on which nothing grew but the remains of the spinach eaten that winter, the luxuriant stalks with their flowers and monstrous leaves.

"How many years is it since we last took a walk together like this?"

Ushigi only swung the saké bottle in its cloth wrapping and smiled back at him. Kyogo seemed to hear the echo of his own voice from somewhere in the quiet temple precincts. They were walking through the stillness alone.

Kyogo didn't particularly expect his friend to answer. His words had been a monologue or a song welling up out of his heart. The scenery about them folded him in its soft embrace. A very Japanese scene in its gentleness.

Aged cedars covered the grounds of the Temple of Perfect Awakening. Together with the pines, they stood in long black-green files, screening the springtime luster of the cherry trees in pale white bloom between them. Kyogo hadn't thought the cherries would be in flower. These were his first cherry blossoms in more than ten years, the first he'd actually seen since he left Japan. And even these were dreamlike in their pallid beauty.

"I never remembered cherry-viewing with pleasure. It

was all right at night, I knew, but otherwise it came back to me as a dirty, crowded business. But it's different in a clean, quiet place like this. I like this temple. The Perfect Awakening, you said it was, hm?"

"That's right, the Temple of Perfect Awakening." Ushigi smiled. "I've had nothing to do since my discharge, so I've taken to reading books about Kamakura. I know all about it now. I could even become a guide. My favorite spots are this place and the Hall of Light at the Kencho Temple. Let's go there after this."

Kyogo looked up at the two-storied temple gate with its thick straw roof soaring high up among the cedars and the pines. The grounds were meticulously swept, and the sand they walked on was lined with the tracings of the brooms. "Are there any monks here?"

"Yes, there are."

"They stay inside, I take it."

"They're at their Zen exercises, I suppose, or out begging alms, or maybe getting drunk."

"Begging? But surely nobody can afford to give them anything nowadays."

"They get something in the country, I think. The farmers must be all right, if the monks are still eating."

"You look like a monk yourself, with your bald head."

"I've thought of becoming a monk. I don't know too much about it, but in the old days it was very common, I think. All sorts of people would renounce the world and enter monasteries. And it was a simple matter to get into one. It's not so easy nowadays, not by any means."

They were in the shade. Beyond it, the air quavered in thin lines of light up from the sun-drenched ground. The path to the cells and dormitories was cut into a flight of steps over the side of a hill, and these steps were still covered with plum petals fallen in yesterday's rain. There was a pond along the path, and a cherry tree beside it was mirrored on its surface. Leisurely goldfish swam beneath the reflection. The two men stopped and gazed down.

"Cherry trees *are* beautiful. I never realized before."

"I can show you spots where the flowers are much better," Ushigi insisted.

"Where they're in full bloom already, you mean?"

They walked up the gentle, barely graded slope, looking into the bamboo thicket, where red camellias lay spread and dying at the roots of the stalks.

"The tomb of the Unlearned, the first abbot of the temple, is just behind here—a simple heap of stones."

"Well, you do know all about these things. You'd make a wonderful guide. If that bottle were only a gourd, the resemblance would be perfect. But I don't care about the fine points. Karma and the Origins are not for me. Just an aimless stroll through temple grounds in this spring weather, and I've had my fill. It's a really Japanese spring, isn't it? Soft and sleepy. Spring was lovely in Europe, but not like this."

The bamboo rustled in the wind. They mounted the embanked stairs and, near the top, saw a gate. Immediately after, their eyes were caught by the reflected brightness of the little garden inside it. This was the Cloister of the Sun of Buddha, and the mausoleum of Tokimune, the great shogun who founded the temple.

"Here we are!" Ushigi announced, in the gruff tone of a tourist guide.

They stepped inside and Kyogo was paralyzed for a moment by the splendor of the scene. A magnolia tree, its white flowers in full bloom and flooded with afternoon sunlight, rose against the dark-blue sky opposite the single blossoms of a cherry tree.

"This is beautiful."

It was indescribably beautiful. The brilliance of the flowers was imaged on the open panels of the mausoleum door. The thick, luxuriant petals of the magnolias, and the light, exhilarating cherry blossoms, clustered like a heap of numberless bright sea shells, drank in the sunlight, and sent forth again from deep within them a subdued and gentle luster.

Kyogo stood and stared. "I had forgotten." He sighed. "Or rather, I never really saw it before—how beautiful the cherries are."

Perhaps it was seeing the flowers against this bright sky of molten blue that made them so exquisite, he thought. But he didn't feel like searching for the reason. It was enough to look and lose himself in looking.

The cherry blossoms weren't white exactly, nor could you call them pink. They had a gentle, delicate color between white and pink. Theirs was a subtle beauty. Their luster issued tenuous and faint from some great depth within them. Foreign plants were different, their colors deep and rich and demonstrative. These reticent and modest flowers hid their hues inside them, almost, it seemed, on purpose.

"We've grown old, we two," Kyogo murmured. "We've become fond of cherry blossoms. They used to bore me, people talked about them so much."

"Oh, I don't see much connection between liking flowers and how old you are."

"There is a connection," Kyogo protested. "Young people don't know how to enjoy flowers. Few of them, anyway. It's an old man's pleasure, as though you could begin to love plants only after you'd used up all your feelings for people. It's the same way with vines and birds—they've always been diversions for the old."

Ushigi knew the cloister cherries were lovely, but

couldn't share Kyogo's intoxication with them. He stood at the base of the mausoleum stairs, facing the central shrine inside, and said a prayer.

"They say the body of Tokimune Hojo is buried under this entrance block."

Kyogo nodded indifferently. He had no great interest in ancient heroes. The flowered branches of the cherry trees attracted his gaze once more, and it seemed to him that the sunlight had changed upon the blossoms in the moment he had looked away.

"How still it is!" And after they'd gone down the hill again, he went on: "I've been making trips to Kyoto and Nara lately. I wasn't especially enthusiastic about the idea, but, you know, it's strange—as soon as I get to one of these places and look around, I find myself drawn to the relics of the old Japan."

"Kyoto and Nara went untouched in the fires."

"Thank God." Kyogo's voice was resonant. "Overseas, I felt that the whole of Japan might well be devastated by the war. It seemed inevitable, a good thing even. It would give the new Japan a fresh start. But now that I'm back, now that I've seen the horror of the ruins, I can't feel that way. Certainly not about the temples and statues in Kyoto and Nara. Thank God they were spared. What else is left in Japan? They may be remnants of a past unrelated to our time. It may be best to put them out of mind. But still, when you've lived abroad without kith or kin for twenty years, and you come back and grope for something that will bind you to your country's soil— It was a complete surprise to me. I don't believe in the gods or Buddhas. What power have these old shrines and temples that they draw me so? Because everywhere else there are only burned wastes and slums, is that it, Ushigi? Maybe a narrow downtown side street or a weather-beaten farmhouse would have done as well. Strange that an expatriate like me should feel this way—as though I were seeking somewhere to rest my soul and to breathe in peace."

Ushigi looked up inquiringly. "Have you been to see your wife and family?"

Kyogo's smile was lit by the evening sunlight filtering through the cedar trees. He answered quietly: "I'll save my feelings for the landscape, not for people."

"What are you saying?" Ushigi stood still. "You haven't gone to see your wife and daughter yet?"

Kyogo's smile was almost imperceptible. "I don't even want to see them. And if I did, it wouldn't do any good."

Ushigi pressed the matter home. "Are you ashamed to show yourself to your wife?"

"No, it isn't that. I'd rather not have talked about it, even to you. My wife has married again, and taken Tomoko with her. It's perfectly natural. I've got to stay out of their way now. Even you must grant that. The dead have no right to come up out of the ground and disturb other people's lives."

The Yokosuka train rushed past on the track beside the street. Its cars were lighted, though the sun was still up, and they could see the black, massed crowd of passengers it was carrying home from work at windy speed. A thin cloud of dust rose from the tracks behind it and floated toward the houses across the way.

"You're pitying me, aren't you? There's no reason to. After all these rootless years the very idea of home has vanished from my mind. You think that heartless, I suppose, but things just are that way, and there's nothing to be done about it. It was hard to bear at first, being away from home, but as I got used to loneliness my own wife and child became like strangers to me. The distinction has grown very faint, just as boundary lines have disappeared from the map, so far as I'm concerned. Especially now that she's remarried—she *is* somebody else's wife."

"I'm sorry for you, Moriya."

"Don't be absurd. I have no intention of giving way to my feelings. I have some affection for others at times, but I know I can't expect anything in return. That's how you get to feel, when you've been wandering about in foreign countries all alone. That's how you *must* feel, perhaps. I remember rainy evenings in country inns, somewhere abroad, when I used to look outside and see the lighted windows in some house, and the whole family together there, husband and wife and children. . . . At moments like that, of course, I would listen to the raindrops on the highway and pity my own solitude, and yearn desperately for my family in Japan. But I grew to hate such feelings. I was just another dirty little Jap, and contempt lay waiting all around me. Why is it, why are the lonely hated? It makes no difference whether you're Japanese or, let's say, Persian. Alone in Europe, and you're bad. Why?"

They were walking through the outer gate of the Kencho Temple grounds. Kyogo went on: "Japanese are too sentimental about their relatives. They either love them too much or hate them too much. That sickens me. It's one evil I've cured myself of, I think. My relatives mean no more and no less to me than the stranger next door."

Flowers greeted them again inside. Two rows of cherry trees spread their branches in the wide interior to form a cloud of blossoms, over which the second story of the high gate soared lightly. The bells began to ring from the bell tower as they entered, and the sound crept quavering through the blossoms and trailed its long resonance behind it. The spring evening was tranquil. Sky and air were like still water, for no wind stirred.

"Bells?" Kyogo turned around. "They're still ringing them."

He was thinking of the bells he had heard abroad—the clear song of the bells in cathedral carillons ringing one after another. And of how different they sounded from Japanese bells.

They walked through the side entrance of the gate to the main temple building and went to the tea room for the worshippers of the Lay Monk. And here they made use of the two-quart bottle of saké Ushigi had been carrying. There was no one else in the bare room. They sat at a crude low-legged table, and Kyogo looked about him. It was a lonely tea room beside an untraveled road, and high up on the wall below the ceiling wooden plaques hung side by side, carved with the names of the members of the group of worshippers.

"It's not of our time, this place." Ushigi's tone was unapologetic, almost proud. "It's for the Lay Monk's worshippers. Except on his death day, there's no one here."

"It's not of our world. It might be a stage set."

And therefore fit for a man like himself, defeated and forbidden public activity. Ushigi almost said it, but didn't. For there had been a tacit understanding between them that topics which might make the conversation painful would be avoided. And especially because he had ranked high in the beaten forces. Silently, he drained his saké cup.

"I suppose so." He sighed. "You say you haven't been to see your wife and daughter yet? Don't you even love them?"

"Love them? Why, yes, I do. But you know how I am. I don't want to make the first approach."

"Lonely fellow!"

"No. You're the lonely one. You doted on your son, like the Japanese father you are, and now—you've killed him in your war. You must really be lonely."

Ushigi raised his eyes, intense with protest. But he said nothing until he had drunk down his saké. "Let's not talk about that!"

There was a finality in the prohibition, but something seemed to melt in him a second later. "Since we're here, I'll say this much. I think he died nobly. And his death is the only thing in the world that comforts me a little for having helped bring Japan to this pass, for still being here to see it, for not being dead myself. He has atoned for my crime. I go on living to no purpose—except one last thing that I must do. When it becomes possible to leave Japan, I'm going to Midway to look at the sea where my son lies drowned."

He stopped, and the silence was deep between them. Muscles twitched faintly in Ushigi's face, betraying the passion he could not master.

"I want to beg his forgiveness and give him my thanks. And I want to tell my son that his father thinks he did well. That's all I want. I think of it as soon as I get up in the morning, and when I wake suddenly in the night, I think of it again. It's the only thing left that I can do, as I am now. My wife too, she's the same way."

"No wonder, if you carry on like that," Kyogo reproached him. "How do you manage to eat?"

"Eat?" Ushigi's nasal tone was satiric. "By selling the furniture. Our house wasn't burned, so there's always something salable around."

"Don't you want to work?"

"I haven't even thought about it. When I must, I'll make the effort, and something will turn up, I imagine. Meanwhile I just sit. . . . So many of my friends died in the war, one way or another. When I think of it and that I'm the only one left alive, I feel ashamed and can't do anything."

"Ushigi!" Kyogo was sharp. "You're wrong."

"Wrong?"

"Terribly wrong. You're still carrying death around on your shoulders. First of all, stop crying."

"Crying?"

"Yes. You're a grown man, and you can't stop mourning for your son. In a woman, that would be all right. But you're a man, and you were a sailor. I loathe these sentiments. Leave the dead to rest in peace."

Ushigi was silent.

"You've managed to save your life, and you don't even value it. You're sulking. Is that right? Let me tell you. You've killed in this mad war, even your son you've killed, and you're still alive yourself. It's half a miracle that you're alive. Don't you want to make something of that life? Don't you want to use it to do something in your son's stead? You and your kind have smashed Japan to pieces, have made people suffer agonies, and—"

"Moriya!" Ushigi sat up, his face flushed.

Kyogo paled a little. "I'm sorry," he said. "But it's as I say. I understand your desire to atone. But that's just some more Japanese sentimentalism. Can you deny it? It's about time we got rid of it. That's what's brought us to this pass. Why can't you shake off death and try to live? What would be wrong in it? If you need some capital, I'll give it to you. As a matter of fact, that's why I came today."

Ushigi stared at Kyogo. "You say you'll give me money?"

"Yes, if you'll put it to use."

"No, thank you." He said it emphatically, then said no more. Kyogo looked into his expressionless face and

remembered suddenly the heavy features of the young
M.P. There was a dull opaqueness about this old friend's
face which reminded one of the other. Kyogo loathed that
quality more than anything else in the world. It marked
a relentlessness that suffocated others.

"Can't you be a little less proud?" Kyogo said softly,
only to hear Ushigi explode:

"It's your money."

Kyogo was taken aback, but kept himself under control. Something chill and dark whirled its icy current
through his heart.

"Ah—" he put down his cup—"so that's what you've
been thinking."

"Let me have my pride. You probably noticed today—
I'm a beaten man, but when I knew you were coming I
felt I couldn't ask you into the house, it would be unpardonable to the dead. That's just the sort of man I
am."

"Oh, that's why you came running from the door with
your bottle and invited me flower-viewing right away. I
didn't think anything of it. That sort of thing is unim-
aginable to me."

"You think it wrong of me. Forgive me, I'm a stubborn man."

"I shouldn't have come. I don't intend to apologize
for myself now."

"I've heard the talk about your having taken all the
blame though not entirely responsible for what happened. But that doesn't—"

"Right you are. I'm a wretch. Stole office money and
ran off without facing the music. And it's only because
Japan has been defeated and there is no Navy any more
that I've been able to come back."

"Enough of that. Let's drink."

Kyogo was getting angrier and angrier with his friend.

And, strangely, his anger didn't seem to be on his own account, though Ushigi was hurting him. He had suddenly seen exactly what it was that made Ushigi like the young M.P.—the inability to feel the unhappiness of others. Ushigi was a fine man, of course. But a man out of the past, out of a Japan that had died already. And he sat there facing today with all his ancient pride, resolved never to give in and never to approve. It was the officer in him; he had lived in a class above and apart, almost in another world.

They climbed the steep path up the hill between the straight, slender trunks of scattered cedars. It was night now, and the moonlight picked out the white walls of the monks' cells, with their black base-panels down below and their strange windows up above. They went through the gate on top of the hill and entered the compound of the Founder's Hall of Kencho Temple. The refectory faced a Zen exercise chamber just beyond the entrance. Countless old junipers branched behind them. Finally, at the end of the prospect, the Founder's Hall itself, the Hall of Light, opened its doors into darkness.

But not total darkness, for a single lamp burned day and night inside, accenting the tremendous emptiness of the interior. They gazed at the flowers in the evening dimness until they came up to the ancient Zen shrine. The light reflected faintly on the paper screens of the refectory in the still, unpeopled night.

"This is the place I wanted you to see."

Only the columns stood on the expanse of plaster-hard earthen floor. The lamp shone deep inside, before the central niche. Yellowish and dim, its light flickered on the temple wall. The moon lit up the bamboo stalks outside the windows.

"There's a statue of the founder or a memorial tablet inside, I'm told, and they offer services to it—but that doesn't matter to me. The Hall itself is beautiful. I love this emptiness. I come here frequently."

Ushigi was being vague, and Moriya felt vexed again. To be sure, this was a quiet temple hall on a spring evening. But in the cities, thieves were prowling among the ruins, and the Ueno subway was crowded with the homeless victims of the war. "But, Ushigi," he thought, "you have no time to think of that. You just live within yourself, convinced that your life is over."

"Want to go back?"

"All right, let's go."

They walked down the cedar-lined unlighted slope toward the two-story gate. People were talking amid the flowers. They walked on and saw them shadowed in the moonlight and heard a child's voice among them.

"You'll be going by North Kamakura station again?" Ushigi inquired.

"Not yet. I'm not angry with you, Ushigi, certainly not for myself, but I do want to talk to you a little more."

Ushigi smiled an old, sly smile. "Don't you think we've talked enough already?"

"No, I don't." There was a stern rebuke in Kyogo's tone. "I don't want to get you mad again, but I do intend to exorcise your demon. And it would be too much trouble to take another trip out here."

"Just forgive me, and let it go at that."

"Trying to escape?"

"Escape? No, I'm not running away. Just leave me alone. I am what I am."

"And by staying what you are, you'll become death's first cousin. . . . You could live easily enough, but you insist on making things hard for yourself. Maybe you think you're being strong, but you're a coward, Ushigi. A craven, small-hearted coward. You haven't got the guts to do anything."

"What are you saying?"

"There's nothing weaker or more helpless than a soldier out of the forces. Have you thought of it, Ushigi?—a soldier or a sailor lives surrounded by bugaboos. I stopped early, and came to see it. I quit the Navy because of cowardice, because there was something in my record I had to be afraid of. It's a life of saluting, isn't it? When I got out and learned to live entirely by my own resources, I was amazed to find I didn't have to be afraid of anyone any more. For the first time in my life I knew what it meant to be free. The very idea was inconceivable in the Navy. When you have to fit yourself into a world of slaves, you can't help being scared all the time. You may think yourself strong, Ushigi, but you're a coward."

"Now that's enough, Moriya."

"No, it isn't. I'm going to say what I have to say. That's how Japan has always been, the whole country, not only soldiers. We've all lived in constant fear of someone or something, hesitant and frightened and subservient. And it's still the same. That hasn't changed, for all our brave new world. Everyone wastes his life justifying himself to something. It's weakness, and the weak can never be free. You pride yourself on your stubbornness, but stubbornness is the weakling's weapon. You're just curling up small inside your shell, too frightened to look outside. You sulk and wish you were dead, but that only proves you don't feel capable of living."

Ushigi didn't fill the pause.

"Look at me. I have nothing to protect me, but there's nothing that I have to fear. If I were in your position, I'd go out and be a signalman; I'd shine shoes if I had to. I wouldn't give a damn what people said; I'd just live. But you're too afraid for your reputation to do that."

Ushigi stood still, and glared, and roared: "Go away!"

Kyogo moved ahead without saying any more, and left

Ushigi behind. His back soon disappeared down the moonlit road. Ushigi walked slowly to his home and when he got there, he found Kyogo had reached it ahead of him and was talking to his wife.

Kyogo looked up at Ushigi with a laugh. "I've laid one unhealthy ghost at least. . . . Hope I haven't polluted your house."

A fresh stick of incense smoked on the family altar.

A DAY IN SPRING

"Mr. Onozaki—a visitor for you."

Onozaki was at the easel, just beginning to get tired. "Who is it?"

"A pretty young woman. I don't know her name." The superintendent's wife, her arms full of the family wash, marched down the corridor humming, and out onto the balcony at the end.

Onozaki's apartment was a large single room littered with painting materials, pots, medicine bottles, his guitar, and potatoes that had tumbled out of their newspaper wrapping.

"A woman?" he asked, though there was no one there to answer him. His eyes were still fixed affectionately on the picture he had been working at. It was based on sketches of a row of cheap saloons on a side street in a suburban market. He had been there frequently of late, and naturally had had to paint it.

He groped for the tin of cigarettes on the table, took one and put it in his mouth, then walked downstairs. A young lady in Western dress was waiting for him, standing on the earthen floor of the narrow entrance. Her back was to him, for she was looking out at the cherry tree just inside the gate. Only a few branches could be seen from where she was.

She turned around when she heard his footsteps.

He had never seen her before. Her hair caught his attention. It was luxuriant in its halo of light from outside, and set in a permanent wave.

"I'm Onozaki."

The girl bowed. "I'm from the magazine *Etoile,* and I've come to ask you to do some illustrations for a novel we're running. Mr. Inokuma tells me you've been in Malacca and know all about it."

He had taken her card, but forgot to look it it. "Malacca!" His eyes were wide open and laughing. "Know it, he says! I loved Malacca. H'm—whose novel is it?"

She named a well-known writer. "It's about Malacca, and he brings in a temple and a Spanish fortress."

"St. John's Hill!" he shouted. It was the hill where the fortress stood. "That makes me homesick. I've still got my sketches of that section; sent them home beforehand, luckily. But what kind of novel is it? Is it the sort of thing I'd be able to illustrate?"

They were still standing on the earthen floor. She looked down and opened her handbag to take out the manuscript. Kohei noticed her rich curls again and finally read her name on the card she'd given him.

"The *Etoile* Company. Miss—Banko, is it?—Moriya."

"I pronounce it Tomoko."

It was the Chinese ideograph for *companion* that Kohei had misread. He nodded happily. "I should have known." When he got really drunk, nowadays, Onozaki would forget everything that had happened. The name Tomoko Moriya meant nothing to him. "Would you let me read the manuscript? Is it very long?"

"Only thirty double pages."

"I'll read it and then tell you whether or not I'll do the drawings. I have done some illustrating in the past, it so happens. It pays as little as ever, I suppose?"

"Oh—" Tomoko was embarrassed. Her wheaten color emphasized her youth and purity. "I'll go back to the office and find out—"

"No need." Onozaki waved his hand broadly. "It's not

the money I care about. I only meant that I don't intend to make a profession of illustrating. Poor as I look, I'm a millionaire, you know, one of the new Zaibatsu. So naturally I can't waste my time on trivial drawings. However, you said Malacca, didn't you? I'm going to read this to see whether or not I can work on it. Could you wait a few minutes? Or would you prefer to go out for a walk?"

"If you don't mind, I'll wait here."

"But I can't show you up to my studio." He looked very happy about it. "The scenery here is too pretty, for one thing. Wait a minute. I'll go borrow a chair for you."

He went into the superintendent's office and came back with a crude affair of twisted wood. "This floor is nasty. People seem to have been shining their shoes on it or something. Take the chair out there under the cherry tree."

Tomoko did so, thinking how strangely youthful the painter was, for all his white hair.

Having sent Tomoko out to the cherry tree, Onozaki sat down at his ease on the stairway inside, spread the manuscript open on his knees, and started reading it. And he read it aloud in a kind of soliloquy, clause by clause. Tomoko was looking up at the branches overhead, but a laugh bubbled up inside her and she had all she could do to hold it in.

"Mm-h'm—Malacca—"

She sat down, turned aside so as not to see him. A little giggle burst out by itself. She bit her lips and tried desperately to stop it, but a fine quiver kept running up and down the arm under which she held her handbag. Young laughter is irrepressible.

"Ahah, now—"

He paid her no mind, but went on reading, changing his tone with each passage. His voice dropped suddenly, and he read to himself for a while. Then he struck the page with his clenched fist and yelled: "He's wrong, wrong! Malacca isn't like this at all. He's a liar! He may have been to Malacca, but he's never seen it. Lies, all lies!" And he stuck his hand into his long white hair.

Onozaki play-acted at least half the time. Not that he was really trying to deceive anyone, but he managed to make his daily routine enjoyable by overemphasizing little things and playing up his reactions with theatrical gestures. Of course, this depended a good deal on who was with him. Acting works with some people, but not with others.

Onozaki clasped his head in his hands in a pose of deep thought. Tomoko was worried. She was sure he meant to refuse the commission. She had had her job at the magazine only a very short time, and was still too guileless and inexperienced not to be frightened by Onozaki's posturing. Her little laugh vanished. She watched the painter from under the blossoms, completely serious. She couldn't even speak.

The weather was still chilly even though the cherries were in bloom. The sun shone, but the air was cold. Onozaki looked at the earnest young girl and the cold, cloudless sky, and found an exquisite harmony between them. Tomoko was lovely as she sat below the blossoming flowers, and in the half-turn of her body toward him the line from her breast to her shoulder around the handbag held between them was feminine and delicate and pure.

"Don't I have any chance of getting you to do it?"

She shouldn't have said that. But Onozaki had decided to take the job as soon as this lovely young lady had asked him. He sighed as though gravely ill, and spoke as if enraged in defense of the distant city he knew so well. "Malacca isn't like this. Really, it isn't. . . .

The colors are rich and exhilarating, intense but mellow. Furthermore, young lady, I am quite certain that there were no post boxes standing on the streets of Malacca. And when I was there it was quite impossible to saunter into a tobacco shop and filch cigarettes."

"Couldn't I ask you to do the drawings as you please?"

"As I please? . . . Yes, yes—paint the Malacca that I know!"

Tomoko was relieved. "If you'll consider it on those terms—"

He dropped the tragic pose finally, and burst into a childish grin that made him an altogether different person. "Of course I'll do it!"

"Thank you! When can I come for them? Our deadline's very close. Would next Wednesday be all right?"

"I'm sure it will." He was being magnanimous. "But you needn't make the trip all the way out here. Your office is in the Ginza section, isn't it? I'll deliver the illustrations myself. And, young lady, I'll do something else. I'm going to do one of the illustrations in color. No, I don't expect you to print it in color. I just want to show you how beautiful and mellow the colors are in the streets of Malacca. That picture will be my gift to you, young lady."

Outside, Tomoko became her usual easygoing self again. Her walk and posture came alive; she moved like a little fish swimming with the current. Her feelings had escaped from stiffness and formality.

The air was cold, but spring had come. From the window of the train, the willows in the long waste of ruins were a warm blur of green. In everything she saw, Tomoko could feel the birth of the new year. She was able to believe that life was beginning right now in front of her eyes, and so she was happy. The infinite pain and sorrow all over postwar Tokyo didn't cloud her heart.

She had her work at the modern dress shop, and now the assistant's job on the staff of the magazine as well. Her income was assured. She had written some fashion articles for *Etoile*, and they had got her the job.

Her mother had always told her that even a woman should be able to support herself, but Tomoko had never believed she could. After the war, however, she had had to try. And, to her own surprise, she had become financially independent. At the same time, she had freed herself from "the family," in fact if not in form. It was a new age, when women could go out to work without shocking anybody. Her mother had had astonishing foresight. But more than that, she had always worried about Tomoko's position in the family. The girl was living in her stepfather's house, after all, and a stepfather was not a father, however strongly he felt his obligations. Why else should this quiet, modest woman, almost tied to the house, as anyone could see, give her daughter such advice?

Whenever Tomoko thought of her mother, something tender would spread through her heart. And her eyes would moisten and her sense of strength melt away.

She was thinking of her mother now, as she clung to a strap in the crowded train. When she was younger, she had been plunged into long terror now and then by the thought that her mother would die some day. The idea would come to her in bed at night sometimes, and she would have to get up and turn on the light, or feel for her mother's hand through the bedclothes. She had to make sure her mother was still lying there or be too worried to sleep. Tomoko would know that she looked frightened. Her mother would open her eyes and scold: "What's the matter with you, Tomoko?" but take her daughter's hand gently in her own. Tomoko would be silent in the darkness, unable to answer. Her mother would say no more for a while, but then would get up, as if nothing was the matter, and come round quietly to sit beside her.

"If you can't sleep, I'll help you, Tomoko!" And she would take her daughter in her arms, as though she was still a baby, and rub away her tears against her own cheek, and say to her: "Sleep darling, sleep well, and grow up to be a big girl soon."

Tomoko got off at Yuraku and started walking back to the *Etoile* offices in West Ginza. But on the way she ran into Tatsuzo Oki, the man she called her father. He was some distance ahead of her, but it was impossible to mistake him. The careful posture, the slightly rounded shoulders in the gray overcoat, and, above all, the deliberateness of his walk, as though every step were meant to demonstrate how important to society this college professor was.

Tomoko ran up gaily and walked shoulder to shoulder with him for a while, waiting for him to recognize her. He had been nearsighted since youth, and his big black-rimmed glasses seemed to weigh down his thin face. They turned toward her suddenly.

"What's this?" He stood still. "I was wondering what young lady this might be."

Tomoko smiled inside the collar of her overcoat. "Where are you going?" she asked.

"M'm!" The crease beside his hairless lips deepened. "A friend of mine—he used to be a newspaperman, but he's been purged—has sent me an announcement that he's opened an *objet d'art* and secondhand-book store in this neighborhood. I'm going to see what's on display. It should be right ahead here."

He launched into another theme. "Secondhand-book prices have really gone high, you know. They're quite absurd. Any trivial novel costs a hundred, even two hundred yen. And scholarly books have become impossible. As for foreign books, if they have any reputation at all, why, you look at the price and can't believe your eyes. And they're climbing rapidly, from month to month. They're quite insane, these prices."

Tomoko interrupted with the remark that would flatter Oki the most: "Why, in that case, Father, your library must be quite valuable."

"Yes, yes indeed. It's gradually become a little property." Oki's self-satisfaction was evident. "We're very lucky it wasn't lost in the war. Books are a scholar's life, of course. But, more than that, I've always had broad interests, so that my library isn't confined to my own field, philosophy. I have volumes in other studies so rare that they surprise my specialist friends. I'm very glad of it, as things have turned out."

Professor Oki had other reasons to feel satisfied. He called himself a thoroughgoing liberal, but the war had shaken him into making a few ardently nationalistic gestures, and the Army had even commissioned him to travel on the continent. Luckily his timidity and nervousness had saved him from any conspicuous exhibition of the strained enthusiasm then current, and of course his activities had been limited to the cultural and artistic fields, anyway. So the two or three books he had written during the war did not subject him to the purge. Whatever the political climate, Professor Oki managed to seem temperate and fair, thus avoiding danger to himself and preserving the esteem of his respectable readers. And naturally there was no Japanese government of any complexion which wasn't eager to appoint this moderate and impartial gentleman to its committees, praising the ripeness of his scholarship and confident that he would never cause any trouble. Professor Oki understood everything moderately. It wasn't likely that the high tide of cultural activity after the war would leave Professor Oki on the beach.

"It's still a bit cold, but the streets certainly look like spring."

Tomoko knew that Oki was very sensitive to cold, he was so thin. "Don't worry, the warm weather is almost here. By next week you won't need an overcoat any more."

"What about yourself, my dear? How's the job going?" Oki was a very modern man and treated the child his wife had brought him as a friend. "Do you find it interesting?"

"Yes, I do. It brings me into touch with all sorts of people." Tomoko was thinking of Onozaki. "Today I went to see Mr. Onozaki, the painter, and asked him to do some illustrations for us."

"Onozaki? . . . Oh, Kohei Onozaki. Yes—he used to run an art magazine. Is that fellow painting again? He's from the old days—made quite a name for himself as a pro-Fauvist art critic after he came back from France, but I haven't heard much of anything about him since then. I thought he was dead. He must be quite old by now."

"But what a vigorous, interesting man!"

"If you ever want to ask a favor of somewhat more important painters than your Onozaki, I'll be glad to talk to them for you. They're all friends of mine."

Tomoko just nodded and smiled.

"And if you like, I'll do an article for you myself."

"Really?"

"Only one, though. I can't waste too much time on a magazine like yours."

"That's mean! It's not so low-class as all that. And we're trying to improve it."

The budding branches of a willow were imaged in the

glass of a show window, large and filled with awkward rows of books. They were at the secondhand-book store Oki had been telling her about.

"Here we are." He peered inside. "Come along, won't you?"

The store was open for business, but wasn't quite in order yet. Young men were standing on footstools in front of the shelves, arranging the volumes.

"Is Fujiwara in?"

While Oki made his inquiry, Tomoko looked at the young men, who had turned toward her when she came in. She recognized one of the faces, and smiled.

"Mr. Fujiwara has stepped out for a while. May I have your name?" another employee asked him, in the deadly earnest tone of an ex-soldier.

Before Oki could reply, the young man Tomoko had recognized said quickly: "This is Professor Tatsuzo Oki."

Tomoko blushed with discomfort. This same young man had told her once, after a brief apology, that Oki's books were a bore. And here was Oki trying to look irritated at being recognized so promptly, but inwardly delighted.

"Ah, Professor Oki?" The first young man was flustered.

After so many years of looking down at students from a platform, Oki was convinced he knew how to treat young people. The secret was to maintain your distance rigidly and talk down to them across it, but at the same time make occasional advances to them, as though the friendship you felt for them but had to restrain were finding its outlet.

"Ah, you've been doing a fine job, I see," he said jovially as he walked over to the shelves. He pushed his glasses up on his forehead, narrowed his eyes in a way he had—they were blurred with old age now, as well as

being very nearsighted—and started looking over the
titles. "Have you got anything unusual?"

The young men, beaming at the chance of talking to
such a famous scholar, answered in series. "We haven't
finished setting the books up yet."

"There's quite a large collection that we bought from
someone of the old nobility. He had to sell because of
the property tax or something."

"The old nobility? There must be books on Japanese
literature and history, then. Maybe some painting col-
lections too, h'm?" Oki laughed suddenly. "Ah-ha! You
have my books too." He took a volume of his own off
the shelf and opened it. Tomoko watched him, then
looked at the young man she had been thinking about.
He was a college student and his name was Yukichi
Okabe. He had been looking into the shop from an
earth-floored room behind it, but came out now with the
tea service and started pouring.

"Please help yourselves," he said, placing the cups and
trays, as he filled them, on the glass top of a display case.
The tea looked weak.

Tomoko glanced at Oki again. He was spending too
much time over his own book. She talked to Yukichi.
"Do you have a regular job here now?"

"No, I'm just on as an extra for a few days. Got the
job through the school." Yukichi grinned. "Rounded up
and sent over as a temporary assistant. I can't even understand lots of these books."

Yukichi had been almost thirty when he got back
from overseas. But he had gone to college, and was spe-
cializing in linguistics. He was earning his tuition by
working in a publishing firm.

"This price is much too high!" Oki was looking at the
sales price written inside the cover of his book. "Five

hundred yen! You're being awfully hard on the readers. They're the poorest class there is nowadays."

"Maybe so, sir, but your readers don't seem to mind. They buy your books anyway."

"When this first came out, it cost three yen. If books don't come down, it will be pretty sad for culture in Japan. I always make it a condition with my publisher that my books sell for as little as possible. With first editions, I always do that." Oki walked busily along the shelves, examining titles. "This is a rare item. There probably aren't too many copies of it in Japan. And it's by no means obsolete, scientifically speaking. As a matter of fact, it's being recognized as more valuable than ever, in some quarters. A rather special book. I wonder who had it."

He put his head to one side. "I suppose he had to let it go to keep alive. He must have felt as though he was stripping himself bare. Scholars are terribly hard up nowadays. You know, a full professor is paid less than a workman no older than a child. It's they who bear the whole weight of the country's scholarship and culture, and they don't make enough to eat."

This was perfectly true, so true that no one in Japan, nowadays, wondered at it. Everyone knew that it was unjust and unreasonable, and that nothing could be done about it. Oki himself was riding the tide of postwar "culturism," and was an exception to the rule. But he was always bemoaning the fate of scholars in general and its influence on culture, in the commonplaces current on the subject. And this was no doubt some sort of intellectual virtue. Unfortunately, lamentation solved nothing by itself. Even a college janitor could *talk* about professors' having a hard time making a living—or so thought Yukichi as he regarded Oki's agitation.

Yukichi looked away from the professor, over the art books in the show window and through the glass plating, into the street outside. The spring sunshine had changed the atmosphere of the block, changed it entirely. The buds on the willow had grown enough for him to see them now, and their soft green reminded him more of young flowers than of leaves. The store was new, but standing between the shelves lined with old books he felt he was peering out from a cellar. That may have been why people seemed to be walking with so much more freedom and life than in winter. A man in a khaki overcoat, a dischargee probably, crouched down to the sidewalk, picked up a cigarette stub, and then passed on.

"Professor Oki, do you have anything new being published now?"

"H'm, yes. They're always coming to talk to me about it. What a nuisance! They disturb my studies."

During this exchange, Yukichi met Tomoko's eye and sent her a sympathetic smile. The spring he had seen in the sunshine outside glowed from Tomoko's youthful body. The piles of old books oppressed her. She was bored. And Yukichi was invaded by the feeling that all men who have come back from war sometimes have— the thrill, right there and then, at that very moment, of having returned and being alive. He looked around him uncertainly as though there was still an anxiety deep inside him that he might wake up on the battlefield again and find he had only been dreaming he was back in Japan. So he was all the happier that spring had come to the streets, and Tomoko looked even more exciting to him.

Little things made him happy. Things so little that most people overlook them would astonish and delight

him. Sparrows strutting on the tracks while he waited
for the train, for example. The sparrows in the city
were underfed and their wings dirty with soot. But
Yukichi loved to watch them. They would alight on the
rusty sand between the tracks, slant their little heads to
one side and examine the neighborhood importantly,
then take wing again unexpectedly, land at another point
on the tracks, and start all over again. They made the
time pass quickly till the train pulled in.

Yukichi saw himself in the sparrows.

"They're alive!"

This was the lesson he'd learned on the battlefields.
When you've been robbed of your will, chained to one
spot you can't stir from, and known that, though you
don't want to die, you may be dragged off to be killed at
any moment, you can't help loving life; you've seen how
brief and bound and imperiled it can be.

Yukichi had read a story somewhere about a convict
sentenced to death who had found a solitary weed shoot-
ing up between the flagstones of his prison courtyard.
He had devoted himself to it heart and soul and spent
all his time watching for its flower, as tiny as a grain of
rice, to bloom. Yukichi could believe that story im-
plicitly. His own experience had taught him to.

Anyone could die; he knew that. On the battlefield
you could propel yourself straight into the enemy's fire
or wait for a shot from the other side to come and finish
you off. That wasn't frightening. That didn't require
courage. But living so as to avoid death—that had been
frightening, and cruel. Some of his comrades had been
amazingly unconcerned about survival. They had seemed
to have no feelings about it. Just as one rarely thinks of
illness while one is in good health. When marching
off to an engagement in which they might well die, they
would either be joking—and it was weird to be joking

then—or grim and silent. It was like living under a sentence of death, signed and sealed but with no date set. They were horrible, those days, with that invisible burden always weighing on the back of one's neck. It wasn't a matter of hardening the will and jumping into the abyss once and for all. It was living day after day under the shadow of death, not knowing whether it would ever come or not, unsure that it was near, uncertain it was far.

The average soldier loved children and flowers and birds. So long as he didn't get drunk on blood and go mad, or fall victim to the compulsion to prove his courage, he cherished timid little living things.

The seal was broken. Yukichi's hands and feet were free. It had been raining the day he landed at Uraga, a veteran. On the train, he had been looking out of a broken window at the young green leaves when one of his comrades shouted something he still remembered:

"Japan's beautiful. Oh, what a beautiful country it is! All these trees, all this grass!"

Only a man who had lived in chains could have said that.

After work Yukichi walked to Shimbashi station, on his way home. He noticed Tomoko across the street walking with a girl about the same age as herself. He didn't know Tomoko well enough to shout a greeting from that distance, so they walked parallel to each other on either side of the empty car tracks, and Yukichi looked at Tomoko as he walked.

The girls were discussing something fervently—with the sort of fervor that only young ladies ever show. The days were growing longer, and there were still some traces of evening sunlight on Tomoko's side of the street. Gleams of sunset shone here and there through the gaps between tall buildings and lit up a glass show window or sent long shadows out behind a sidewalk tree or passer-by. They were plane trees and hadn't budded yet. Their black, naked branches twisted in the sky, dancing. The girls passed by a candy store, its windows spread with gay colors, to stop in front of a flower shop. The plate glass was clouded, but Yukichi could imagine the bright spring flowers inside.

The girls stood looking for some time, but didn't go in to buy anything. They walked ahead, talking as fervently as before. A trivial thing, but it made Yukichi happy. Japan was beaten, but peace had come. The girls were proving it, unknowingly, by the way they walked and talked. And this was a very urban sight. Hundreds, thousands of other girls, in other parts of Tokyo, were probably doing exactly the same thing.

"Mr. Okabe!" Someone called him, and Yukichi recognized a young student who was, like himself, in the Philology Faculty, but the Japanese Literature section of it. Yukichi was older than his fellow students because of his service, so everybody at school called him Mister.

"Hello there."

The young student had no coat, but wore an old uniform and clogs on his feet. His paleness completed the picture of the struggling student. With him was a genteel, light-skinned young man of the same age, twenty-three or twenty-four, wearing a suit and flashy topcoat.

"Hello, Mr. Okabe. You've done some publishing work, haven't you?" It was the pale one. He turned round to the youth in the topcoat. "Let me introduce you. This is Toshiki Okamura, another college student. He and I have decided to set up a company to publish magazines and books. I think we might ask Mr. Okabe for his advice, Toshiki."

Toshiki took out a card and handed it to Yukichi, and spoke with his usual calm. "You have some experience in these matters, sir?"

Yukichi wondered who this young man might be. He was slight in build, at least five years younger than himself, and looked like a child, yet spoke in such a mature way.

"If it's convenient for you, we'd like to invite you to dinner and discuss this with you over our food."

Toshiki sounded less and less like a student. He seemed to know an amazing number of people in this part of the Ginza. Much older people stopped to greet him, as well as some obscure young men, and even some women.

They started talking as they stood there, and Yukichi promised to wait with them for one more student. Finally a girl in Western dress came up to join them.

"A young lady from the Toho Movie Company," Toshiki introduced her. "She likes beer."

The woman curled her painted lips into a smile. She was a fleshy modern type, with an excellent physique.

"She was walking alone recently and got caught in one of those prostitute round-ups. The police put her in the truck and took her away, and were going to send her to the Yoshiwara Hospital. But I got a doctor friend of mine to write a medical certificate for her and managed to get her out of it."

The woman didn't even look embarrassed. She just pouted her lips again and laughed as though the story was not about herself and she didn't consider it a surprising event for Tokyo nowadays.

"You mustn't be so careless as to walk around by yourself in a Western dress," Toshiki said. "They drag off every woman like that they see. They don't bother to find out whether she's a prostitute or not."

"A tragic thing," the student of Japanese literature broke in. "They can't even protest."

"It's like fate. It's awful for the women."

Yukichi was irritated by the feminine delicacy of Toshiki's speech. Maybe he thought it refined, but it was terribly annoying. You'd never hear it from a man who'd been drafted and suffered in the war. He wouldn't have the leisure to use words that way. Toshiki belonged to the next generation, just coming of age. He'd been one or two years too young for the draft, and the surrender had saved him.

Toshiki's over-gentle speech got on Yukichi's nerves more and more as the evening wore on. He couldn't help thinking what a tremendous gap a few years' difference had put between them.

"You'll need paper to publish. Can you get any?" Yukichi was controlling his dislike for Toshiki. After all, he was older.

"Yes," Toshiki said, "we have money. Of course we're going to use black-market paper. We'll put out books that can sell, and pay for them as we go along. That should work out. I have an excellent patron—a woman, but no man can match her. There's no worry about money. I'd like to introduce you to my aunt some day."

It was past eight when Yukichi reached Yokohama, where he lived, and walked out of Cherry Tree station. Occupation trucks and automobiles, one after another, were passing through the darkness of the square, their headlights gleaming, and Yukichi had to wait awhile before he could cross the street.

The wind had fallen with evening, and the weather had grown warm. But for the crowd of homeless workers who gathered every night in the space between the Central Ward Government Office and the Embroidered

Bridge, winter is much longer than it is for people who have overcoats. They were there now, collected in groups on the sidewalks and empty lots. They had lit fires to warm themselves, and stood or squatted in chill black circles around the surging red flames.

They had the blank look of Chinese coolies. There were intelligent faces among them, and refined old men who might once have headed considerable households, and youths who would pass for students if they wore scholastic uniforms. But when you had seen them, not on a spring evening like tonight, but on a stifling summer day when the sky was still red with sunset, coming back from a day's labor, too weak from hunger to stand, and sitting down on the curb in crowded rows, you had to admit, however little you liked it, that Japan had its coolies too. Some of them were almost naked. Others had taken off their shirts to hunt for lice.

To Yukichi the most painful sight was the khaki shirts and pants turned pitch-black with dirt. He had had to live in khaki so long that now he had an instinctive aversion to the color. He was sure it was the most depressing of all colors to Japanese eyes. And these men, the most wretched victims of the war, had nothing else to wear, and even these khaki clothes hung on them in rags, as they sat empty-eyed and silent on the roadside. They looked like things, not men. From his life in the Army, Yukichi knew that when a man had fallen to the lowest depth, his heart remained still, whatever happened. It was closed even to despair. Like a piece of stiffened rubber, he waited to crack, but unhappily went on living, only to know cold and hunger and thirst at their severest. And then the absent, impenetrable look of the coolie was engraved on his face.

Across the bridge, the row of stalls under the pent-roof of the unwalled market on one side of the street

and the small houses across the way crowded toward
each other, to leave a narrow black tunnel of a street
between them. The market was a sinister place when the
shops were closed, and Yukichi didn't want to walk
through it. Instead he marched down the middle of the
car tracks, hearing nothing but the sound of his own
shoes. But suddenly, inside the market he had thought
empty, someone coughed and scratched himself and
moaned in troubled sleep.

"Oh—it's cold, cold."

Walking along the wooden street wall of the Occupation Army Barracks, Yukichi thought of the young student he had met today. The only reason Toshiki Okamura had for going into the publishing business was that
books were selling well. He saw no social meaning in
printing books, and recognized no responsibility.

Yukichi had pointed it out to him, and Toshiki had
answered, puzzled: "But it was in order to make money
that I decided to go into this. It's the same way with
other lines. In business it's better not to consider superfluous matters. Am I mistaken?"

Toshiki was remarkably bold and self-confident, for
all his polite and delicate way of talking. Yukichi was
an older man, but felt he had run into a stone wall.

"I've heard that left-wing books have an excellent
market, so I intend to print a lot of them. I've been
around to the teachers at college and asked them for
assistance. They all say they'll be happy to help. Nowadays, having a book published means a great deal to
a college teacher financially. I think the best way to
handle them would be to advance part of their royalties when we sign the contracts."

Nowadays there were students, Yukichi had heard,
who coolly walked out of the lecture hall after the professor had arrived. Toshiki talked politely, but what he

said reeked of boldness. Students who had been given the right to contradict their teachers were also free to use them.

"Why don't you publish one of Tatsuzo Oki's books? They say he demands fifteen per cent royalties where most people get ten or twelve per cent, but you can be certain of selling every last copy. The Tokyo intellectuals criticize him for this and that, but he has a solid set of readers, especially women, out in the prefectures who believe in him as if he were God."

Toshiki jumped at the idea, took out his notebook, and jotted down a memo. "Is Professor Oki also a leftist?"

"He can be anything. His color changes with the season. But he tries to keep an impartial, virtuous position, and never stumbles off his cloud. He's an absolutely safe man whatever happens, so I think he'd be good for you. Since he never runs any risk himself, he should fit in with your commercial objectives."

Yukichi immediately regretted having made the remark. This degenerate certainly had the cheek to call on Oki. That was all right. What Yukichi reproached himself for was that Toshiki might meet Tomoko there. He didn't want that to happen. He had a vague feeling that it shouldn't.

After the last war a European had written a novel, *Bachelor Girl*, about young women whom wartime experiences had masculinized. Perhaps this war had not only strengthened masculine tendencies among young women, but also produced a breed of feminine men. Toshiki reminded Yukichi of a famous degenerate who was appearing in Ueno Park dressed as a woman. That was an extreme case, no doubt, but Toshiki was not entirely unlike him. The war had not only given Japan its tragic class of coolies. It had also created a strange new variety of human beings.

THE DIAMOND

"Mr. Onozaki! Mr. Onozaki!"

He finally noticed Saeko's smiling face. "Ah, you."

"What were you so lost in thought about? I knew it was you all the way down the block."

"How stupid of me!" His face broke into that boyish look of his. "I could never forgive myself if I hadn't seen a woman as beautiful as you walking straight toward me. But I did see you, you know. I just didn't recognize you. I thought you were some magnificent young lady—"

"Thank you so much. There's no tax on talking, is there? But you'd do better to visit an optometrist and get your eyes tested. I really think you should. Your vision seems to be far gone already."

"Nothing of the sort. You're altogether wrong." And he made one of his theatrical gestures. "It's spring, that's what's the matter."

"It blurs your eyes?"

"I'm a wicked man. Unlikely as it seems, Mrs. Takano, I'm on my way to—what do you call it?—a rendezvous with a beautiful woman. And when en route to a rendezvous, a gentleman must make believe he doesn't see other women, no matter how lovely they are. He's got to pass them by—it's courtesy to his sweetheart. Incidentally, thanks again for that party awhile back. I trust the miniature gentleman is in good health?"

"The miniature gentleman? Oh, you mean little Toshi. He is a miniature gentleman, isn't he?"

"Impeccable. As though he'd just stepped out of a tailor's show window."

"Careful. I'll tell him what you say."

"He won't get mad. I suspect he'll like it."

Saeko couldn't tell whether Onozaki was joking or serious.

"Look at any of these postwar gentlemen. They're all standard models out of the show window. People who can neither destroy nor create. Have you ever seen one of those advertisements in American magazines— hat, suit, shoes, and *shoe soles*, all neatly matched for you, and lined up prettily on the colored page? A complete outfit for so many dollars. And you can get one by money order, even if you live in the wilds of Texas. An arrangement that leaves nothing to be desired. We'll have it in Japan soon. I intend to live a long time and enjoy myself watching the development of the miniature gentlemen. It'll turn out as I say."

They were talking on a crowded, busy block in Ginza, each defending himself with one arm against the people pushing by.

"Mr. Onozaki," Saeko interrupted, "shall I guess the name of the beautiful lady you're going to see?"

"Please."

"Tomoko Moriya. Am I wrong?"

Onozaki's eyes widened. "Remarkable!" he blurted, but he saw her method right away and turned over the parcel he was holding under his arm. It contained the illustrations for the magazine. "Master detective! Madam Sherlock Holmes! You just read the address here."

"Is she pretty?"

"Absolutely."

"How old?"

"Oh—twenty-one or two. Maybe a bit younger."

"Let's walk," Saeko urged quietly, and started off beside him. It didn't seem to bother her that she was going in the wrong direction.

"Say!" Onozaki twisted his neck. "Do you know this girl?"

Saeko tilted her head and smiled a melancholy smile. "A little. She's the daughter of a friend. I've never met her. Would you mind if I went with you, Mr. Onozaki?"

"Not at all!" Onozaki hadn't caught the connection yet. He'd forgotten all about Saeko's inquiry at the party.

"You're delivering some paintings?"

"Illustrations for a novel. And do you know what they're about, Mrs. Takano? Malacca, our Malacca. I've painted that hill you and I visited together."

"Really?"

"It's like a dream now, but I liked that town more than any other place in the South."

"Is that where you sketched the ruins of an old church while I drove through the town?"

"That's it. That's the place—remember how quiet it always was, as if it were dozing?"

Saeko thought of Heeren Street, the empty blocks flooded with noon sunshine and lined with Chinese mansions. And the thick lacquered doors, always shut, in the gates to the silent and, so far as one could tell from the outside, uninhabited houses. But she had been in one of them, in a cool, shaded room, where she had met Kyogo Moriya for the first time and talked with him. He had been wearing a Chinese robe. She remembered what they had been speaking about, almost word for word. Kyogo had predicted that Japanese women would abandon the kimono when the war was over, and she had disagreed.

"The weather's changed, hasn't it? You get warm walking."

"Yes, indeed." Onozaki looked at her solemnly. "Especially wearing that thick wool overcoat."

Etoile had its offices on the third floor of a small building in the Shimbashi district that had survived the war. The paint on the walls of the staircase was dirty and the badly lit corridors were like murky tunnels.

"Dark, isn't it?"

Saeko didn't answer.

Onozaki felt an anxiety under her silence and turned around to look at her.

"Mr. Onozaki, please don't introduce me. Say I just met you and happened to come along."

"Why?"

"No reason, just so. I'd like to observe her quietly— see what sort of person she is."

"I don't understand. You've gone out of your way to come."

"I want to avoid making any unnecessary trouble."

"Well, here we are at the third floor."

They walked down the corridor, reading the company names on the frosted-glass windows of the doors on either side, till Onozaki found *Etoile*. They opened the door and walked into a narrow room lined with desks. More than ten people, men and women, were standing or sitting at their work.

"Is Miss Moriya here?"

A round-faced girl at the desk nearest the door left the mail she had been sorting and got up to answer him. "She hasn't come in yet, sir." Young as she was, she had learned to use lipstick, apparently by watching her elders. Her mouth was a startling color.

A young man at another desk filled in. "Miss Moriya only works here in the afternoons. She's usually at the Dandelion Dress Shop on Fourth Street in the mornings."

"I've brought the magazine illustrations Miss Moriya

ordered. It's not necessary that I see her personally. If
there's anyone else who—"

"Ah!" Another young man, bespectacled and sitting
next to the window, got up and came over. "Are you
Mr. Onozaki?"

"Yes. I'd promised to bring them today, so here I am."

"I'm afraid we've put you to a great deal of trouble."
He showed them to chairs. "Forgive our cramped quarters."

A hill of books filled one corner of the narrow room,
and the walls were plastered with advertising posters.
Some of the employees were shouting into their desk
telephones. The place was lively enough, but Saeko
found it a strange litter of squalid people and dusty
books. She had been expecting to see Tomoko, and the
girl's absence made the office a pointless, over-crowded
confusion.

The workroom at the Dandelion was in the rear, so
they called it "Backstage." A wooden partition divided
it into a Japanese room, where the sewing machines
were, and a Western room with a triple mirror where
customers had their fittings.

Tomoko worked at a large plain wood table next to a
full-length triple mirror. In the mornings the sunlight
poured in from the window to the east of her. The freshly
cut material, piled up in waves on the table, was reflected
in the mirror, a mass of gorgeous colors. Tomoko herself
seemed a mass of colors as she sat there, motionless for
long stretches, studying the design in front of her. The
room was quiet in the mornings, the machines were
silent. It was spring, and the window was open. The lace
curtain that dimmed the intense sunlight would catch
the breeze now and then, float lightly in, swell, and re-

turn slowly to the window. Tomoko had taken off her jacket, and the bright reflected network of the lace would sketch itself on her left sleeve for a moment and withdraw.

Tomoko took up a pencil and made some changes in the pattern of the bodice on the garment. It was a dress for early summer she was designing. Their customers seemed to have more money in summer. That was their busiest season.

The woman who ran the Dandelion had been a schoolmate of Tomoko's mother. Her husband had been purged out of his post in the government service after the war, and the little property they'd had had been taken by the new taxes or frozen by other regulations. She had decided to try a woman's luck at getting money enough to live on, and the Dandelion was the result. Those of her friends who were also in sight of destitution and the younger wives and girls in her family had been mobilized into the venture, and Tomoko had come along.

Tomoko's mother had grasped the chance to resolve her long, secret anxiety about Tomoko's future. Her plans for the day when her daughter would have to leave Oki's house and support herself had borne fruit at last.

Tomoko had become one of the most valued workers at the Dandelion. She didn't come to the job, as so many women did after the war, out of pure necessity and totally unprepared. She had been trained to the work and loved it. Since she was a child, she had dreamed of going into business so she could repay her mother for all her kindness, and might have done so by herself if the Dandelion hadn't opened.

She was happy in the job. It gave her a chance for commissions to ghost fashion articles for magazines, and the older women in the shop, complete amateurs at business, had to get Tomoko to help them with their problems. They came to rely on her and were soon treating her like a mature woman.

The Dandelion was managed by a group of older women, all friends, all graduates of Women's College, and mostly war widows. Tomoko specialized, with pleasure, in designing, and occasionally did some sewing. Most of the women only took turns as salesladies, and Tomoko stood out among them as the youngest and most valuable. As she sat at her table working, her concentration and earnestness reminded one of a young girl over her textbooks.

Someone opened the door from the shop without warning. Tomoko was startled and turned round with the look of an angry child. It was the chief saleslady. "Pardon me. A customer for you." She turned to the lady behind her. "I hope you'll forgive the mess in here."

The customer walked in, and Tomoko rose to greet her. Her eyes opened wide in surprise. The woman's dress was well made. Tomoko could see that at a glance. It fit perfectly and was worn even better. But it was more than that that attracted attention. Tomoko was thrilled by the woman's sheer beauty. It was a cold, even somewhat frightening beauty. The face was clear-cut, with large eyes and delicate, firm nose and mouth. She looked slender, but the curves softly outlined in the nap of her wool dress were not without fullness.

The big eyes smiled at Tomoko, then glanced calmly about the room. "What a nice room you have!"

"Oh, no. I'm always ashamed of the way it's littered up."

Saeko viewed herself in the triple mirror from every angle, turning on the wooden floor amid the bright dance of the slanting morning sunlight. Her eyes came back to Tomoko in a gentle smile. "You know Mr. Onozaki, the painter, don't you, miss?"

Tomoko felt oppressed by the question and blushed. "Slightly."

"I was with Mr. Onozaki a little while ago, at the *Etoile* office. He said he was delivering some pictures. I've just left him, as a matter of fact. I even know your name already. Miss Tomoko Moriya. What a lovely name it is! And more than that, Mr. Onozaki told me how beautiful you were—he was singing your praises, you see."

"The illustrations are ready?"

"Yes, we delivered them together. But you work here as well as at the magazine, don't you?"

The saleslady opened a cabinet and took out some bolts of cloth. "She's just a girl, as you see, but so earnest at her designing! And our customers' favorite. They all ask for her. She has a remarkable talent, young as she is. She just looks at a customer and thinks something up, without any trouble, that we could never dream of. We may wonder about it at first, but when it's made up, it always turns out to be an original dress, and in the best of taste. It's really incredible."

"I'm envious of your work." Saeko was glancing at the design on Tomoko's table. "May I see it?"

"Oh, please don't. It's not finished yet."

"Let me see it anyway."

"I've only sketched in the outline." The blood had rushed to Tomoko's head and showed in her face. But she still couldn't keep her eyes from Saeko's white profile. The light skin with its soft, lustrous, almost greenish tinge, and the part between the glistening black hairs, were compelling, fascinating even to another woman. It was a few minutes before Tomoko could turn away her eyes.

"For summer, already?"

"Yes, just a try." Tomoko laughed. "I want to design

a bathing-suit for this summer too. The people at *Etoile* say they'll get a movie actress to model it, and run the picture as a frontispiece."

Even Saeko enjoyed the girl's enthusiasm. "You're doing really first-rate work. It makes me jealous. Young people nowadays *are* different, aren't they?"

The saleslady had piled the materials from the cabinet on the table, and was waiting for Saeko to look them over. "As you can see, we have nothing very good in the way of cloth."

"That can't be helped nowadays." Saeko smiled tactfully. "Why, even at the theater, I'm told, they have to see what's left in the wardrobe before they know what play they can put on. They can only do the pieces they have costumes for, so it's the costume manager, not the actors or the writers, who decides the program. Luckily, the costumes for the lead parts were sent out of the city during the war and they still have them. But the cottons for the smaller parts were all burned, and that's become a real problem now. Miss Tomoko must be having the same trouble. I suppose there are lots of times when you can't do the work you want to do because you can't get the material you need."

She was going through the bolts of cloth one by one. It was impossible to guess her background. Even the stone in the ring on her white finger told you nothing. It was nothing so ostentatious as a diamond—just a cat's eye, severely inconspicuous.

"Would you put this aside for me? It's for winter, though."

"You certainly do have fine taste. Goods of this quality aren't to be had anywhere in Japan, and won't be coming in for some time yet."

"It may be a bit loud for me, though."

"Not in the least. Someone I know brought this piece

back from a trip to England years ago and let us have it recently because she needed some ready cash. You can be sure of the quality. It's genuine English cloth."

Saeko interrupted. "By the way, Miss Tomoko, I'd very much like you to come to my house, when it's convenient for you. I have some cloth at home I'd like you to look at and decide what should be done with it. You shall be my adviser on Western fashions."

It was cloudy the next morning, as it so often is in spring, and looked like rain. Tomoko left the house with her raincoat. But the low clouds hung in a windless sky all day. By late afternoon the rain hadn't come yet.

Tomoko followed Saeko's instructions to South Takanawa, a residential area spared by the war. It was a quiet enclave of wooden houses, and even the trees looked old. There were no ashes and no ruins. Nothing had been burned down here, but a desolation hovered over the place. There was little light, of course, on this cloudy day, but more than that, the uncared-for walls and shrubs and gardens accounted for it. No one had money enough since the war to bother about such things. Here and there a cherry tree in full flower stretched its branches over an old wooden street wall with gaps between its loosening planks. The flowers looked heavy suspended in the gray sky.

From somewhere along the lane the tones of a samisen floated through the sleepy air. Tomoko was in another world from the busy, crowded everyday outside. What a vast difference there was between places the war had touched and those it had spared!

Tomoko had been wondering what sort of house a woman with Saeko Takano's sense of style would live in. Her taste in Western clothing was perfectly mature. She had gone far beyond copying the style book and imitating foreigners. Her dresses were in good taste and she wore them as if born to it.

Tomoko found the sign with the single name "Takano" written on it at a simple gate down the block. It consisted of two wooden panels, each attached to a high, unadorned pillar. The panels were open, revealing a wide front garden. Old trees, untrimmed and unaligned, spread their branches between the gate and the house entrance. The house itself was fairly large, in Japanese style, and the door in the entrance was of time-worn latticework. There were three more name-signs on it, with men's names. Saeko had probably given lodging to some war victims. It was the custom at large houses at the time.

At the lattice door, Tomoko heard the samisen again and a woman singing to it. The voice was skilled and melodious and, to Tomoko's amazement, sounded like Saeko's. The song was an old piece, something in the Kiyomoto style.

Tomoko rang the bell. A young maid came out and received her ceremoniously. She rolled open a panel of the screen door to the interior, and Tomoko knew for certain that the music and the singing were in this house, upstairs, and that the voice was Saeko's.

The maid showed her down the corridor and into a Western room that opened off it, then went toward the back of the house. It was an old room, but bright, because its windows looked out on the garden and trellised wisteria. The pictures on the wall were by well-known painters of the modern schools, and the furniture was in the latest style.

The samisen stopped. Lines of rain glittered white in the sky over the crowded trees of the garden. Saeko was saying good-by to a guest, a woman apparently, at the entrance.

"My! It's started to rain, I'm afraid."

Tomoko had been waiting barely a minute when Saeko came in. She was wearing a Japanese lined robe with a dark-blue, almost black, splashed pattern, and an obi tied around it. She hardly seemed the same person Tomoko had met yesterday. The obi, Tomoko could tell, was a Ryukyu Islands style, white cloth printed in a complex flower design.

"I'm sorry to have kept you waiting." Saeko was smiling. "My music teacher's been here. . . . I'm very glad you've come. This is an old house, as you can see, and a bit gloomy on a day like this."

"You wear Japanese clothes too." Tomoko looked as though she had just recovered from amazement. "I'd assumed you only wore Western dresses."

"It depends on my mood. . . . Oh, yes, I'd asked you to look over some material, hadn't I? Must that be today?"

"Why, no. I can come back again."

"Let's take our time about it, h'm? There's something I want to talk to you about."

Saeko was looking at Tomoko, now and again, almost staring, with a depth and intimacy in her eyes that hardly seemed suited to a young lady who had just dropped round from a dress shop. "You *are* lovely—and very much like your father."

Tomoko lifted her eyes. It was a moment before she felt surprise, and then not too much. She had no reason to take Saeko literally.

The rain was silent. It soaked into the matting of the veranda beneath the trellises without a sound.

"Miss Tomoko, I have a favor I want to ask you. . . . Would you accept a position with me, as a sort of secretary? You needn't do anything in particular. Just be with me. You'll be free to go on with your own work, and can help me select my clothes on the side. I have a Chinese woman in my household who'll continue doing the actual dressmaking. She's an excellent *couturière*. You'll only have to decide what sort of thing I should wear. You're working at that magazine, I know. I've just given some money to a set of young people who are setting up a publishing house and I'd like you to go in with them. Do you think you'd like that? Your salary would be higher than where you are now—and quite apart from what you'd get as my secretary and fashion adviser. I want you at any price. That's a terrible thing to say, I suppose, but I'm a willful woman. Can't I make you come to me?"

Her eyes sparkled mischievously, and she added something Tomoko couldn't understand: "But you musn't tell your father for a while."

Young women are full of life. It seeps through their pores. But along with it goes an indefinable uncertainty.

Tomoko looked at Saeko, surprised. Her eyes were clear, transparent—there was no experience, no past behind their bright innocence. But Tomoko still thought that Saeko meant Tatsuzo Oki when she spoke of her father. No other possibility had occurred to her.

"Your father has reason to be angry with me. I had no idea of hurting him. . . . It was during the war. There were some wicked people—I got him into serious trouble without meaning to. I felt terrible about it, but I'm sure he's angry with me. So—" a smile spread over Saeko's face—"so I'd like you not to let your father hear about me for a while, not until the right time comes. The right time will come. Then, why then—but first I want to win your friendship, Tomoko. Do you promise?"

"Where did you know my father?"

"Singapore."

Tomoko's eyes opened with even more surprise.

"I met him for the first time at a place called Malacca
—a quiet little town on a beautiful stretch of seacoast.
He was a fine man, and kind. He showed those years in
Europe. He wasn't like other Japanese—more modern
and aware; and he had such interesting conversation.
He's finally come back to Japan, I understand."

Tomoko stared at Saeko. Her eyes seemed to fill her
whole face. Her skin was turning pale. A reply had been
forming in her mind, but it had vanished now. She
hadn't had time yet to decide how to take what Saeko
was saying, and what she should think about it.

Impulsively, as though something were pushing her,
she blurted: "The man you met—did he speak to you
about me?"

"What are you saying, Tomoko? You haven't seen
your father yet?"

Tomoko shook her head, but said nothing. She shook
her head violently, disturbing her glistening thick black
hair. Her arms began to tremble, and she strove to control them. A hard glitter came into her fixed eyes. Shock
distorted her lovely lips and nostrils.

Saeko realized that Tomoko couldn't be lying, but the
question came involuntarily: "You mean it?"

The rain grew audible. Tomoko sat white and motionless, like a thing of stone. Only her fingers moved. She
held them clasped on her lap, but they seemed to have
taken on a life of their own. They shook with agitation
and Tomoko could not make them still.

"It's incredible. Your father's come back to Japan and
you don't even know where he is?"

"That man—" Panic showed in Tomoko's face. "I'm
ashamed to say it, but—I can't remember the time when
I called him father. I was three or four when— When I
say father I mean the man who's father to me now. The
other—I've only seen pictures of him, and that so long

ago I can barely remember what he looked like. If he should suddenly come up to me, I'd only be bewildered."

"You don't remember him?"

"No! Not at all." And suddenly Tomoko looked as though she were going to cry. "Mother's married again, too. . . . He mustn't come. He's got to stay away. Poor mother—he mustn't make her suffer any more. I don't know anything about it, but—he mustn't hurt her. Mrs. Takano, you say you know him. If you should see him, tell him that, please. Poor Mother, she's suffered enough." Tomoko buried her face in her hands and broke into sobs. Her shoulders rose and fell with her deep breathing.

Saeko looked away toward the rainfall in the garden. The thin, hazy springtime rain scattered in fine drops over the fresh colors of the garden trees. Sitting there as though deeply moved, Saeko felt quite another emotion burst out of her heart with a pang, and start along her veins to spread through her body. A smile came momentarily to her face as she looked out the window. The emotion that filled her now was confidence and pride as a woman.

"Tomoko." Her voice was carefully modulated, gentle but demanding. "Your mother is your mother and you are you. Surely you can see that it's out of consideration for your mother that your father hasn't come to you. What else could keep him away, now that he's finally returned to Japan? Tomoko, I want to be like a mother to you. I want to show Kyogo Moriya what a splendid young lady I've helped bring up. Or don't you like that?"

Tomoko didn't answer.

Saeko stood up and went over to her. "Your father could talk about nothing but you when we were together in Singapore. He was lonely, Tomoko. A gentle, feeling man—there was nothing military about him. I was crying when I came away from seeing him. There was white in his hair, and he couldn't go home. He had no choice but to spend his whole life wandering through foreign countries. He was suffering, Tomoko, suffering so much that he spoke about it to a woman like me, just because I happened to be there. . . . He was wondering what you were like—you were so young when he last saw you." Saeko bit her lips. Tears were flowing silently down her cheeks, and they were real.

Tomoko felt Saeko come closer, lean over, and put her hands softly on her shoulders. The odor of a rare perfume hovered about Saeko's clothing. And underneath the clothing, Saeko's flesh, pressed against her, was alive with a strange excitement that troubled Tomoko. Not since childhood had she felt another's body so close, except her mother's. The arms were around her shoulders now, and there was something more sensual in the embrace than mere affection. Tomoko squirmed beneath it.

"You seem like my own flesh and blood to me, Tomoko." Saeko's tone was warm.

Tomoko's body was shaking as she looked up, her face almost touching Saeko's. Passion and intensity had changed Saeko's features. She looked like another person.

"Your father is really a good man."

Under Tomoko's unblinking stare, she became herself again. She looked aside for a moment, released the girl's shoulders, and took her hands. "You must meet him. There'll be no danger, if you see him alone. I'll know where he is soon and arrange for you to meet him without anybody knowing. It will be all right that way."

"I'll have to think about it. I'll let you know."

"But why?"

Tomoko couldn't answer.

"Don't you understand how lonely your father must be, even back here in Japan?"

Tomoko nodded submissively.

"Well then, please do as I say. I'll keep behind the scenes. I'm just going to make it possible for you to meet him. You have nothing to worry about."

"But I—" Uncertainty showed on her face again. "I can't decide what I should do. And—I don't like having secrets from Mother. Not secrets like this, anyway." She stared into space, and tears welled up in her eyes again.

"Still worried about your mother?"

"Mother's done so much for me." Her voice was low. She seemed on the verge of tears. "Since Father left, she's given her whole life to taking care of me. She even got married again for my sake. I've come to realize that." She could not believe that her mother had ever really loved her imperious stepfather.

"Are there any other children?"

"I have a younger brother, but he's still a child." Tomoko was seeing her mother's situation more clearly than ever, and how helplessly she had been driven into it. Tomoko had never thought about it so seriously before. She could see it now with such depth and clarity that she felt the pain of it in her own heart. "Mrs. Takano, I don't want to meet him. Forgive me, I can't."

"I understand." Saeko's eyes were as definite about it as her voice. "I shouldn't have spoken about it. I've made you unhappy. I didn't mean to, you know."

"Of course not."

"Don't misunderstand. I saw into your father's heart when I met him then. I wanted to tell you about it. I didn't think— Women are such fools!"

"Please don't reproach yourself."

Saeko didn't miss the traces of agitation on Tomoko's

face. She was still a girl, and her strength was mostly talk. If she actually met her father, things would turn out differently. So Saeko knew that she would have another chance and would be able to make better use of it. She smiled innocently. "Enough of this. Let's forget all about it. I'd like you to look over the cloth. But before that, what about the first thing we discussed? Will you become my secretary?"

"I don't think I'm qualified. Really, I don't know anything."

"That isn't the point. I want you to be mine, one way or another. You know how capricious I am. That's why I'm asking you. You needn't worry about your qualifications."

Tomoko was silent.

"I'm not asking you to come and be with me every day. There are many times I want to be alone, too. And I have a husband, even I, and sometimes go and stay with him. The best thing for you to keep busy at would be that publishing house. They're all young students there."

"Thank you very much. But I'm obligated to the people at the company I'm working at. I can't leave suddenly."

"How good you are! I'm glad of it. But you can advise me on Western fashions. That should be all right. Why don't you just do that for a while, and take on the other work when you come to know me and see that I'm not an evil, lying woman? But, work or no work, I do want you to be my friend, Tomoko, willful and self-centered though I am. Or, to put it better, I've decided not to let go of you."

Saeko was being excessively kind. Tomoko saw vaguely that it was for her father's sake. She realized too that she had been drawn to Saeko herself, very strongly for the little time she'd known her. She had never seen a woman living so freely, in every sense of the word, and that in itself was a strong attraction. But when she thought of her mother, she hesitated.

"I really don't know how to answer you."

"Cheer up. Look! The rain's stopped and the sun is shining. Only little Tomoko's weather is still uncertain."

And indeed the sunlight was splendid on the dripping branches of the garden trees. Here and there amid the leaves of an evergreen, lustrous even in winter, fruit grew red like flowers.

When she got back to the magazine office and started speaking to people, Tomoko realized that she wanted to be alone, untroubled by anyone.

Her father had disappeared before she was aware of the world around her, and now, suddenly, he was back in Japan, or so she was told. The initial shock had worn off and she felt capable of using her own judgment again. But something had entered her heart that had never been there before. It was like a blind spot impeding her vision, or a shadow near her that kept getting on her nerves, so that her eyes turned naturally toward it. Tomoko was in this state of mind as she stood talking to her co-workers about the magazine.

It was in the train on the way home that Tomoko realized that the surrender had cleared the way for her father's return. The thought added the shocking weight of reality to what had still been an indefinite idea.

This was no abstract notion. It was solid fact. And somewhere, sometime, she would see her father face to face. She was looking down, her body swaying with the motion of the car, but raised her eyes at the thought. They were full of surprise. The evening train was packed. It was not impossible that her father, Kyogo, was somewhere in the crowd. The idea came to her mind. She became conscious of it, and realizing she was losing her self-control, pulled herself together.

What was so surprising about it? And what reason had she to cry? There would be nothing wrong about going to see her father. She had no need to worry. She would only be going in order to stop him from making Mother unhappy. The responsibility would be entirely his, not hers. Nothing held her back. She was free to meet her father, as any person might.

She closed her eyes and smiled to herself. A feeling she had not expected stirred and spread in her body. A faceless, bodiless father had entered Tomoko's heart and occupied a place there he would never leave again. It was a strange thing, but not an unhappy one. Indeed, her heart was dancing. There was white in his hair, Saeko had said. The words came sharp and clear into her consciousness.

Tomoko was imagining her father in the way that a young mother, feeling her baby growing and moving in her womb, tries to imagine what he will look like when he is born. Her father had come into her heart a mere shadow. She was trying to give him a face, and put clothes on him, and guess his age. Embodying this invisible form step by step was very much like her designing work. It made her happy, and a smile came of itself to her lips.

The stars were clouded as she walked home down the road. Inside the gate, lamplight shone from the Western window of the guest room next to Oki's study. He had a visitor.

Tatsuzo Oki, like the scholar he was, led a secluded life in the Western part of the house, coming to join his family in the Japanese rooms only for meals. Tomoko went in by the lattice door of the side entrance and walked to the kitchen to say hello to her mother, who was working there.

"I'm home, Mother."

A European tea set was standing ready before the cupboard.

"You're just in time, my dear. Would you take this into the guest room?"

Setsuko, Tomoko's mother, was the sort of woman who wouldn't let her picture be taken, and hated appearing before guests. Tomoko waited while her mother put sugar in the tea. Since the war, they'd had orders from Oki to use real sugar only in his own tea or coffee, and to give the guests saccharine. Tomoko watched her mother doing so, and felt unhappy. A teaspoon with a special design went next to Oki's cup.

"Who's here?"

"A newspaperman."

Tomoko knocked lightly at the guest-room door.

"Come in," Oki answered and glanced at her for a second. Then he turned back to his guest, who was taking notes in pencil on a paper pad, and went on discoursing in his usual rapid, condescending speech: "Reform is impossible unless the Academy of Arts is given more authority, and its influence strengthened. It must not remain what it is at present—a place of retirement for antiquated gentlemen. It must be placed above the bureaucrats and enabled to perform positive work. But, in fact, the master-disciple relationships and nepotism of the feudal members have become an obstacle to reform, and—"

"Now, wait a minute. Wait a minute," the newspaperman protested.

But Oki came down on him with all his weight, as if he were debating seriously: "After all, the establishment of a healthy academicism is the first necessity in Japan. Democratization is the second step. Unless civil decisions control the bureaucrats, the work can not go forward.

Culture is politics too. It's the technique we have to acquire. Of course our littérateurs and artists have always
tended to avoid politics, in the tradition of Oriental scholars. But that will no longer do in this age of democracy.
The artistic genius may be permitted his solitude and
unhappiness. But it's the generality that's important.
The generalization of culture and art, I mean. And that
is politics, is it not? To bring up the most immediate
problem, the members of the Academy must demand
seats in the Diet."

Tomoko left and went up to her room on the second
floor of the Japanese section to change her clothes. Oki's
tone was vigorous enough, but what he was saying
sounded empty and incoherent. Tomoko had a secret
tonight. Her mother had given her a tightly sealed packet
of letters and photographs to take with her as her own
when she married or left the house. Tomoko meant to
open it in privacy and look at the pictures of her father.
She switched on the light and opened her pocketbook to
get out the key to her cabinet. A small object wrapped in
paper slipped out. Saeko had handed it to her as she was
leaving her house. Tomoko opened it casually and found
a diamond the size of a soybean sparkling luminously in
her hand.

THE HOUSE OF PEONIES

The next Sunday, it was too warm to wear a coat. Tomoko had decided that the diamond was an improper
gift and was walking to Saeko's to return it as politely
as she could. When she reached the house, the car was
waiting in front amid the fallen cherry blossoms on the
road, and Saeko was on her way out through the garden.
There was a young man with her.

"Hello, Tomoko." Saeko looked much younger in
Western dress. "You've come just at the right time. If
you're free now, come along with us part of the way. . . .
Oh, this is Toshiki Okamura. He's doing that publishing
work I mentioned to you. And this is Tomoko Moriya."

"You're going on a trip?"

"A little one, in line of duty." Saeko smiled enigmatically. "Come along as far as Yokohama. Toshi here will
bring you back with all his usual chivalry."

"Where are you going?"

"To my husband's place." Her voice was crisp. "Wives
have some duties, even under the new constitution."

Tomoko was still puzzled, but she couldn't very well
mention the diamond at that point, so she decided to
accept the invitation.

"Yokohama's been built up wonderfully, I understand," Toshiki said. "They have an American town
there, and pleasant places to walk, and there must be
some first-rate dance halls and cabarets. Why don't you
stop there awhile yourself, Aunt Saeko?"

"I'm not traveling for pleasure today. Though I may
see some peonies in bloom." Saeko turned to Tomoko,

who was sitting on her left. "My husband's an unusual man. He has no profession and he's never had a job since he left school. But he does raise peonies. It's the only thing he can do, and he does it very well."

Tomoko was wondering how to bring up the diamond. The peonies were a surprising note. But as she pictured the large luxuriant blossoms in her mind, she realized how much they resembled Saeko.

Toshiki interrupted her thoughts. "Moriya . . . This must be the daughter of that man I went looking for."

Saeko kept looking ahead at the front seat and said coolly: "Oh, that business—you needn't bother any more, now that I've met Tomoko."

"Mr. Moriya's been in Kyoto all the time."

Saeko said nothing.

"Admiral Ushigi sent me a postcard after my trip to his house to let me know the name of Mr. Moriya's hotel in Kyoto. Ushigi writes very elegantly. Too elegantly. I could barely make out the gist of it."

Saeko continued to ignore him. She was looking out the window, and suddenly changed the subject. "Look, you can see the ocean from the Tokyo-Yokohama Highway now. Everything's been burned down clean to the coast."

It was a long and desolate stretch of ruins. A few shacks had been built, and in the remains of factories the burned and rusted skeletons of machines lay monstrous in the spring sunlight. There were no flowers, only the dead black trunks of the trees. Here and there a concrete wall stood undamaged in the rubble.

"Toshi!" Saeko sounded sharp. "Are you making any progress with publishing? You've got to work at it steadily, you know. I won't stand for any nonsense."

"I'm taking care of it, Aunt Saeko."

"So." She nodded her head. "As I told you in the first place, you just can't run a business with only students."

"But Aunt Saeko, you say that because you don't know what young people are like nowadays. We're different from the men who went through the war—the generation just before us. We've had to think about how to make a living, whether we wanted to or not. We're serious about working. We may be in school, but we've learned how to live in society already."

"A little too soon, perhaps. It makes me uneasy."

"That's because of your ancient ideas."

"Isn't he impolite? Calling a girl my age ancient." Saeko smiled toward Tomoko. "But, you know, I loathe cheap machine-made cloth, no matter how modern it is. I'll take rugged homespun, any day. You understand me, Tomoko. You could take some Japanese summer-robe material and turn it into a Western dress that would be perfectly chic. Even Kurume-pattern cloth makes a blouse that's far more suitable to Japanese women than any printed stuff. Don't you agree? No modern material has that deep-blue color. French women would jump at the chance to wear it. But Japanese women are afraid to—a blouse of that material might look remade from last year's wardrobe."

"It depends on who wears it, Aunt Saeko."

"I was thinking of Tomoko. It would be perfect for you, Tomoko—that rich blue would stand out beautifully against your white skin. You're not one of those women who would drape around themselves a piece of shiny cloth thin enough to flap in the wind and think they're in the height of Western fashion."

Tomoko blushed. The words tumbled out. "But it's yourself you're talking about, Mrs. Takano."

Saeko kept the rudder of the conversation in her own hands all the way to Yokohama. Tomoko never got a chance to mention the diamond.

"Where shall I drop you?" Saeko smiled as though she

were planning something amusing. "Poor me! I'm headed for hours of boredom, peonies or no peonies. But you two . . . I have it. I'll leave you on top of a beautiful hill where you can get a good view of the harbor."

And so she did. The steamers in port had anchored their vast hulks half within and half without the wall of buildings that lined the concave shore. The sea stretched still and bright, asleep beneath the great sky and the heavy light of spring.

"Well, good-by, Tomoko. See you again."

And the automobile drew away along the quiet hill-top road. Tomoko was alone in this unexpected place with a man she had just met. She was silent. Her eyes followed the car for a while, then turned toward the ocean.

"Aunt Saeko's like that. She does whatever comes into her head," Toshiki said. "She's a queen. I wonder which, though—queen of hearts, queen of spades, or queen of diamonds?"

The joke brought only a faint smile to Tomoko's lips. She was going to return the diamond the next chance she got. She knew which Saeko was—she was queen of diamonds.

"Shall we walk? Scenery doesn't interest me too much, no matter how good it is. I get much more fun out of meeting people than contemplating nature."

"Are we near a station?"

"You feel lost, huh? Aunt Saeko enjoys doing that to people. But we mustn't let her win. Let's have a good time instead of worrying about it. The joke'll be on her. Isn't that a good idea?"

The war had been here too. There were empty spaces on the hill from which you could look down on the city below. Some prewar Western houses were still standing, and some new ones had been built. They had iron railings entwined with rose vines, or low painted wooden fences. The people on the streets were all foreigners. And new streamlined automobiles drove past in both directions, unendingly and almost without sound.

"What about going dancing?" He asked her while she was thinking about getting her father's address in Kyoto from him.

She lifted her head in surprise and shook it in refusal. "I'd rather stay outside and walk."

Toshiki laughed softly. "Well then, let's walk hand in hand, like those Americans over there."

Tomoko was shocked. "Absolutely not!" She shook her head again, and her thick hair flew from side to side.

"You'd be embarrassed? How old-fashioned!" Toshiki looked like a child when he laughed. "Isn't it the privilege of the young? Everybody's doing it."

Tomoko walked on without saying anything. She still wanted to ask about her father. There was a pain in her chest now.

"Look, the violets are in bloom."

Toshiki was looking at a grassy stretch beyond the sidewalk. It had been a private garden before the war. The house had disappeared, and the grass was growing wild on the level stretch of lawn that looked across a valley to the neighboring hill. There were still some giant tropical lilies amid the grass, and a basin was set in the ground like a vast flowerpot. The garden showed the sea from another angle, glittering over a shoulder of the hill.

Toshiki went in to look for violets. "Look at all the different kinds of things growing here. It used to be a foreigner's garden, I'll bet. There must be flowers here."

Tomoko went in too and stood among the widespread low-bending boughs of a hemlock. It was too hot in the sunlight and she wanted the shade.

"I'll take a smoke." Toshiki chose a spot where the grass was thick and sat down.

The hill across the valley was covered with trees. Western houses, newly built to judge by their bright red-tiled roofs and freshly painted wooden walls, followed one another innumerably along the contours up and down the hill. The colors were unusually rich for Japan. A broad highway cut into the mountainside had apparently just been opened to traffic. A long line of jeeps moved along it like insects.

Tomoko walked over to where Toshiki was sitting and looked across at the colorful scene. The white wash hung up to dry in some of the gardens sparkled and flapped like flags. She finally made up her mind. "Where in Kyoto is my father living?"

Toshiki looked around at her. "What? You don't know?"

"I don't know where the hotel is. He hasn't written."

"I'll give you the address whenever you need it."

Tomoko thought of Toshiki coming or phoning to her house to tell her, and changed color. "I'll come to your place to get it."

"Welcome. Here's my office address on this card. . . . Come on, sit down. Get off your feet. . . . Lovely day, isn't it? That must be a skylark singing."

It was a silent, shining world. The only things that moved now were the jeeps going up the new road.

"Tomoko."

She didn't answer.

"Have you ever had a love-affair?"

"No."

"What about necking, then? Ever done that?"

Tomoko blushed and shook her head.

Toshiki stretched out his arms and grasped her hand. "Let's kiss. . . . But don't tell Aunt Saeko."

She turned around to find Toshiki's light-skinned face almost touching hers. His eyes were shut and his lips pursed up expectantly. And disgustingly. Tomoko did something she had never done before in her whole life. Her right hand was free, and she slapped it against that face with all the strength she could muster.

Toshiki let go her hand in amazement. He wasn't angry. He was laughing. His cheek was red where she had slapped him. "You little savage!" But he was perfectly calm. His laugh was sulky, but his composure hadn't been shaken in the least. "All right. All right. Let's make believe it didn't happen. That was just a warm-up, Tomoko."

"I'll be going now." She stood up.

"Stop that. Don't be a child. I'm not angry."

Tomoko couldn't find an answer.

"What happened, after all? We're alone. It's trivial. It doesn't mean anything. The good weather had me feeling a little springlike, that's all. When it was all over, you'd have found that nothing much had happened, and that you and I were just the same as always. It doesn't mean anything. Don't take it so seriously. We're both young."

"Excuse me. I'm going."

"Let's go together. You don't know the way. This is an Occupation Army area, and the morals have been modernized too." He was too unperturbed not to dampen Tomoko's anger. The only thing that seemed to worry him was that Saeko might find out. He reminded her again. "You won't mention this to Aunt Saeko, will you?"

"No! You can be sure I won't talk about it."

"It's entirely meaningless, you know. Just something to laugh about."

Tomoko pulled herself together and looked at him.

Her excitement had cooled. He seemed even younger than herself, and he could do such a thing without feeling ashamed about it. His callousness was more than impudent. It was unnatural. And when she remembered that face with the eyes shut waiting confidently for her to put her lips on his, she felt sick to her stomach.

"Let's go along Coast Street. It's a beautiful walk."

"Pardon me, but I'd rather walk alone. I want to do some shopping."

"I'd be in your way? . . . All right, as long as you're not angry any more. But do you really think a woman should go walking alone in a strange neighborhood?"

Tomoko walked by herself until she heard a loud voice behind her and looked around. It was a man in shirt sleeves. He was waving to her. The laugh and the white hair told her at once that it was Kohei Onozaki.

"I thought it was you." He laughed like a boy. "Quite a surprise to meet here. I was hungry, so we stopped here to get some *wan-ton*. Come in."

They went into one of the Chinese restaurants that lined the Street Below the Mountain. Onozaki had been looking out the window when he saw Tomoko walking by, and had dropped his chopsticks and gone out to call her. The young man with him, Yukichi Okabe, had stayed at the table. He greeted Tomoko now with a friendly smile.

"You know him, h'm? He's been guiding me all over Yokohama today, and I've been making sketches."

Tomoko knew that Yukichi lived in Yokohama.

"What about some *wan-ton* for you? It's delicious. Yokohama's really the place for *wan-ton*. The broth is wonderful."

Tomoko refused and watched the two men go back to their bowls with gusto.

"He's doing a painting for the color page of a magazine," Yukichi told her. "But Mr. Onozaki insists on looking for the ugly places. They're all he'll paint."

"Pretty places have no meaning," Onozaki announced. "I don't say I won't paint them, but these American scenes look transplanted from the United States. It's not only here. All the damaged cities in Japan are the same. The new sections have no individuality yet."

"Well then, let's go up to the Heights when we get out of here. Yokohama looks different from up there. You can see the parts of the city that are still standing from before the war."

"Local patriotism! But, you know, those coolies really astonished me. It's just as you say, Yukichi, Japan has its coolies now, too—and its thieves' markets. Japanese are different, we used to think; that sort of thing couldn't happen here. There's one delusion smashed to pieces. People are exactly alike when they're pushed to extremes —all people in all countries. We have the proof before our eyes, nowadays."

Onozaki shook his head mournfully. There was bitterness on his face. "We're no nation of gods. People are identical in identical situations. But the very fact that I lament so at every example of corruption shows that I'm still too sentimental. The idea that Japanese are different is still rooted in my head. But we're not, are we? We're a people who can do nothing to save ourselves unless some outside force moves in to change our lives. Are we always going to be that way? The most shameful thing is that we don't even regret it. All we can do is make up arguments to excuse ourselves. Those we have aplenty. We can't overcome our tendency to follow the leader. We're too proud of our borrowed plumage to have opinions of our own. A whole people rushed into the national uniform when the war started, and into aloha shirts when it was over—and hardly noticed the difference. That's how we are, Miss Moriya, the perfect citizens for a dead nation." He spoke with vehemence, then started sipping his *wan-ton* noisily. He was a big eater and had a giant physique. Throughout, the gentle look that showed how much he liked people had never left his face.

"It's no easy thing to live." He was almost sighing. "Of course, there's a reason for it. Everything was smashed in the war. A people who had never known defeat were horribly defeated. Everything was fouled up, and they were helpless. All their faults showed up at once. Germans or Frenchmen wouldn't behave this way. Even a baby knows enough to get up when he tumbles down. . . . M'm, that was good! I'm full." He smiled and lit a cigarette.

"Mr. Onozaki," Yukichi said, "are you really that desperate about Japan?"

"About the Japanese, I am. I love Japan. It's the individual Japanese I detest." Onozaki's face got red, and he fell into his exaggerated way of talking and gesticulating. It was in Paris that he had got into the habit of cornering someone after a meal and talking him to death. But he found it as good for his health in Japan as in Paris.

"The Japanese must be made to suffer more. That's how I see it. They've got to be pushed down mercilessly. They've gone halfway down now, they're suspended midway and feel that the worst is over and that they're all right now. That idea must be knocked out of them, or there'll be no revival. They're thinking they can scrape through. They're cowardly and stupid, with no national confidence or pride. They've got to be pushed down to the very bottom and made to suffer. Any man opens his eyes when he's had his fill of suffering. He bares his teeth and gets mad. That's it, he gets mad, and it's only

getting mad that can save Japan. Look around you, nobody's angry. They're all laughing like idiots. It's pathetic. How many people are there even now who are
really angry about the war? It's over, they congratulate
each other, and laugh, laugh, laugh. Horrible! People
have got to learn to be as angry at what happens to
other people as at what happens to themselves."

Yukichi had been listening quietly to Onozaki's ora-
tion. He spoke now, with a laugh. "Maybe I'm your
angry man—a little bit, anyway. I went through a lot
in the Army, and I'm angry at the war, of course, but
at the other things too. And I suspect lots of Japanese
are, more than you think. They *are* angry, at their fellow
Japanese and especially at the way they've gone to pieces.
So I can't feel so desperate as you, Mr. Onozaki. The
war really hurt me. I had to leave school and interrupt
my studies. But that doesn't mean that my life in the
Army was as meaningless as most people say. Maybe
I'm thinking selfishly, maybe I don't want to recognize
the complete uselessness of a part of my life I was forced
to go through, but so far as I'm concerned I think it
helped me in some ways, painful as it was."

A quiet, gentle smile came to his strong face. "There
are lots of men who really enjoyed life in the Army. They
had a wonderful time. I get angry at the people who can
only talk about the painful, hideous side of the war now
that it's over. I was a student, and it really injured me.
But I lived through it. I didn't die, thank God, and I've
come back. I did nothing bad, nothing I have to repent
as a human being. I suffered for a number of years, but
it's over now, and it doesn't especially bother me today.
It was a terrible experience, of course, but I think it's
been of some use to me for my life. I'm not the only one
who feels that way. Lots of my friends do. I'm sorry for
those who died in the war, but I'm not at all unhappy

now. And the way I look at Japan as it is today may be a bit different from the way Mr. Onozaki does. It's my awful egotism, perhaps, but I'm indescribably happy to be alive. And my life matters to me, it will as long as I live, just because I know what it means to live in a combat area wondering whether you're going to die today, whether you're going to die tomorrow. And in my life now there is no compulsion, there are no orders. So I'm eager to live the way I want to until I die. I probably wouldn't feel that way so strongly if I hadn't gone to war."

"M'm, yes." Onozaki nodded happily.

"So even from my own selfish, personal considerations, I'm not so discouraged as Mr. Onozaki by the demoralization of the Japanese. I'm confident the Japanese people can remake themselves, even if they have to start from the lowest depths. Things are really bad now. But what makes things bad isn't the people so much, it's the situation. I've lived through much worse. So when I go to bed at night now, I lie down and turn off the light and enjoy myself counting up all the reasons I have for being happy. I'm back in Japan. I'm sleeping on cushions. There's a roof on my house, so I don't have to worry about getting up if it rains. Such things make me happy. Silly little things, but life in the Army makes you that simple."

Yukichi led Onozaki up to the hills in the Heights, where he could sketch, and Tomoko walked along with them. They made her forget the unpleasantness with Toshiki.

The road passed to the right of the Negishi racetrack, away from the ocean, over the hills, and down into numberless little valleys. From it you could get a bird's-eye view of Yokohama on its low plain intersected by canals and highways. Onozaki would stop every now and then to sketch something, and Tomoko and Yukichi would stand at the side of the road, or sit down on the grass in the shade of a tree, until he was finished.

The scenery was varied. Some of the hills were round, grassy protuberances straight out of a Hiroshige landscape, while in other spots the ground was shaved off abruptly in a precipitous descent. And the city spread in the distance covered with spring haze.

"The slopes around here all have animal names," Yukichi informed them. "Pig Slope, Ox Slope, Monkey Slope, Badger Slope. There may actually have been monkeys and badgers living here way back before the area was inhabited. These slopes used to be much more heavily wooded. They looked lonely and sinister even in the daytime."

They were all steep slopes twisting down into valleys immediately below. Steps had been cut into some of them and little stone shrines built on others to the deity of roads. Down in the valleys they could see the thatched roofs of ancient farmhouses. Red camellias were conspicuous in the bamboo thickets.

The modern city, spread out far below, with tall buildings sticking up at odd points on its streets, seemed lifeless from the hills—a cemetery of concrete and stone. Tomoko could hardly believe that hundreds of thousands of people were living down there, each living his private, particular life. Onozaki had been speaking about those lives, not comfortable, many of them, in this postwar city, and spent for the most part in shacks and flimsy hut-like wooden houses. And each of those houses was filled with the pain of living, babies crying, shrill women yelling, ration lines forming forever, and insoluble problems piling up one on top of another.

"I was born down there, where this hill ends." Yukichi

pointed out the spot. "The house has disappeared—
burned down in the war. It was near a temple they
called Red Gate." He was smiling happily. "Everything's
changed completely."

Tomoko noticed that Yukichi was plucking out hand-
fuls of grass, unconsciously it seemed. He must feel like
a man who's just recovered from a long, stubborn sick-
ness. He must just have realized again, this very minute,
that he wasn't on the battlefield any longer, that he
was back in his peaceful home, that he was sitting on
the grass in spring sunshine. That's why he looked so
happy.

"What a lovely day it is!" It was Onozaki calling to
them from where he was drawing. He was looking at
the sketch he was working on, his face almost frighten-
ingly intent. In the sky near the mountain across the
way, a single kite was circling, showing them his brown
belly once in the course of each leisurely evolution.

Saeko caught glimpses of a broad arm of the sea on
her left as she rode on. It would appear for a moment
and then vanish again. The foreigners who had come
to live in Yokohama toward the end of the last century
used to call this inlet Mississippi Bay. After leaving Tomoko and Toshiki in Yokohama, Saeko had driven down
the coast, and had just come out of a tunnel cut through
a mountain. The broad highway went on to Kanazawa,
of woodcut fame, to end at Yokosuka. It had been built
for military as well as civilian use and was one of the
best in Japan—a perfect road, solidly paved in reinforced
concrete.

The country became mountainous immediately beyond the tunnel, sloping down gently to the sea. It was
country scenery. The houses that soon came into view
beside the road were old-style farmhouses with thick

straw roofs and paper-screen doors facing the streets, hidden, toward the mountains, behind thick, luxuriant hedges of coral and camellia trees. There were hothouses on the southeastern slopes, where carnations were grown, and Western houses on the profusely wooded hills. For, shielded by the mountains to the north, the soil here was of moderate temperature all year round. A stretch of level ground running straight into the sea was covered by houses that had been villas in the old, peaceful days, and had now become the ordinary homes of a quiet residential section. There was a village temple atop another mountain, thickly wooded and curving south to the sea like an inverted rice bowl. It screened a stretch of ground against the winds in a sort of tranquil valley.

The car stopped here and Saeko stepped out and spoke to the chauffeur. "Thank you. Be here to pick me up at nine o'clock tomorrow morning."

A black-lacquered wooden gate faced the street. It was shut. Saeko pushed open a small side door and walked in. A slight young woman opened a paper panel in the entranceway and stepped down onto the old-fashioned ceremonial block, her white socks flashing under her kimono. She fell to her knees to greet Saeko formally. "Welcome back."

"I've neglected you people terribly, I'm afraid." Saeko smiled and looked down at her husband's mistress. "I'll go around to the side entrance."

"Oh, please come in this way. You're an honored guest."

"No. It's all right. I'll go round."

Saeko walked around by the kitchen to the lattice door of the side entrance. She stood there a minute looking toward the garden. Otane, the mistress, had rushed through the house to let her in. She appeared now on the earth floor of the entrance, wearing wooden clogs, and opened the door.

"How are the peonies doing? Are they in bloom yet?"

"Two or three flowers. It's still a bit early."

"I suppose so. But let's go see them anyway."

Otane took her place as a servant behind Saeko as they walked along.

"Are you going to have a big crop this year?"

"It looks that way."

"Well, good luck." Saeko's attitude toward the younger woman was unchangingly impersonal. "How is your master?"

Saeko was asking about her husband, Nobu. It was before the war that she had found out about the intimate relations between Nobu and Otane, then a registered geisha in the fashionable amusement district of Akasaka. She had gone to the girl's parents herself and arranged to bring her back, and Otane had been Saeko's employee ever since.

The house had been built by a raw-silk dealer as a vacation place. He had been caught short by the stoppage of trade when the war started, and Saeko had picked it up cheaply, foreseeing the need of getting out of the city. The property was a narrow strip of ground, but faced the sea and had a garden laid out on it. Peonies had been planted on the southward slope. They were supposed to be descended, through several transplantings, from an old peony garden in Kanazawa which had been famous for its flowers until its disappearance in the last century. The shrubs had been in bad shape when they moved into the house, but Nobu, whose health was none too good, was an amateur gardener. He had taken care of them and brought them back so well that now they produced beautiful large blossoms every year.

The flower garden was on two levels. There were many

branches on every shrub, and they had been trained apart
so as not to overlap. At full bloom there would be more
than a dozen flowers on each shrub—a lovely sight. But
now only three blossoms, and they half open, shone in
the sunlight. They were white or pale red.

But from where Saeko was standing with Otane,
they could see the ocean through the sparsely flowered
branches. It was blue and bright in the radiance of the
setting sun, and at peace, with the stillness of the spring
afternoon. A giant steamer was just passing, headed out
to sea from the point of Cape Hommoku, its paint glittering in the slanting sunlight.

"How peaceful," Saeko whispered suddenly, and
looked at Otane.

Otane had regular, doll-like features and a full young
body. Coming to live here hadn't changed her beauty,
but it had taken the vitality out of her, so that all one
noticed now was her uninteresting personality.

"Is his health all right?" Saeko was asking about her
husband again.

"Yes. But he still won't go out. He hates the crowds
on the trains."

Saeko laughed. "Well, please rejuvenate him a little.
It's too soon for him to get old. Why, he used to be a
crewman at college."

The mountains had pushed their shadows out over
the sea, and the wind turned cold. They went back to
the house to look for Nobu. They found him sprawled
on the sofa in the hall, reading an old paper-back novel.
He got up when he saw them. "Bring some coffee,
Otane."

It was an order. He took out a cigarette and lit it, then
turned to Saeko, a frightened smile on his face. "You
must be very busy these days. I have my troubles too.
I can't live in this house on ten thousand yen."

Born the younger son of an aristocratic family, Nobu had gone to Peers' School and to a private university. He was a handsome man, and had once been the rage among the women of the Ginza. These physical attractions were unimpaired at the age of forty. For he was still the fop he had always been, and took such minute care of his person that he kept himself looking young.

"What a world it is! You hire a gardener for two days and he robs you of a small fortune."

Saeko looked away from her husband to the sea outside, and smiled. The ship she had seen from the garden had moved a fair distance ahead, and its colors had changed in the sunset. Glass or something on deck glittered intensely.

"That's how things are."

"But the world's gone mad. One daren't go outside."

"The safest thing is to practice Kiyomoto music with Otane, isn't it? I haven't achieved a steady income yet myself, and whenever I think of trying something I find myself paralyzed by orders and regulations. I'm still living on my capital, you know."

"Why don't you sell one of the diamonds?" His voice had that spoiled-child quality she knew so well.

"There aren't any left. What with the property tax and everything, I've had to sell them all already."

"That I don't believe. They're still around some place, aren't they?"

"They're some place certainly, but I don't have them. The world's changed, Nobu. There's no way of getting money any more except by working for it yourself."

"The easiest way's to open one of those smart restaurants, I understand. That's right in your line, so I thought you might have somebody running one for you."

"I may do that, if I can. But even if I do, customers like you just don't exist any more. Come on, now, you've done exactly what you wanted to do most of your life. Consider what's happening now your punishment, and resign yourself to it. You're not so badly off. Lots of ex-customers are waiting on tables nowadays. Things have reversed themselves."

"You mean I should be glad I sowed my wild oats when they came cheap?"

There was a wry smile on the handsome, manly face, but Saeko stared back at him unmoved.

"You certainly picked the right family to be born into, seeing that your mission in life is to amuse yourself. But the world's changed now, and you'll just have to learn to restrain your desires. You're lucky you can waste your time growing peonies, you know. Plenty of noble houses are really in trouble."

Nobu answered in his native Tokyo style, barely moving his lips. "It sounds like the Last Judgment."

"You should go out a little and see what's happening."

"I know perfectly well what's happening, without going to see. It's hard to believe human beings could become so grimy and so crude. Why, there are no manners any more."

"Of course, your manners are perfect." Saeko looked out at the clouds, red with sunset over the ocean. "You should at least go to see how the world's changed outside. You'll get old and out of date unless you do, you know." Saeko had picked the words she knew would hurt her handsome husband the most. "Sticking here this way is like staying in the shade all the time. . . . Look at Otane, how old she's become in the last year or so. It's pitiful, a girl that age with no color in her face."

"She's useful nowadays anyway. Her background's made her acquainted with the pawnbrokers." Nobu spat it out, and changed the subject. "Aoyama's been annoying me. He wants to talk to you and get you to accept some proposition he has. He's in debt again, I think. The store in Shibuya isn't drawing customers the way it did at first. Even the monthly rent's become a problem, he says." Aoyama was his older brother.

"That's what comes of rushing into things one doesn't understand. Is there anything your relatives can do?"

"He says he must see you."

"And he used to talk about me as if I were the devil's lady." There was a cold smile on Saeko's face. "My in-laws are beginning to visit me in Takanawa already. They seem to have forgotten they once called a family council to make you divorce me. How polite they've become! And that they should ask me to suggest a match for Haruko—it's overwhelming!"

She paused, but Nobu was silent.

"What a set of egoists! They show their true colors as soon as they're in trouble, and come to see me, every one of them. It's amusing to watch them. Of course they never mention money to me directly, but you've just got to look at them to see it isn't Haruko they're worrying about. They're talking round and round the matter and slowly circling in to attack. Is it money Aoyama wants? Is that what his important proposition boils down to?"

Otane was serving supper to Saeko and Nobu as they sat facing each other. Saeko didn't ask Otane to join them. She didn't care especially what happened when she wasn't in the house—whether Nobu ate alone or shared his meals sociably with Otane.

Since she had brought her husband's mistress into the house, Saeko had been independent of Nobu's authority. She had been a model wife early in their marriage, and her husband's friends had admired her submissiveness. But at that very time she had been carving out the position she wanted. Her uncle-in-law had been in the Imperial Military Council, and was one of the old men of the Navy. She had used his connections to make the trips to Singapore possible. But it was her own boldness that had taken her there alone during the war. Step by step this quiet-looking woman had asserted her individuality and become too strong a person for her husband, and even for his troublesome relatives, to control. Saeko had by her own efforts amassed the money that set her free, while her husband and his family and friends had seen their ancestral houses shaken to the foundations by the landslide of the surrender, and the foundations themselves fatally cracked by the postwar taxes. Saeko's daring had just managed to save Nobu's household from following the others over the cliff, so that while all the other stars in the family had lost their luster, his seemed to sparkle with extraordinary brilliance. "Thank God at least Nobu has a good wife"—his parents and brothers and relatives envied and commended him, now that they had been reduced to living from hand to mouth. For none of them had built a life for himself by his own ability. They had lived in a world where all they had to do to maintain their position was to use the connections to which they had been born or which they could select at will in society. So, naturally, they had all gone down together, like a set of ninepins, in a spectacular collapse that was not without its grandeur.

Nobu pleaded for them. "They're all very pleasant people."

Saeko didn't bother to deny it. "So they are. Pleasantness comes from long polishing—they've had time to learn how to conceal their true selves skillfully."

Saeko herself didn't know how long her heart had been so impenetrably frozen against her husband. She could look at him and see a perfect stranger. They sat facing each other, and their conversation was purely routine. The things about him that had won her affection in younger days now came near to awakening the opposite emotion. His beauty had come to seem a superficial attractiveness covering a total lack of character, and the perfection of his attire little more than proof of his emptiness within.

It wasn't the affair with Otane that had made her feel this way suddenly. Had her taste improved over the years? Or had Nobu become unexciting to her as she realized that he would be satisfied to spend his life keeping up appearances? No, it was none of these things, exactly. It was simply that the passage of time had stripped him of the halo that had once adorned people of his class in her eyes. In reality, he was nothing but a lazy, selfish man. He had been born to the conviction that he could while his whole life away doing nothing. It was a deep-rooted conviction, and he was glad he had it. He had grown to manhood slowly, with aristocratic nonchalance, and his upbringing had left him incurably apathetic. There was a disgusting languor about him, as though his pride were chronically diseased. He was the sort of man who was irresistible to women who looked no further than the face and body, but that in itself was sickening to Saeko. She had come to see that what was lacking in Nobu was the sense of being alive. His older brother, Aoyama, was much the same, another handsome, dandyish fool.

Saeko said good-night and went up to her apartment on the second floor. She undressed, put on a chemise, and sat down at her dressing-table to take the pins out of her hair.

The door opened suddenly and Nobu's reflection in the mirror startled Saeko.

"I'd like to talk to you a minute," he announced from

the doorway. "I didn't want Otane around. I thought it might be embarrassing."

"I'll put something on. Wait in the next room."

"Pardon me for bursting in, but, after all, I'm—"

"Never mind that. Please do as I say."

There was only a thin piece of silk around her body. Saeko felt ashamed suddenly and blushed. Nobu had looked away, but stood there waiting. She walked over to the bed and wrapped a light kimono around her. She spoke as she was picking out an obi. "Can't this wait until tomorrow morning?"

"No. It would be better to talk about it now," he insisted. "It concerns Otane. I want to send her away. . . . I want to throw off this whole slovenly existence I'm leading now. That's what I want to talk over with you."

"I hardly see that it's any of my business. But aren't you being rather hard on Otane? She's served you faithfully all these years."

"But her life never meant anything anyway. What about me? Do I have to go on dragging the sins of my youth with me the rest of my life? They become a pretty heavy load at my age. I realized I was wrong at the time, but my friends all acted that way, and I was young, so I just slipped into it. . . ."

"If you can talk so selfishly about it, it's plain you still haven't repented what you did. Of course, it takes a human being to repent." Saeko finished tying her obi and turned around toward him. "Let's go into the next room. This place is a mess."

"Saeko!" He looked into her face, his eyes intense. "That's not nice of you. This is your room, isn't it? I'm your husband. How can you order me out? . . . I'm sorry from the bottom of my heart. You don't understand how I've suffered these six years. I've tried to tell you, but you just wouldn't listen."

"You're breaking your promise now. We made an agreement, and you can't change it when it pleases you. And be kind enough to leave that door open."

"You're cold, Saeko—to stay angry so long about a trifle."

"I'm not in the least angry. I have nothing to be angry about."

"You say that, and torture me like this?"

"Torture you, indeed!"

"Saeko, I didn't want to say it, but a woman is a woman."

"Are you trying to get me really angry? Are you trying to make me say what I'd rather not say?"

"Don't get angry! Don't get angry! That's all I ask."

The color of fear on his elegant face provoked Saeko to speak. "You who crushed the feelings of my youth, you come here now and speak this way? And think of Otane, if you will. She's not like me. That poor creature's been trained to accept this kind of life and think herself lucky to have it. She's given herself to you entirely, with utter faith—and you want to get rid of her now she no longer suits your convenience. It would be an abominable thing to do."

"But—if you gave her a decent sum of money, she'd be glad to go back to her parents."

Saeko burst out laughing. "I shall most certainly do nothing of the kind. I refuse, definitely. I find it a very amusing idea. Who's buying what?"

"All right. I can manage to scrape that much together myself."

"Tell me—when you've sent Otane away, with whom do you intend to go on living in this house?"

Nobu paled. He understood well enough what she meant, but was too choked with humiliation to speak.

"Aren't you being cruel? Otane's a good, simple

woman. What a shock it'll be for her! And have you thought what things are like outside now that you're pushing her into the streets?"

"That's why I'm giving her the money."

"Has she agreed to this? Or is it all your own idea? When I first found out about you and her, the only reason I felt I could forgive you was that at least you loved her. But if you slighted my feelings out of pure whim, if you tell me now that everything you've been saying is a lie—aren't you making it all the harder for me to bear as a woman? I've left it all up to you. I've stayed out of your way."

"But you were all wrong about it. You're completely mistaken about what happened between us."

"I know nothing about it and don't want to! The man is responsible in such cases. Otane and I felt embarrassed toward each other as women, and you and she were shy of discussing the matter because you both knew that what you were doing was wrong. Well, good night now. Think it over. If this is what you intend to do, it's absurd to complain about needing more money."

Nobu's eyes flashed, and he shouted: "Saeko! You're in love with someone!"

"What?"

"You are! You must be!"

"I'll leave it to your imagination. Of course, I don't know what may happen in the future, but surely you can see how improbable it is that I'm in love now. I go in for things the whole way. If I were really in love with someone else, I wouldn't be at all in the mood to go on feeding a purely nominal husband and his Number Two. You can be sure of that, can't you?"

Nobu said nothing, but he put his arms around her shoulders and pulled her toward him. They were strong arms, the arms of an oarsman, but Saeko pressed her

two hands against his chest and bent her body back
bow-like to ward him off.

"Saeko, it's you I've always loved. Really, from my
heart—"

"Take your hands off me. I'll call Otane. The plain
truth is you're saying that because you want money."

"Saeko! Don't say things like that!"

"Never mind. I know you and your blood and your
background. Things have gone badly for you, haven't
they? But stop this disgusting, unmanly display. Instead
of these attentions, give me Otane's consolation money.
Then we can separate for good. I hadn't thought of it
until you mentioned it, but there is a man I could fall
in love with. I want to go to him."

The strength ebbed out of Nobu's arms. He stood stiff
and spiritless. His face sagged, pale and ugly, with his
mouth open. Saeko took her chance, walked out the
door, and called Otane's name in her ordinary tone.

"Forgive me, Saeko, forgive me. You shouldn't torture me so cruelly." Nobu was whining like a beaten
puppy. "If you're satisfied, let's leave things as they are.
I'll try to bear it. . . . But don't get angry. Please don't
get angry."

Saeko was listening to the stillness of the house. Otane
wasn't coming.

"Just try to act like a man," she said irritably. "But
I seem to be more manly than you, don't I? Good night!"

Nobu was slow to move. Saeko had reached the point
where she could have loosened her sash and lain down
on the bed right in front of him. She could have undressed, indifferent to his presence. She had always taken
good care of herself, and her body was still young. It
always gave her confidence to look at it in a full-length
mirror. The man's slowness was irritating her beyond
endurance. She felt there was nothing too cruel for her

to do. Nobu apologized one last time and finally went out. She didn't even bother to lock the door behind him.

"Aah!" She sighed out all the feeling she'd been holding in, and sprawled her thinly covered body on the bed, throwing out her arms and legs. She could feel the dark stillness of the peony garden outside her window. The waves broke at intervals on the pebbled shore, but the sudden sounds only made the night more quiet.

Her eyes were shut. She could hear her troubled blood. Her mind was calm. It had come out of the incident indifferent. But she was becoming conscious of the weight of her extended body.

Her heartbeat quickened suddenly. She had moved her arms and legs deliberately, and then realized that her new position was the same as the one she had taken automatically that night in Singapore after parting from Kyogo Moriya. She thought about it, comparing the two positions in detail as though reviewing a school lesson. She lay still, her eyes closed, and the sense of fulfillment she had had that night seeped into her body and lured her mind into a trance. She was like a sponge growing heavy as it takes in water. At the height of fullness, she bit her lip and moaned low.

He was so much older than she, and he could make her feel this way! Her inner eyes stared at this fact in growing surprise, while the inhuman loneliness of the way she was living now shadowed her heart. She had nothing in the world to fear now. But what would become of her if she went on as she was? Kyogo Moriya hated her, there could be no doubt. She thought of these things, and something like a tremor of fear ran up and down her almost naked body.

She sighed, sat up, and turned off the lamp beside her bed.

MOTION

When Tomoko tried to give back the diamond, Saeko pushed her hand away and refused to take it.

"Keep it. They're useful sometimes!" She smiled, and what she said touched Tomoko's secret thoughts. "That diamond is one of the tears that dropped from your eyes when we talked about your father. It was so beautiful! I was to blame for your crying, so the diamond is yours."

The reasoning was strange, but it was delivered with Saeko's usual charm. Tomoko started saying once more she couldn't keep it, but Saeko cut her off. "Well then, just keep it for me." And she handed her a concert ticket. "Will you come with me? They're playing my favorite Tchaikowsky quartet. Mr. Onozaki brought them for us."

On the morning of the day of the concert, someone came to visit Oki while Tomoko was getting ready to go to the shop. It was her turn to bring in the tea. She walked into the study as usual and found Oki talking with his visitor. It was Toshiki Okamura. She was horrified.

Toshiki looked up and saw her too. The very formal way he greeted her showed he hadn't expected to find her here. "Thank you for your company the other day. Do you live here?"

Tomoko had paled with shock. She was afraid that Toshiki might talk to her in front of Oki about her father in Kyoto. She barely said hello and rushed out of the room.

Oki listened to his young visitor's request, rejected it flatly, and stood up waiting for him to leave. He looked out the window and the new green of the garden shone with distorted reflections in the glass of his spectacles. But his visitor made no sign of leaving. He sat there calmly till Oki turned round and addressed him in his highhanded, authoritative tone.

"It's my policy not to let new firms publish my books. Be kind enough to accept that fact. I have my regular publisher, and there's really no use in your coming here on that matter."

It just didn't penetrate. The soft young face stared on at the professor. "But couldn't you even let us have one book, professor, just to help young students in their work?"

"I'm very sorry, but if you're in the publishing business you must know how Japanese readers are. A book published by a reputable firm sells much better than a book by the same author put out by an unknown company. Actually, what you're asking me to do is to hurt my own interests knowingly. Well, I won't. Please understand that."

Toshiki was unperturbed. "What about a royalty of twenty per cent and an advance, half payable when you sign the contract? The general rate is fifteen per cent, I think. Unfortunately, I've only brought fifty thousand yen with me, but you're welcome to it, if you don't mind the amount."

"It's not a matter of money, young man." Oki's tone was chilly and commanding. "It's a matter of my standing as a writer. My books must be published by a well-known firm. That is my policy."

"Nevertheless, there must be some way—" Toshiki wouldn't take no for an answer. He had no doubt that he would have his way eventually. He was too resilient to have been dented in the slightest yet. "If everyone felt like you, sir, new publishing houses could never get good writers. Wouldn't that be a tragic thing? I think so."

"You can look elsewhere, but you'd better resign yourself to not getting me."

"But it's you we need, sir. If you weren't Professor Oki, I wouldn't be talking to you this way. We want one of your books to get our company off to a good start. Thanks to your reputation, sir, we'd be recognized immediately."

Oki was worn out by his feminine but remarkably strong opponent. Very few firms would be ready to hand over tens of thousands before they even knew what book one would give them. If he hadn't respected his own authority so much, he would have been willing to accept with a vague promise of a book in the indefinite future. But the sense of his own dignity possessed Oki like a chronic disease, and he would not let himself be treated lightly.

"You tell me this is a student outfit, a sort of extracurricular company. Isn't it a little odd for a set of students to have that kind of money at their disposal?"

"We have a backer, sir, who tells us we can have as much as we need to build up a first-rate company. That's why I dared to hope for a book of yours, sir. We want people to see that Professor Oki has given a book to a firm of young people to help the new generation make good. What about it, Professor Oki? Just one."

"You are persistent!" Oki looked out into the garden silently. The glasses on his pointed nose imaged the green garden trees again. Oki always looked cold when he had his glasses on. "It is difficult to make an exception. I have obligations to others. But since it's a student company, I should give it some thought, I suppose. I could make a collection of short pieces—not fragments, I mean, but articles I've written for various magazines. That would make a volume—a sort of anthology of my simpler cultural criticism."

Toshiki was triumphant. "Would you do that for us?"

"I can't do it right away. I'll have to polish them up a bit, even though they've been published already. That will take time. I'm writing a new book now, and I'll have to work on this in the intervals. It will probably take two or three months."

"That would be perfect. I should be inexpressibly grateful for the honor of publishing one of your books, sir."

"All right, I'll do it." Oki smiled. "You've finally made me capitulate, haven't you? The terms you mentioned will be satisfactory. I'll leave the size of the printing and that sort of thing up to you."

Toshiki picked up his new briefcase and laid it on his knees. He took out the money. Oki was signing the receipt.

Toshiki interrupted him. "By the way, Miss Tomoko asked me to get some information for her—the name of Mr. Moriya's hotel in Kyoto."

"Whose hotel?" Oki tried to appear unconcerned as he looked up at Toshiki. The young man was evidently well pleased with what he was doing, even proud.

"Mr. Kyogo Moriya—Miss Tomoko's father, who's been abroad so long."

Oki stopped writing and stared at Toshiki for a moment, his high bald forehead deeply creased. But he went back to his signature without saying anything. "Here you are." He held out the piece of paper and looked out into the garden again. He wore his customary expression of universal indifference. A coward from childhood, Oki had constructed this mask over the years as a defense. Only his very nearsighted eyes occasionally betrayed his nervousness.

Toshiki took out his notebook, tore off a page, and wrote the name and address of Moriya's hotel on it with his ball-point pen. "Would you be kind enough to send for Miss Tomoko?"

"No!" Oki snapped in his habitual tone. "I'll give it to her." He took the slip, raised his glasses to his forehead, and read it, speaking to Toshiki the while. "That book—I intend to do it as quickly as I can, so I'd rather not have you people troubling me about it. . . . Did Tomoko ask you for this?"

"Yes, sir."

"What's your connection with this man Moriya?"

"I have no particular connection with him. One of my relatives happens to be a former Navy man and he arranged for me to get the address from ex-Admiral Ushigi."

"So there are still some of them around!" Oki's tone revealed his intense dislike for the military.

"I understand that you were in North and Central China during the war yourself, sir," Toshiki remarked casually.

"They asked me to go. It was way back. My work had nothing to do with the war—cultural business, you know. I ate some delicious Peking dishes, went to see a few classical plays, and that sort of thing."

Oki saw Toshiki out to the entrance. He didn't return to his study, but rushed down the corridor to the Japanese section of the house. "Setsuko!" he shouted.

Tomoko's mother appeared from the kitchen instantaneously and looked up into her husband's frightened face.

"Has Tomoko left yet?"

"No, she's still here. She said she was leaving right away, though."

"Come here a minute," Oki ordered and walked into the study. "Close the door behind you."

Oki was plainly in a bad mood. He sat down in his chair, folded his arms, and stared into the garden, an offended look on his face. Setsuko stood there waiting for him to speak.

"Setsuko!" he started in a high-pitched, insistent voice. "Did you know what Tomoko meant to do?"

"Tomoko? What is it? I don't know anything about it."

"Is that so?" He examined her face. "You must have known. I can't believe a nice girl like Tomoko would act this way without telling you about it."

The cruelty at the base of Oki's personality was now brutally apparent. He did his work in the early morning hours nowadays when there was no one around to disturb him, and he had just finished a short essay he had been asked to write on the home under the new constitution. In it he had pointed out that the new home was founded on the family members' respect for one another's personalities. Oki always believed what he wrote, and he had laid down his pen feeling it was a blessed thing to be living in the beautiful world he had just described. Blessings came cheap in Professor Oki's world, for he wrote, by preference, of things as they should be. And his writings were always on the highest level and in world dimensions, so full of Beauty and Goodness and Truth that they had implanted an unshakable confidence in many a reader who lived too far away ever to see the professor in person or observe his private life. But it was a concrete domestic problem in which Oki was now engaged, and universal standards did not apply. Of course, the fact that the professor's actual life presented a few minor exceptions to his general ideas was no reason for his readers in distant corners of Japan not to respect his thought as thought. It may be of some phenomenological interest, however, to point out that the readers of books do have a tendency to confuse a man's intellectual product with the man himself.

Oki felt not the slightest need to manifest his principles here. Rather than his principles, it was his personality that he exercised freely and frankly with his family, overcautious though he was in outside relationships.

"Of course I don't know what sort of person this fellow is. I've never met him." And he showed his wife the slip of paper. "Would this be the Moriya who was Tomoko's father?"

Setsuko changed color, as if an invisible hand had slapped her in the face. It was an effort just to go on standing there.

"It appears that this man you told me was dead has returned unannounced to Japan. Or rather, now that he need fear no punishment for the vile crime he committed, he has been able to come back like a gentleman, I suppose. Japan is in such a pitiable state that no undesirable can be denied entrance. He can't hurt the country too much. But what's his return going to do to this household?"

Setsuko put her hand on the back of the chair and squeezed it hard, unconsciously. She was trying to bear up under the merciless, relentless gleam that came from behind her husband's glasses.

Oki realized that what he had been saying was rather vulgar. He didn't feel exactly that it was intentional, but that he had been made to say something vulgar, and it was all Setsuko's fault. Kyogo Moriya was Setsuko's former husband. It followed of a certainty that it was

Setsuko who had brought this misfortune into his household.

"I wish you'd say something." Oki clicked his tongue irritably and then burst into a rage. He was shouting, unable to control himself. "I needn't tell you that it isn't out of jealousy of that man that I'm talking to you this way. That would be vulgar. It's true, then, that you didn't know anything about this?"

"Not a thing."

"Tomoko was acting alone? . . . I suppose Moriya got in touch with her some way. I'd rather not speak about this at all. But I must concern myself with the peace of this household. What do you think we should do?"

Setsuko shook her head. She had no idea what they should do.

Oki remembered something all of a sudden. He had been yearning to run for the House of Councilors in the next election and had sent feelers out in all directions. He became excited again. What would happen if some newspaper found out that his wife's former husband had committed a disgraceful crime, fled abroad, and come back now that the surrender had changed everything? Such a romantic event would be sure to attract interest. Tomoko's picture would be in the newspapers, and maybe his wife's too. He himself would receive unwelcome public attention. Divorce and remarriage were commonplace enough, but this was more than that. His enemies would be delighted, and would use the incident in the election campaign. They would see to it that everybody knew about the scandal in the home of Tatsuzo Oki, the so-called "man of character."

The strength ebbed out of him suddenly, and he started gasping with pain. Setsuko trembled. "I'll have to forget about the House of Councilors. I'll be dragged through the mud if I put myself before the public. And I've been so careful. But now—"

"I don't know how to apologize." Setsuko cried low, as though she were being beaten.

"Your apologies won't do me any good." Oki wasn't angry. He was too much in the grip of his natural cowardice for rage. "What's Tomoko thinking of? Does she mean to leave us and go to that man?" His voice grew louder. "You mustn't let her do anything rash. After all, she owes me something. I've raised her up to now, and she must be aware of her obligation. You mustn't let her go off on her own, without my permission. Do you understand? That's the most important thing. She mustn't try to get in touch with him behind our backs. Shall I give her a talking-to, or will you?"

Of course it was Setsuko's job, as the natural parent, to talk to her daughter. It would be more painful for her, but that wasn't the point. Oki moaned something faintly about how dangerous it was for him to get angry, and Setsuko understood her duty. She didn't even raise her head.

Tomoko should have left for the shop already, but Toshiki had worried her and she was still in the house. She had seen her mother being summoned into the library. The worst was going to happen, she was sure of it, and she had stayed in the kitchen as if nailed to her chair.

She had sat there unhappily, trying to divert her mind from the anxiety of waiting by designing a suit for the father she hadn't met yet. It was the only thing that helped.

Tomoko had looked at the photographs. They showed her father as a young naval officer, so young that it was hard to think of him as a father. He looked more like an older brother. The pictures had brought a smile to her face and made the idea of her father even more exhilarating. She felt a pleasant tenseness now. She knew it was wrong of her to be acting so without telling her mother, but the pleasure she felt was irresistible. Her youth gave her an unconscious strength. It stirred within her provocatively. She was ready to challenge the decision her parents would reach in their discussion. She was anxious as she waited, to be sure, but also expectant.

The study door opened and her mother came out. Tomoko started from her chair. She looked into her mother's face and gasped. It was more than white. It was like a porcelain surface in winter.

Setsuko looked smaller than usual. She tried to smile in her ordinary way as she turned to Tomoko. "Haven't you left yet, dear?"

She took a cup from the shelf, walked over to the sink, turned the tap-handle, filled the cup, and drank it down. Her hands were shaking. "That was good." She rinsed the cup, wiped it, and put it back. Her movements were almost automatic. "Yes, yes." She was speaking to herself. Without looking at Tomoko, she walked into her own room.

The sound of her voice lingered in Tomoko's ears. Tomoko had been terrified by the way her mother acted —like a mechanical doll. She felt an anxiety such as she used to have when a child and worried so much that her mother might die that she couldn't sleep at night without making sure Mother was there. But this was an even deeper anxiety. It impelled her into motion and sent her, almost entranced, after her mother.

Setsuko wasn't doing anything, just standing in the middle of her room, dazed. She looked startled when she saw Tomoko at the door.

Tomoko was unaware of her own actions. She joined

the fingers of both hands on her chest as if praying or worshipping her mother, bowed her head, and sobbed.

It was a minute before her mother spoke. "Come in, Tomoko. Don't stand there. . . . Grown-up people don't cry like that. Look at me. I'm not crying. . . . And I probably have much more reason than you, Tomoko."

Her strength came back to her when she saw her daughter before her. More than strength, perhaps, it was an intensity of purpose, as though she had resolved once never to cry all her life long. Pain and unhappiness had become mere incidentals of life to her. And at the end, when she was dismissed from this world, if there were no one else to give her a word of thanks, she would be ready to tell herself that she had labored well.

"Come on, Tomoko, you're a big girl now."

But what was she to say after that? She was still too confused to know. It had come too suddenly—as though a strong wind had struck her in the face and were stifling her. The only thing that would give her relief would be to busy herself about some everyday household duty. She bent down to pick up a scrap of thread from the rush-matted floor, and wound and unwound it about her fingers. Her fingers were trembling unnaturally.

But Setsuko seemed unaware of what she was doing as she spoke. "Please think of Taro. He's still so little. You're his older sister, so—you mustn't do anything thoughtless. Couldn't you just make believe nothing had come up, and go on living quietly as you have been? What would be wrong in that? Please don't do anything rash."

Tomoko's head was still lowered, but her mother saw her nod. "What it's all about I don't know, not even I, your mother. It just happened, I suppose, and not because anybody wanted it to—that's how it must be. When you're older, Tomoko, you'll understand me better. I have no choice. No matter how unbearable things become, I have to stay and endure it. Please help me, Tomoko."

Tomoko made an effort to control her tears. And she no longer concealed her face, but looked up at her mother.

Setsuko had dropped the piece of thread and lost it. She didn't have the energy to look for it. "Tomoko, I know that you're going to leave us some day and live as you will. I've brought you up so that you could." The words stuck in her throat and tears welled up inside her, in spite of all she could do. "And so—and so—"

Setsuko was unaware that her voice had changed to the high, insistent tone that Oki used. A sad thing for a woman, but Setsuko didn't know it. "When you do, Tomoko, you'll be free to go where you like and meet whom you will. But now, now, Tomoko, you must think of your brother and of me. Do you understand me, To-moko?"

"Yes." Tomoko's voice was clipped. "I'm thinking only of you, Mother."

The door to Oki's study opened heavily, and the sound reverberated down the hall. "Setsuko!" came the shrill call once more.

"Hello there!" Onozaki greeted Tomoko from the entrance of the Concert Hall, where he was standing. "I'm very glad you could come. How did you like our day in Yokohama? Yukichi should be here tonight. A son of an old friend of mine has just been made first violinist. This is his first appearance."

He was as cheerful as ever, having a wonderful time all by himself. "Mrs. Takano should be here any minute. I'm waiting for her. Mustn't forget to pay one's respects to the queen of the financial world."

Tomoko waited with him. The fresh green foliage of the park trees swirled and billowed vividly in the dim evening light. An endless stream of elegantly dressed men and women climbed the stairs.

"Yukichi's a fine young man, isn't he?" Onozaki was evidently very fond of him. "Of course it would be better if he could see that there can be no culture or anything unless human poverty is wiped out. But he has a rare seriousness and steadiness for a young man nowadays. They're all scatterbrains."

Saeko came walking up the stairs in a pure white dress. Onozaki raised his arms over his giant frame. "What an honor! Thanks for coming."

Saeko smiled at Tomoko. "It's quite summer already, isn't it? I'm glad to see you here. You weren't too busy, then, I take it?"

The meaningless remark brought back into Tomoko's mind what had happened at home that morning. She hadn't really been able to get over it. There had been heaviness in her heart all day. She felt bound somehow, and firmly. She noticed how beautiful was the single purple orchid pinned to the breast of Saeko's sheer white dress, but her mood was too flaccid for her to give it more than a moment's attention.

"Have you been all right since I saw you?" Saeko asked as they walked upstairs together.

As Tomoko answered, she wondered why it was that Saeko's company made her father in Kyoto seem so much more real to her. Perhaps because her mother had just forbidden her to see him. Saeko and the orchid on her breast, Saeko's lovely body itself, seemed to suggest her father. It was because Saeko knew so much more about her father than she did, she decided, and felt a certain displeasure at the fact.

As she came out of her reverie, she looked at Saeko

and was surprised yet again at how very beautiful the woman was, even in the midst of this glittering crowd.

"Let's stop in some place on the way home and have something cold to drink."

"Cold beer, you mean, h'm?"

As Tomoko listened to this very typical city evening exchange, she was musing about how important her father had become to her in the little while since she had heard of him. The place he occupied in her heart was more than permanent, it was growing larger with every hour that passed. She was anxious about it.

The music started, and it was beautiful, but Tomoko could not keep the tears out of her eyes. They came faster and faster. Only the platform was lighted. The crowded seats were in the dark, and even Saeko, sitting next to her, probably couldn't see that she was crying.

The music was one of Tchaikowsky's string quartets. Tomoko didn't follow it all the way through. Her grief became too strong for her at moments, and the music simply vanished from her ears.

Oki's selfishness and timidity rose before her suddenly like a wall. She had to break it down or suffocate. For all his noble reasons, he was a cold, self-centered man. Her mother felt the weight of his arrogance more than she did, and felt it every day. Mother was a weak person. And the fact that she'd brought a child with her into her second marriage had put her, sensitive as she was, under an obligation that made her even less able to defend herself.

Tomoko thought of her mother as she had been this morning, and her tears became uncontrollable. The music would end soon, and the lights go on. It would be impossible to hide her wet cheeks. Tomoko was in a panic. Oki was a monster to have tortured Mother so about something Mother had nothing to do with. It was a contemptible, inhuman thing to do. He could think only of himself. There was no sympathy in him.

An altogether different anxiety rose suddenly in her mind, and Tomoko was deaf to the music once more.

At intermission, Tomoko followed Saeko out into the broad, crowded lobby. Onozaki and their other acquaintances hadn't come up to them yet.

"I'd like to talk to you about my father."

Saeko stopped the little fan she'd been using. The scent of her perfume came to Tomoko's nostrils.

"You don't think my father would come to our house, do you? It would be terrible if he did. I could write to him, but I'd rather go to Kyoto, if I can, and see him. I want to talk to him."

Saeko looked at her, intense and serious. "If you can, you say. Do you have the courage?"

Tomoko was quite calm. "I do. But no one at home must know about it. I've been ordered to Karuizawa by the magazine—I'll tell them that at home, and they won't think anything of it."

They caught sight of the painter threading his way toward them through the crowded lobby. His white hair made him conspicuous from afar.

Saeko put her fan over her mouth. Her lovely features opened into a smile. She spoke softly. "Yes, do that, Tomoko. I'll go with you."

"Really?"

"But your father mustn't know. I'm afraid of him."

"How hot it is! Real summer weather." Onozaki was beside them, his face red.

❀ ᘛᘚ XIII ᘛᘚ ❀

THE PAST

When anyone asked him why he came, Kyogo Moriya's only answer was a smile.

He had come for the first time when the double cherry was in bloom, and since then had spent two days every week in this Kyoto hotel, over the weekend usually, but not always. On his first trip the leaves had been budding on the trees; later he had seen them in their early green; and now they were in the full color of midsummer. Most people avoided Kyoto in the summer because it was so hot, but that was just when Kyogo chose to come.

The hotel people observed that Kyogo didn't come on business, like the other guests, and never had a visitor. Either he would go out walking by himself, or spend the whole day quietly in his room gazing out over the Kamo River. But he wasn't what you would call a strange fellow. If you talked to him, you found that he was a cultivated person, gentle and considerate, and able to converse about all sorts of things. He was just beginning to be old. They understood that he lived in Kobe, waiting for the China trade to start again, and meanwhile had nothing to do. At any rate it was certain, because he himself had told them so, that he lodged with a Chinese family on the Heights in Kobe. That was where he came from every week—"because Kobe is a dreary sight since the fires. I prefer the view here in Kyoto, with everything still standing. It's pleasanter and much more restful," he would say with a quiet smile.

He went out walking often, apparently to see the old

temples in the suburbs. They knew that he was back from overseas, but he never talked about his family, and never brought anyone with him.

Nowadays, of course, the war was responsible for all kinds of unhappiness in people's lives, and so, occasionally, the women would ask each other: "I wonder whether he lost his wife." For the loneliness that they could see in Kyogo, used as they were to summing up their guests, was a consequence of something more than the age he showed by the streaks of white in his sideburns.

When he stayed in, he would sit alone in the rattan chair on the porch upstairs, reading a book, or just looking at the river bed below and the opposite shore. That couldn't be very interesting, they thought. But when they asked him: "Aren't you bored? Why don't you go somewhere today?" he would turn around and laugh and say: "It's too hot. And, anyway, I'm not bored. I enjoy doing nothing, like this."

And his cheerful tone would seem to assert that his was the right way to enjoy oneself in Kyoto.

The scene from the balcony was beautiful with mountains and water. He could see the Eastern Mountain, thick with trees that gently enfolded the great temple roofs and pagodas. But even the ordinary-looking road on the opposite bank of the Kamo River had something of the charm of the old capital for Kyogo, so that he never tired of watching the oxcarts and people on bicycles passing along it.

The river itself was lined with willows. Kyogo had come to appreciate their beauty during these trips. He remembered seeing the bright buds swelling on the willow branches in spring, and now, in midsummer, they had turned into innumerable filaments that hung from the willows like old-men's whiskers and interwove into rich green masses holding the shade within them. These willows had a delicate beauty such as Kyogo had never been able to find in Europe, and he felt that he could look at them forever. And these were old willows beside water.

He had seen other old willows in Kyoto, spreading at will in the town, their branches sweeping down to cover the shop roofs, and he knew what a rare sight this was nowadays, something you could see only in Japan, in an ancient city the war had spared. But still, these willows that flanked the road along the Kamo River were unique. They gave a cheerful rhythm to the city as the branches of each separate tree waved together at every gust of wind or turned into so many clouds of smoky green when it rained. Of course, Kyoto was the willow-cherry capital, and there were cherry trees as well as willows along the river. But at this season the cherry trees were dark, for half their leaves were dead. It was the willows, all along the foreground of the scene before him, that set a gay summer color against the blackish tones of the pine-covered mountains in the background.

Right below the willows, the Canal of the Lute flowed deep in its narrow channel, and its bright surface reflected mirror images. Every day one could see the women of the city walk down the low stone steps from the road to do their washing in the cool shade of the trees, next to the great weed thickets that flourished along the channel, right here in the middle of the city.

Beyond the willows was a row of shops, each on the ground floor of an old-fashioned Kyoto burgher's house, with latticed windows on the upper floor and a square tiled roof high above. All the roofs in the long row of houses were the same shape, but of different sizes and at different heights. Even the large roofs seemed light, because these were wooden buildings in pure Japanese style. In all his European sightseeing Kyogo had never seen such buoyant architecture. It was exhilarating to look at them.

Kyogo remembered how, on some of his trips to Kyoto, when he had just been walking around the city instead of visiting the old temples, he had come upon some back street lined with old houses, and had felt something like love for it. He thought of the old houses, for example, on the street of the Temple of the Original Vow in the western quarter, and of those on Elder Sister Lane in Muromachi. Their windows were covered by frames of wooden bars projecting into the street, and the carved doors in their entranceways were shut, so that one could not see what they were like inside. They were badly lighted and uncomfortable, no doubt, but they were wonderfully peaceful and made the street around them tranquil. Some of them still had the traditional ocher painted on their window bars.

He was also fond of the streets on which only little temples stood, surrounded by their terraces and earthen walls. They seemed deserted to Kyogo when he peered inside through the gates; but the shrubs in the front gardens had been stirred into luxuriance by the summer heat, and in some of the entrances the hibiscus bloomed white against the burning sky. And he enjoyed the walk from High Terrace Temple to Clear Water Shrine, up the stone-graded sloping streets between antique shops, bamboo carpenters' shops, and the gates of peaceful villas. As he walked, the deeply wooded Eastern Mountain towered straight above him and he could also glimpse it at the ends of the lanes that threaded between the walls of private houses.

People say: "Kyoto boasts one thousand three hundred temples of all sizes, small as the city is." It might be better to say that there were thirteen hundred temples here precisely because it was Kyoto. Some of them were inconspicuous little shrines hidden away among ordinary houses on ordinary streets.

Kyogo hadn't seen all the temples in Kyoto, but at one time or another he had visited all those that were famous for their beautiful gardens; and he had also been to distant Nara and had gone through the temples there and seen their beautiful Buddhist statues. And in all of them he had had the feeling that something was missing. There was a dry, lonely atmosphere in these temples, such as one felt in a museum. There was nothing alive in them. He was very glad that they had escaped damage in the war, of course, but they had very little meaning left for the modern world, and even the cleanest of them smelled vaguely of decay.

In France and Italy, Kyogo had seen old cathedrals that were still filled with the life of the people. Men and women who lived near them came in great numbers to kneel and pray in their dim interiors, and even the irreligious tourist was careful to remove his hat and to move about silently so as not to disturb them at their devotion. The European cathedrals really seemed like places of worship, not, like so many of the temples in Kyoto and Nara, national museums, where art that had once had religious significance was kept on display for tourists whose ancestors had once come to worship there. In Japan, the more famous a temple was, the more guides and the fewer monks one would find in it. Going into one of them from the summer sunshine was like stepping into some deserted old house, vast and damp-smelling and desolate. And coming out, perhaps onto a modern street where trolleys ran, you would feel that the temple you had just seen had lost all contact with the life going on in the city around it.

Once in late spring Kyogo had stood on the terrace of the Clear Water Shrine, looking down at the city

through incredible banks of purple mist that rays of sunlight specked with gold. The startling beauty of that
mist had moved him deeply. It was the very purple of
Japanese paintings. Nowhere else in the world had Kyogo
seen such soft and gently nuanced tones. In the dry climate of the Mediterranean coast there were a greater
range of colors in the sky and more variety in the clouds,
but only in Japan could one see anything so gracious as
that brilliant, deep, mellow-colored mist trailing in the
sky and blurring the great roofs of the temples and the
modern buildings on the ground below into vague masses
of shadow.

The peak of Mount Atago stood clear above the mist,
lit by the glow of the setting sun, which still filled the
upper sky while the evening crept up from below. As the
color of the mist darkened, the lights began to come on
in the streets of the city, outlining distinctly its famous
checkerboard pattern.

It was because of this magnificent view that Clear
Water Shrine was still alive, Kyogo thought, as the
temples of Kyoto passed through his mind. Others, like
the Moss Temple and the Temple of Dragon's Peace,
still lived only because they had especially beautiful
gardens. Kyogo thought of the poem in which Verlaine
had called his Paris a desert of stone. Kyoto, and Nara
too, might be called a desert of old temples. The temples
stood there intact, but the life had dried out of them, and
only the natural beauty in which they were set saved
them from total ruin.

But there was something in Kyogo himself to which
these desolate temples appealed. Through the long years
abroad he had never thought he would come back to
Japan, but ever since his abrupt return he had felt more
and more drawn to the old things, the things that were
from the past. Actually that meant Kyoto and Nara, for

they were about all of the past that the war had left standing.

Kyoto and Nara were what the guidebooks called places of historical interest, and Kyogo understood how meaningless they had become in the life of modern Japanese. Perhaps, as some people said, the surrender had made everyone suddenly indifferent to the Japanese past. But surely, even before that, the hard struggle to make a living in the modern economy had robbed people of the leisure for useless retrospection. The young people, especially, had lost all faith in their country's history. They would consider Kyogo an idler, and what he was doing a waste of time. Kyogo was aware of it. He knew that a young man nowadays would feel much happier on the floor of a dance hall than on the beautiful carpet-thick moss in the garden of the Western Fragrant Shrine. The young wanted only to push ahead, and the past of Japan could not hold them back. Still, every now and then, when he was walking along a quiet country road to some temple, Kyogo would catch sight of a group of young people who seemed to be headed the same way, and he would be tempted to start a conversation with them.

But why did he care how the younger generation felt about these few remnants of the old Japan which had escaped the fires? There was nothing sentimental about Kyogo. He should have been able to be indifferent about what would happen to Japan in the future. He had no reason to be concerned about the postwar generation's feelings for the Japanese past.

But it made him happy, in his walks around Kyoto, to find shops selling antique furniture or *objets d'art* wherever he went. It hadn't struck him seriously yet that families were selling these precious things in order to live. He simply knew that in a city where there were plenty of antique shops the people still had leisure to long for the past and to take care of things that were about to perish. In his European experience, too, Kyogo had noticed that the more deeply civilized a country was, the more antique shops one would find in its cities. In the unimportant countries there would be none.

Occasionally he had come across antique shops in the poorer sections of Kyoto, in really medieval buildings, low-eaved and well lighted, their old sign-curtains hanging tattered and discolored in front, and he had wondered sometimes whether they had any customers. They couldn't attract tourists in this part of town, where most of the buildings looked like warehouses or old-style homes. Probably what business they had was with people who lived in Kyoto. They hardly looked like stores—the braziers and serving-tables, bowls and old furniture inside seemed to be there for daily use, not for sale as *objets d'art*.

Kyogo had no house to furnish and there was nothing in these shops that he needed, but sometimes he would stop at one of them, out of some vague impulse, and look around. The dealer who came out to serve him would be no old man, out of touch with the modern world, but a young fellow in a shop apron, his pale face suggesting that he rarely left the store. If Kyogo happened to inspect some dyed-pattern plate and run his hand over it, the young man would rouse his interest by telling him where it was kilned and that it was much more than a century old. If Kyogo was interested in dye-ware, they still had some real *shonzui* there. Kyogo knew little of such things, but the shopkeeper treated him as though it was a matter of course that he should know all about ceramics. And Kyogo was surprised and charmed by the minute care the shopkeeper took of every old charcoal-scuttle box and reed pot-rest, as though even these things had a value and an excellence of their own. It was wonderful, he thought, that there were Japanese who could still pay such delicate attention to common things. It was a tiny part of Japanese life which he had almost forgotten.

Kyogo had grown used to Europe, so that after his return he was able to see what a really meager and impoverished life the Japanese had had through the centuries. Of course he understood that the war was responsible for the extreme poverty of the moment. But surely the Japanese people had never known luxury, never in all their long history. That came home to you when you looked at the buildings that had represented dignity and grandeur for them, like the temples in the old Western Capital of Nara. The Phoenix Hall at Uji was beautiful too, in its classical style, but it seemed a very small and narrow beauty if you had seen the vast cathedrals of the West. But the ancient Japanese had lavished their resources on these temples, and if they were so unimpressive, you could guess how much chance the individual had had to satisfy his desires in private life. The castles from the feudal period were certainly magnificent, but they only made you feel the more keenly the meagerness of the life with which the townspeople and even poorer commoners, on whose heads the system rested, had been forced to content themselves. You didn't have to seek out the back streets to see this. It was clear just from the way the old houses here in Kyoto were built, with their interiors invisible from the street, with hardly any exposure to the sunlight, and so cramped that adjacent houses had to share a single wall.

It was because they were so poor, Kyogo saw, that the Japanese had discovered a world of beauty unknown to Western æsthetics and called it by names suggesting melancholy and unfulfillment. They had been denied the luxury of really satisfying their human desires, so they had suppressed them and found ways to enjoy poverty.

Kyogo had become too much a foreigner to appreciate the old teahouses. The pure moss garden of the Western Fragrant Shrine and the rock gardens of the Temple of Dragon's Peace interested him because of their different beauty; but here too he saw the taste of a people who had learned to bear the meagerness of their lives by cultivating a fondness for simple things like herbs and plants. Only a people who accounted luxury a vice and poverty a virtue could have planned these exquisitely neat gardens. The average Westerner would not understand why they were beautiful. Kyogo found them strange himself, and preferred bright, luxurious gardens. The garden of the Golden Tower Shrine, for example, even a Westerner would recognize as beautiful. There was a garden that really seemed made for human enjoyment! There was none of that Japanese tortuousness about it; it was free, spacious, and bright. No other garden combined such elegance of style with so much practicality. It was well watered and wide open to the sky. The building, too, was of such a luxurious architecture that it was hard to believe it was the work of Japanese. They had even covered it with gold leaf. Of course, it had been designed in the days before ink and water drawings, the tea ceremony, and Zen had come in. Was that why it was so magnificent?

Young people in Japan since the war were so uninterested in history and knew so little about it that they were certainly becoming more and more insensitive to what had been good in the old Japan. Times had changed, and they were not being taught to see these things. Soon young people would look at the restrained beauty of the gardens of the Dragon Peace Temple and the Western Fragrant Shrine and see only somewhat unusual gardens.

The purity of feeling in the style would become steadily more alien to them. They would be as Kyogo was now, able to see only what was physically there. In a little while (if not, indeed, already) they would find the gardens of the Golden Tower Shrine less beautiful than the lawns and artificial fountains and regular tree-lined paths of a Western-style public park, laid out like a geometrical design.

Clearly the Japanese past was losing its hold on young Japanese. Now that poverty had gone beyond the point where it could be considered a virtue, it had turned into the worst of evils, and the Japanese were becoming unable to see the beauty allied to it. Later, when poverty had been overcome, they might create an altogether different art, freer and broader than the old.

Kyogo thought of Toshisada Ushigi and that flower-scented night in spring when they had walked through Kamakura to see the temples. He smiled. Ushigi was infatuated with the past. He lived in an entirely different world from the young generation of postwar Japan. Kyogo himself stood between the two. He did not belong to the old Japan, nor was he one of those who were going to create something for the new Japan. He could see both worlds just because nothing bound him to either.

And it was with the belief that nothing would bind him that Kyogo made his trips to Kyoto. He was merely reminiscing about the old Japan, perhaps because of his age. Or perhaps he was moved by the nostalgic attraction to the past which might be expected in one who had come home to his country after so many years abroad. He felt some love for the old streets he walked through and noticed with a sad little smile that even in this ancient capital the girls, even the older women, were wearing Western dresses now.

Poverty was changing the customs and the character

of the Japanese. It was said that the new generation had rejected the past and immediately gone rotten, but poverty was the reason. Kyogo remembered a broadcast of one of those street-corner public-opinion polls. The question was whether the bureaucrats had been successfully democratized. The public complained bitterly about how impolite the officials were. And then a young fellow of twenty who worked in the District Office came to the microphone and said that naturally you were impolite if you had to live on a thirty-six-hundred-yen base. And if you didn't get a raise, you wouldn't get any politer. He talked in a brutal, bellicose tone, and didn't even watch his language.

Kyogo couldn't forget the broadcast. It had showed him how much of the grace had gone out of Japanese life. Nowadays poverty had only an evil effect, even on Japanese. It had made everyone terribly impatient. The young man was probably an extreme case. His immaturity and inexperience made him childishly incapable of the sort of nonchalance a foreigner would have shown in the same situation. A Frenchman or Chinese might have said the same sort of thing, but he would have cracked a joke or made a pun while doing it. But the young Japanese just blurted it out without adornment. Postwar Japan was really a desert. The young were devoid of subtlety—as one might expect of a generation stripped of its past.

These ideas would pass through Kyogo's head as he sat idle and alone at the hotel, the unbroken sound of flowing water in his ears and the green of the willows across the river in his eyes. Downstairs, his landlady might make a phone call and he would overhear her.

"Hello, Harugiku. Could you come over right away? Oh, thanks. Well, then—I don't want to rush you, but could you make it early?"

Her soft Western drawl was soothing to the ear. Kyogo would feel suddenly that he was in the old Kyoto of the days before the war, and that everything was normal.

Kyogo never became sentimental. But he would sense an indescribable, delicate atmosphere enfolding his body, and feel, wonderfully deep down, that he had come back to Japan. He didn't mean to let anything bind him, but something like a mist or an ether was stealing into his heart insensibly and satisfying his longing for the old Japan. It hadn't been a bad country. But it was ended now. That made him sad. He felt sorry for the young savages who were growing up in these postwar days, ignorant even of what had been good in the past.

As soon as Saeko reached her hotel in Kyoto with Tomoko, she told the maid to call up and find out whether Kyogo was in. She ordered her not to give their names.

Saeko waited for the answer as eagerly as Tomoko.

Their hotel was near the Southern Zen Temple. Formerly the private villa of an Osaka industrialist, it had been licensed as a hotel after the war. The rooms were luxuriously laid out, and water flowed through the garden, sounding like rain even while the sun shone on the green leaves. Beyond the elegant garden shrubs they could see the mountain on which the Southern Zen Temple stood.

The maid came to make her report. "He'll be there day after tomorrow, you say?" Saeko confirmed the message, and turned to Tomoko with a smile. She looked relieved. "The day after tomorrow will be all right, won't it?"

Tomoko inclined her head doubtfully. She still seemed unsure of herself after coming all this way.

"You don't have to see him right away, surely. If you're in a hurry, they probably know his Kobe address at the hotel, but—we don't know what his arrangements are in Kobe. It would be best to wait here, I think."

Tomoko was convinced, and nodded her agreement. But she thought of her mother back home, and it troubled her that she would have to be away for three whole days. "You're sure it won't inconvenience you to stay so long, Saeko?"

"Don't worry about me." Saeko laughed lightly as she turned away and fixed her eyes on the lake in the garden. The brilliant green leaves cast a beautiful reflection on her white skin. She was glad that the meeting with Kyogo wasn't to take place immediately after their arrival, without any preparation. This respite would give her a chance to compose herself. For Saeko had felt the strain as though she had been coming to meet Kyogo herself, not arranging for Tomoko to meet him, and now she could breathe more easily. And, of course, Tomoko was going to see Kyogo alone, and she and Saeko were leaving right after. That was the plan; but, it was not impossible that Kyogo and Saeko, being in Kyoto, might come face to face somewhere, unexpectedly. And for Saeko, the thought of such a possibility brought with it, secretly, something like a temptation not to let it hang over her head, but, instead, to gather her courage and go herself to see Kyogo. Involuntarily, she drew in her breath.

At night they left the sliding door open; the sound of flowing water still rained into the darkened room and through the mosquito netting around the bed where they lay. Saeko's voice rose above it. "I must seem a strange woman to you, Tomoko."

A light was shining somewhere in the garden, and Tomoko could still make out the white circle of Saeko's face in the darkness and see that she was lying with her arms around the pillow.

"I've done all sorts of things, and seen all sorts of people—and the only person I've ever been afraid of is your father. There's a reason, Tomoko."

The sound of spring water was strange to Tomoko, and it kept her wide awake. She was thinking how different Saeko was, lying next to her here in the dim light, from the gay and fluent and utterly unapproachable person she had always seemed before. She sensed the weight of Saeko's body in the darkness and knew that her flesh would be womanly to the touch.

The white netting stirred slightly in the thick summer night.

"It's just like rain," Saeko said of the continuous sound of the water flow, and then went on: "You must think it strange of me to come all this way and still insist on keeping out of your father's sight. But I have a reason, Tomoko."

Tomoko said nothing.

"The truth is, I hurt your father once, without meaning to at all. I'd met him accidentally in Singapore. He was hiding out in the Chinese quarter, but I knew that some people in the Navy knew where he was, and I didn't realize there was any secret about it. I was careless enough to talk about him around Singapore and the story got to the Military Police, somehow. . . . It was a terrible time, just when things were going very badly for Japan in the war, and the M.P.'s were even more nervous than usual. Your father was the sort of man who talked quite freely against the war, and, even worse, the Chinese family he was living with had English connections, so things became serious. He was put in the M.P. prison. When I heard that he was safe and had come back to Japan, I felt better, but I've suffered terribly for what I did—it was really inexcusable, and ever since then the very thought of it would keep me awake all night. War is a horrible thing. People were capable of doing things then without a second thought—things that seem utterly fantastic to them when they look back now.

"But your father was magnificent. He spoke out clearly against the war, right in the middle of it all. Such a good man!—and to think that a woman's silly thoughtlessness, however unintentional, should cause him so much trouble! I still can't excuse myself. . . . How angry your father must be. He has a right to hate me, I've resigned myself to that, but there's a wound in my conscience for what I did, and that won't heal.

"When I met you, Tomoko, and realized that you were Moriya's daughter, what a thrill went through me! I felt you were someone close to me—that's the only way to put it. God or something had brought us together, I believed. Evil woman though I was, I wanted Tomoko, at least, to be my friend—I wanted it desperately, it's all I've been able to think about. So I must know, Tomoko— can you forgive me?"

"I can't see that you need forgiveness. I can't believe that you're the sort of person you say you are."

"Really? You forgive me?"

Saeko slid over to Tomoko. She took her hand gently and folded it into her nightgown at her breast. "Can you understand what I have suffered, Tomoko? I had to tell you about it sometime, I felt. Only I knew what I had done, no one else. Even your father doesn't really know, I think, but I couldn't keep it from you, Tomoko."

Saeko stopped talking and pressed her face down into the sheet. She seemed to be crying hard, and Tomoko could see her shoulders in the dark-blue nightgown rise and fall violently with her sobs.

Saeko had kept hold of Tomoko's hand when she turned over on her face, and now it was flat under her body and the weight of her quivering breasts. The intimate contact made Tomoko uneasy.

Tomoko had tried to listen receptively, but Saeko's words had just brushed over the surface of her mind and left her strangely unmoved. It was rather to the touch of Saeko's warm skin and throbbing breast that she reacted with a sense of trouble. What came to her mind, surprisingly, was those diamonds. And her uneasiness, which had had nothing to settle on, suddenly deepened, and she tried to pull her hand away from Saeko's grasp. But Saeko tightened her fingers around it and wouldn't let go.

"I wonder whether you can understand. I've really suffered. I daren't ever see your father again."

Tomoko was still wondering exactly what Saeko had done, but since her father had been able to come back to Japan unharmed, she was sure that nothing that had happened in the past would matter to him any longer. "I'm sure you needn't feel that way," she answered. "You're not the sort of person to do anything really bad."

"Do you mean that?"

"Yes."

"Thank you, Tomoko. Then you'll defend me if your father is still angry at me, if he should ever say he can't forgive me?"

"I'm not sure I understand. But whatever I can do— But there'll be no need for that."

"I just want you to promise me. . . . I'm thinking how terrible the war was. People couldn't live by normal human feelings. They did cruel things and got horrible ideas. Look at me. I went away overseas by myself, like a man— into a man's world, and there I saw human ugliness and vileness and perversion until I couldn't stand it any more. It's not an easy thing to live. Soon I had become the manly creature that you must think me now. But what I really want, Tomoko, is to be a woman. If only I could relax, like a woman, if only the time would come

when I needn't feel I should have been born a man—
that's what I long for. They say I'm stubborn, that I
won't accept defeat. It's true, but I'm the one who
suffers most for being that way. Only to you, Tomoko,
would I confess my weakness this way. I'm showing you
the Saeko that begs for pity. Go and see your father,
Tomoko. He's a gentleman, a good man. But I'm afraid
of him. So much afraid that it took courage for me to
come here with you, a great deal of courage."

Tomoko had been listening in silence, but she broke
in now. Her tone was so simple and innocent that it surprised herself as she spoke.

"Saeko, don't talk that way. Come with me to see
him. It will be all right."

"I can't do that. You mustn't even mention me when
you see your father. Not right now. I mean it, not a word
about me. I forbid it."

"But it's strange—your hiding yourself this way."

"Oh, I'll meet him sometime, somewhere—I'm sure of
that," Saeko said quickly. "You understand—after I've
worked up the courage." She sounded as though she had
put on a smile. "I'm a coward, I know. When it comes to
your father, I get the strangest, cowering feeling. I'm
awfully afraid. You must think I've done something
terrible."

What had she done to make her this anxious about
it? Tomoko didn't know yet, but she was more and more
suspicious. Saeko was different tonight. There was so
much passion in her voice that her story sounded confused. Tomoko had been listening to her with a constant sense of oppression. She couldn't wholly believe
what Saeko was saying just because of the feeling with
which she said it. Somewhere in her story Tomoko
smelled a lie. And Saeko's extraordinary intimacy seemed
designed to conceal the falsehood. It made Tomoko un-

easy too. It was so unlike Saeko. Tomoko burst out: "What should I do?"

And Saeko, turning around to face her, surprised Tomoko by repeating the same words, earnestly: "What should I do?" Then, quickly: "I'm sorry, Tomoko!"

Suddenly she grasped Tomoko by both arms. The touch of her fevered body told Tomoko that her mood had changed completely. She seemed gay now, even playful. "Forgive me. I've troubled you so much, and about nothing. It doesn't matter as much as I said, probably, but it was only for your sake that I made this trip to Kyoto, so you mustn't mention me to your father. I insist on it."

Tomoko didn't answer.

"Promise me, Tomoko."

"All right. I promise."

"Forgive me—I've been talking so strangely to you. But let's be friends, h'm? Give me a hug, Tomoko, with all your strength. Hug me so tight that my bones crack. Please, Tomoko."

Tomoko couldn't hold it in. "You frighten me, Saeko."

Gently, Saeko let go. "I'm sorry, Tomoko. I wasn't thinking. You don't understand this sort of loneliness yet, do you? And for me to act so, your masculine friend—it's absurd."

The next day, when Tomoko got up, Saeko looked her usual serene and cheerful self in the bright morning sunlight.

❀ ∿∿∿ XIV ∿∿∿ ❀

THE GARDEN OF
GROVES AND PONDS

After the automobile entered the Street of Wood Merchants, along the edge of which flows the Steep Rapids River, it drew close to the luxurious border of plane trees along the sidewalk, slowed down, and presently stopped. When Tomoko read the name of her father's inn on the lantern hanging at the eaves over the entrance gate, she suddenly felt a pang of hesitation.

"Is this it?" Saeko asked crisply. Although she was aware of the danger of coming upon Kyogo by chance, now that she and Tomoko had arrived safely, something resembling disappointment accompanied her sense of relief.

"You go ahead," she told Tomoko. "But let's make the night train if we can."

The car started off, and Tomoko, gazing after it, saw Saeko through the rear window turn around, gently raise her hand, and make a signal.

Tomoko once again looked up at the vermilion lettering on the lantern. The long narrow alley, at the most three feet wide, was not at all like the entrance to an inn. Paved in granite, it led deeply inward between the tenements on either side. The porches of these tenements were spread with rush mats, and some women were sewing there. Through the narrow doorway of one, she could see a chest of drawers in an inner room. Farther along the cramped alley was a stone well, and a baby carriage had been left ready. The eaves on both sides jutted out unevenly, as in an ordinary public alleyway. At the extreme inner end, where Tomoko ran into a lattice grille, she found the entrance to Kyogo's hotel.

Once she reached the lattice, Tomoko began to compose herself. At the right of the entrance was a kitchen in which she could see several maids standing on the bare board floor, working. She called out from in front of the lattice, as custom requires, and a middle-aged woman who seemed to be the landlady came out and greeted her in the soft, mellow accents of Kyoto.

"So you want Mr. Moriya. It's a pity, but he left here just a short while ago." Then, in a voice somewhat louder than necessary, to show her authority, she called out to the kitchen: "Where did Mr. Moriya go? . . . Oh, to the Golden Tower Shrine? It was just a short while ago, wasn't it?"

She turned back to Tomoko with a smile and said, watching her intently: "He went alone, so I suppose he's gone by streetcar. If you take a taxi from here, you'll be sure to catch him. Shall I call one for you?" When Tomoko asked her to do so, the woman arose briskly and went to the phone.

Tomoko thought that perhaps it was fortunate that her father had gone out. She had gradually grown uneasy about meeting him for the first time in so public a place as a hotel, where she would have to go through the formality of giving her calling card to one of the hotel's staff and asking to be announced. Still, if she followed him to the Golden Tower Shrine, suppose there were a great many sightseers there? She doubted that she would be able to tell which one of them was her own father, for she had seen only a photograph of him as a young man.

Apparently the landlady was sending for the taxi immediately, for she said: "Yes, that's right. Please come at once," and then hung up.

Tomoko was not yet fully aware of the boldness of her conduct. She had really come to Kyoto solely because of the intense desire to spare her mother unhappiness. She was determined to do anything for her mother's sake. That was the only source of her courage.

From the window of the taxi she saw by the roadside the sacred stone archway of the Shrine of the Heavenly Gods of the Northern Fields. The car sped along the wide paved road and approached the lovely tree-covered park known as Pine Mountain. The neighborhood was gradually becoming more suburban and beginning to offer vistas in which, here and there, paddy-fields could be seen. Soon the car turned into a street that lay just beyond the corner of a small house, and stopped in front of the entrance to the Golden Tower Shrine.

Probably because it was a sweltering afternoon, there was no one else in sight, and a solemn stillness surrounded the temple's precincts. A gravel walk passed through a wood of large camphor trees in which a few other species were mingled, and reached into the gateway of the temple. The shade of the trees made it cooler along the walk. The song of cicadas could be heard faintly, seeping through the silence.

Tomoko crossed a small stone bridge and passed through the gateway. There was a low pine tree with twisted boughs in the foreground, and beyond it stood a large white building that appeared to be the quarters of the chief priest. All was hushed, and there was no sign of any human being. Moss covered the ground prettily and spread onto the path, which was edged with thin ropes to restrain trampling sightseers. Picking her way along the paving-stones, Tomoko arrived automatically in front of the guide's office. An aged man with an air of boredom was alone in the shed, and gave her a ticket upon receiving the admission fee.

"You go in on that side," he said, and merely nodded toward the entrance.

"At last," thought Tomoko, feeling slightly tense. Could her father be here already? Or would he arrive later if he was coming by streetcar?

Tomoko had no idea how she would address him when the time came. Nevertheless, she felt calmer and more composed than she had expected she would. Indeed, beyond mere composure, a feeling of active defiance had started to come over her, as if she was about to call him to account. She would do it not only to shield her mother; it was for herself too. She was disconcerted because her determination was tempered by a stirring of fondness for the image of her father, even though she knew she should show no sign of affection. She should think merely of safeguarding her mother without bowing to her own emotions.

The leaves, ruffled by a light breeze, glistened in the sun. A pathway running between an earthen wall and a hedge brought her unexpectedly to the bank of a pond. The triple pagoda roofs of the Golden Tower, which she had seen in pictures and in photographs, presented their serene and graceful shape to her. Since she was standing in the cool shade of the luxuriant trees behind her, the garden, flooded with the rays of the afternoon sun, was made brighter by contrast. Even when we come upon something beautiful without particular preparation, we still respond to its beauty.

Instinctively Tomoko looked around her to see whether, in this radiant scene, there was anyone who might be her father. A man who looked like a guide was sitting in the shade of the Golden Tower, but there was no one else. She supposed that the usual crowds of sight-seers were kept away by the heat in the city.

Boughs and branches basking in the sun were reflected on the water around the inverted image of the three-storied tower. The reflection was so clear that one could count each glistening pine needle. The outfall of the pond was at her feet and murmured faintly but constantly. The stillness filled her with an impulsive desire to look about her. The garden was so bright that it was almost impossible to describe.

Tomoko moved closer to the Golden Tower. The gold leaf still left on the underside of the third-story roof and on the upper part of the pillars was so somber-hued that it did not appear to be golden.

The guide was wearing *mompe*, a baggy wartime type of Japanese trousers. He rose and approached her, for he had no reason to suppose that she was not a tourist. "Please take off your shoes," he said, "and come inside."

After she had done so, he began to explain the various images of Buddha which were placed in a gallery facing the pond. She listened to him reluctantly. When he finished with the images, he explained the positions and æsthetic significance of the elegant stepping-stones in the pond. Each isle, with its small pines and moss-covered rocks, was distinguished from the others by a special name, such as Crane-and-Tortoise Isle, or Field-of-Reeds Isle.

Somewhere in the distance a hen cackled.

As she listened to the prosaic and monotonous explanation, Tomoko's attention constantly wandered across the pond to the path by which she had come. When he finished his account the guide promptly returned to his seat in the shade; Tomoko remained standing in the gallery, which had a small roof that jutted out over the pond, and gazed at her surroundings. She noticed a carp swimming, and peered into the water at it.

It was a large black carp. As it turned adroitly, its back showed a golden glint. It continued to swim leisurely and to circle around. Countless small young carp were swimming in the same manner, making ripples on the surface and disturbing the slime on the bottom, which rose like scattered tinsel. The water eddied gently and made the sun's dazzling image lengthen and shorten.

A plank ran along the handrail, providing a seat. To-moko sat on it and looked once more toward the garden's entrance. There was still no sign of anyone coming, so, vacantly, she gazed across the pond or watched the carp.

The water, eddying to the movement of the carp, was reflected on the rafters and underside of the roof, and the reflections moved slowly and softly as if they were bits of waste silk. A ray of light glancing off the water played brightly on Tomoko's breast. The old guide now dozed on his seat in the shade, resting the tip of his fan on his knee. Tomoko grew gradually uneasy because no one came; she had promised to try to take the train that night, and the ticket was already in her handbag. She even thought of sending a message to her father at his hotel, telling him the reason for her visit, and of leaving without meeting him. But within her stirred a sense of the destiny of her mother and herself in this world, and an unspeakable loneliness came over her.

The same black carp was still swimming slowly in the shallower waters of the pond. Then, as she glanced upward, she noticed a man standing on the spot where she herself had halted and looked this way a short while ago. He was wearing a white suit and a Panama hat, and was looking at the pond.

When he heard footsteps, the old guide opened his eyes. He behaved as if Kyogo's face was already familiar to him.

"It's hot, isn't it?" Kyogo said to him gently.

"Yes, it's unbearable," the guide said automatically in his Kyoto dialect, and merely sat upright. He omitted his explanation of the wooden images and the stepping-stones.

Kyogo looked into the building, on whose eaves reflections from the water were dancing; he saw Tomoko sitting in the gallery. He had sensed someone there. And, finding in that shady place, where old golden Buddha images were arrayed, a typical modern and urban-mannered young girl, he looked at her with an expression of amusement.

Tomoko had been staring in his direction, but upon meeting his eyes, she turned her gaze to the garden. Her body remained motionless, and to Kyogo her dress was only a blur of white.

Without taking off his shoes and without climbing up to the gallery as other sightseers would do, Kyogo stood in the shade, took off his hat, and merely gazed at the pond.

Tomoko thought of getting up and going to him, but, as if nailed to her seat, she could not move. In a little while, giving a slight salute to the guard, Kyogo started to walk away. His white-suited figure disappeared behind the wall.

Moving without conscious thought, Tomoko rose, crossed the gallery, and came to the place where she had left her shoes. As she started to walk along the thinly wooded path, she saw Kyogo standing at another spot, watching the pond. She drew nearer, but she found herself incapable of acting boldly; she was conscious only of the pounding of her heart. Were she to continue, she would pass just behind her father; since she could not summon the courage to speak to him and to reveal her identity, she thought she would most likely walk past him in silence.

Then, as if he sensed her presence, Kyogo glanced back over his shoulder and looked at her. "Excuse me," he said gently, "but do you enjoy visiting places such as this?"

Tomoko stopped short, staring at Kyogo in amazement, and was unable to reply.

"Forgive me," said Kyogo with a smile and in an even gentler tone, "I should have added 'at your age.' Do you live in this city?"

Tomoko shook her head.

"You come from another city? Are you from Tokyo? What places have you visited since you've been here in Kyoto?"

Tomoko noticed the way her father was treating her. She was suddenly quite amused. She smiled at Kyogo, and as she did so she felt much more at her ease. "I haven't seen any other place yet."

"Aren't you here in Kyoto to go sightseeing during your school vacation?"

"No, I'm not here to go sightseeing, and I don't go to school any longer. I've already been graduated."

"Oh, I must beg your pardon then," said Kyogo ceremoniously, as if he was laughing at himself. "I never can make even the remotest guess about the ages of young people like you. I was convinced that you still went to school."

He suddenly fell silent and strolled peacefully by her side along the path through the wood. The branches of the trees were well trimmed, the garden resplendent.

"May I ask how old you are?"

"I'm twenty-two."

Kyogo gazed at her with new, deep intensity. "So a girl of twenty-two would look something like you? Isn't that so?" Then he added: "What an old fool I am."

Veiling her glance, Tomoko had been dispassionately observing Kyogo. She no longer doubted that he was her father. It seemed to her like a dream that here, walking beside her, was the man about whom she had speculated when she saw photographs of him in his youth, and whom she had pictured in her mind from Saeko's words. She was a little surprised at finding him younger than she had imagined. Before meeting him, she had secretly anticipated some sentiment of attachment toward him, but she could not yet say she had any such feeling. She was somewhat bewildered, and her emotions still were pent up. Yet in spite of this, her heart was light. Maybe it was partly because Kyogo, though he had a keen look in his eyes, was gentle and had a taste for quiet things. She was glad he had actually turned out to be a decent person, just as Saeko had repeatedly described him. But that was all she felt, and it was not as if these were the feelings of a daughter toward her father.

They went around to the rear and came upon a spot where spring water, trickling through moss-covered rocks, had formed a little well. "They say this water was used for the Shogun's tea ceremonies," Kyogo told her, "but I don't know whether it's true or not." A tender expression came into his eyes as he asked: "What are you doing now, since graduating?"

"Dressmaking." She paused, then continued: "I'm also helping to edit a magazine."

"At your age!" Kyogo looked at her in astonishment. "Well, well! That's very good! Since my time, things have changed a great deal for Japanese girls. I've lived in foreign countries for such a long time that I feel as if I were Rip Van Winkle. Wherever I go in Japan, I'm astonished by the great changes that have come over everything I see. Particularly, I have no idea what thoughts are passing through the minds of young people like yourself, boy or girl." He laughed, and then asked: "I'm afraid it's rude of me to ask such a question, but I wonder what kind of home you come from."

"Do you mean my family?"

"Yes. What is your father doing?"

"His occupation?" Tomoko, suddenly feeling as if she were being swept along by some unknown force, answered clearly: "Father was in the Navy. Formerly."

"The Navy?" Kyogo exclaimed, raising his eyes and looking at Tomoko's face. "Well, well," he murmured. Although she couldn't fathom the meaning of his exclamation, his voice reverberated deeply and was charged with complex nuances. The words aroused a faint agitation in Tomoko's mind. Had her father sensed something? Their talk was broken off. The silence of a summer afternoon dropped heavily around them.

There was a spot where water poured down onto a cluster of rocks. Although the drop was too small to merit the title of waterfall, a notice board indicated that it was called the Dragon's Gate Falls, and the rocks on which the water poured, the Carp Stones. The two had now reached the face of these falls. The branches of a maple tree cast a light shadow on the ground.

"In any event," said Kyogo slowly, "your father is in good health, isn't he?"

Tomoko fixed her large eyes upon the masculine face she believed to be her father's, and nodded firmly. She believed that she had managed to do this quite deliberately, though only a moment earlier she had been on the verge of disclosing everything in a torrent of words.

Then she noticed how poised Kyogo was, and that his face was serene. Whether because he was a polished gentleman or because he wished to be considerate to a younger person, his eyes were kind, his courtesy never-failing, and his perfectly balanced and tranquil feelings apparent from the very beginning.

"I'm glad to hear that," said Kyogo without moving. "Too many people have died."

All at once an irrepressible smile played on Tomoko's face. A faint touch of malice lurked somewhere within her. She had begun to think that her father, standing there before her serene and well-built, was an amusing and touchingly weak character because of his very mildness. "He still doesn't know I'm Tomoko." This thought alone was sufficient to make her feel strangely light-hearted. Even her expression was brighter.

She moved her lips as if she wished to say something. Her eyes, which were turned toward her father, had acquired a mischievous and artless sparkle, and were like the eyes of a child who is planning some prank.

"I used to be in the Navy too," her father started to say. "Since I had a daughter of your age, there cannot be much difference in the time when I and your father were at the Naval Academy—"

Tomoko interrupted him suddenly. "Father!" The word slipped effortlessly and readily from her lips. "I'm Tomoko."

Kyogo stared at Tomoko. He was wordless.

Tomoko's profound emotions had come bursting from her. Once she no longer contained her lightheartedness, it became uncontrollable. Her father was staring at her doubtfully, in a way that made her feel she was watching the unsure motions of a blind person whom she wanted to take by the hand and comfort. Her father seemed gradually to grasp the meaning of her words.

"I'm Tomoko," she repeated. "Don't you understand?"

Kyogo's eyes were moist, but he showed no sign of

disturbance either in his bearing or in his countenance. To Tomoko his placidness appeared no less than elegant.

"You shouldn't surprise a person," he said in a mild voice. He was still gazing at Tomoko. The expression in his eyes changed only by growing more intense. His lips trembled slightly.

"To think that I didn't know," he murmured. And at that instant a shadow of gloom passed over his face. Confronted with affection, suddenly a feeling of sadness, of pensive dreariness, of the sorrow of living in this world, had placed its weight upon his soul; only by great self-restraint could he put a brake upon his emotions. He spoke as if he had played an unworthy comic role in front of his daughter. "You must have felt terrible," he said heavily. "I really knew nothing. I hope you'll understand it couldn't be helped, and please forgive me."

Frantically, Tomoko shook her head. The light glinted from her abundant, permanent-waved hair. Her face still shone. "I knew at once that you were my father. Really. Just at a glance."

"Let's walk," suggested Kyogo. Always it had been like that when an uncontrollable emotion had swelled in his heart, even when he had been living abroad; and now the habit suddenly and automatically took hold of him. Walking was a matter of rousing his physical self. The exercise would shake him free of his emotions.

"Do I look like anyone's parent?" he asked fiercely.

The girl laughed gently and nodded. "Yes. Now it's really clear you're my father."

"You think so?"

"Father, what did you think of me? You thought I was someone else's child, didn't you?"

After hesitating a bit, Kyogo said: "Yes, I did." Then he asserted: "Of course I did. The Tomoko I knew was only four. She was just a child." He closed his eyes momentarily as he trod along the pavement of the narrow, sloping path. "How you've grown up!" he murmured.

At the crest of the slope there was a tea-ceremony house with alcove posts of sacred bamboo which was one of the attractions of the Golden Tower Shrine. It was called the Lovely Evening Arbor. Kyogo had no interest in it, however, and when they passed the place he didn't take enough notice of it to point it out to Tomoko. They merely followed the path and went out through the small gate at the garden's end.

"When did you come?" Kyogo asked.

"I've already been here three days."

"Alone?" Kyogo must have been thinking of her mother. "Or is someone with you?"

"Yes, a friend." Saeko's image crossed Tomoko's mind; all at once she felt uneasy. The memory of the way Saeko's features became tense and her tone agitated when she spoke of Kyogo disturbed her former tranquillity.

"And when are you leaving?"

"I'm taking the night train tonight."

"In such a hurry?" A sudden sigh escaped from Kyogo's lips. "If you would like to, let's have dinner together." Then, unaware of the fatherly manner he adopted, he added: "Shall we invite your friend, too?"

Tomoko hastily shook her head in a gesture of refusal. "No, she's busy," she answered. "She has other engagements."

"Do you know her through your work?"

"Yes, she's connected with it in a way."

"But really," said her father, restraining his secret excitement, "how can a girl like you make a living by working?"

Tomoko laughed with cheerful innocence. "Oh, somehow or other," she replied with happiness in her heart. "It's not necessary for me to work. But mother had the kindness to suggest that I do something."

"I see." Kyogo had pulled out a cigarette and had stopped to light it. "Your mother's well, isn't she?"

The lighter caught fire with a faint but sharp sound. There was something modish and elegant in her father's manner as he flicked his lighter and brought the flame to his cigarette. She glanced at the hair at his temples and noticed traces of silver. He inhaled deeply; then, breathing out the smoke, watched it fade away into the woods.

"I haven't the right to say this," he said suddenly, "but I am very happy that I was able to meet you."

Tomoko said nothing.

"But—you shouldn't have come. Does your mother know about this?"

Noticing a new sternness in her father's eyes as he looked at her, Tomoko shook her head.

"Then your mother doesn't know. You mean to say your coming here was just your own idea?" Kyogo fell silent for a moment; then he asked in a thick voice: "Who told you about me?"

"It must have come through Mr. Ushigi."

"Oh," Kyogo responded in a clear tone, "I see. That man, was it?" Then he added: "Fathead."

Tomoko was surprised to hear him use the word.

"What's the matter? Good heavens, I meant Ushigi, not you!"

They had come to the front of a small temple. A row of slender paper lanterns with the characters meaning Stone God of Fire boldly painted on them hung there pointlessly and, in the quiet of a summer afternoon, gave the place an air of desertion.

"Everyone lives in his own queer way," said Kyogo.

"Ushigi, and I too. I don't suppose you understand yet, but we're like these lanterns. We hang dangling in this world, and there's something sad about us. But it's not that anyone else made us that way. It's ourselves, we ourselves. Honestly."

His voice began to ring out. To Tomoko it seemed as if his blood had begun to circulate more rapidly, spreading a new vivacity throughout his body; even his complexion all at once appeared younger.

"I confess I'm an egotist and a wanderer. I've trained myself to live without feeling too much sadness or loneliness. I'm outside the pattern of ordinary people. I want you to realize this. You may think I'm speaking queerly. But these are my true feelings, so there's nothing wrong in having you listen to me. Abroad, I was always alone. Once I'd grown used to it, I didn't feel lonely any more. It was the course I had chosen. I could do nothing but go straight ahead. What's more, living in this world is not a matter of trying to iron out your relationships with others; to the end it is a matter of struggling with yourself. I'm a man who's lived with that belief. That's why —that's why, in the eyes of others, I seem heartless and cold. The fact that I'm speaking to you in this way at our first meeting proves that I actually am. But that's how I'm made. It's bad. It's truly bad. Yet now that you've come to have a look at me, thinking of me as your father, though in every meaningful way I'm not, what sort of person have I got to show you? I can't use make-up at this late stage."

Tomoko said nothing.

"Look at me: a man who has calmly deserted his wife and child; a heartless egotist; an old man who's already become indifferent to human emotions. That's my balance sheet. To be alone—that's my wish." Despite the determination of his words, tears abruptly welled into

Kyogo's eyes, and he added in a heavy voice: "You shouldn't have come, my dear."

Her father was speaking slowly. His voice was quiet. There was no insistence in it. Yet its sound waves, invisible to the eye, pierced her heart. It was as if, in spite of the fashionable, foppish appearance of his person, the true strength that lurked below had overcome these barriers and broken through to the surface. Tomoko, however, was not misled.

She had been listening to him with undivided attention and without blinking, and now her spirits lifted and she even began to feel exhilarated. Her father was strong; this she felt above all else. He was stating straightforwardly matters which must be as distressing to him as they were to her. In spite of the pitiless words that he had spoken, Tomoko's eyes were shining.

"I'm a cruel father," said Kyogo. "I know you came all this way just to see me. But it's bad for your mother. It was wrong to do it. You shouldn't do anything that's wrong."

Feeling that she need make no explanation or excuse, Tomoko nodded submissively.

"To tell the truth, what I should have done immediately after I came back to Japan was to go to your mother to apologize humbly. I still believe that's what I should have done. But it turned out that I couldn't do it. You understand this, don't you?"

"Yes, I understand."

"The dead shouldn't disturb the living," said Kyogo with a laugh. "You know something? The name of Kyogo Moriya has been erased from Japan's census register. He's dead. By law, a missing person is considered dead."

Tomoko found herself saying lightly: "There is your grave, Father."

"Yes, so I've heard. I've heard there's a grave. That's why I didn't appear before you either. Any ghost would hesitate to appear before a daughter like you. Partly it was a matter of social decency. But it also can be called my punishment. Some day I'll at least go to visit my grave. But what a strange relationship between father and daughter! Awhile ago I spoke your name for the first time. I spoke it timidly, not knowing whether it was all right to use it or not. Yet Tomoko is the name I myself gave you. I chose it because it means Companion Child. It meant that you would be a life's companion to us, the young couple we were then. I suppose you didn't know. Companion Child! But now, Tomoko, you're your mother's companion. Your mother is the one who has done the most for you, and your place is beside her. As for me, I've already said I'm all right alone. Your mother—please treat her gently."

They had descended a flight of stone steps and had reached the path through the wood near the temple's exit. No sooner had Tomoko brought herself to nod in reply to her father's words than tears streamed into her eyes; unable to hold them back, she covered her face with her hands and stood there crying. Not in the least in grief for herself, but for her mother, she wept aloud like a child.

Kyogo picked up the handbag that had slipped from under Tomoko's arm onto the gravel walk. It was made of glossy black leather and did not seem very modest for one belonging to a young girl. It was heavy, as if chock-full.

"You mustn't cry," Kyogo told her firmly. "It's all right to be angry. It's not proper to cry. It's all right to get mad and hit me. You have a right to be angry. Now let's walk. You're going to let me be your father until we part tonight, aren't you? You should do as your father says."

Tomoko could not speak.

"Cry no more, my dear."

Tomoko shook her head; then, sobbing, said haltingly: "It's not—because I feel sorry for myself—that I cried. All of a sudden—I felt sorry for Mother."

"Thank you," said Kyogo, deeply moved, but not losing his calm tone. "I'm happier than I can say that you've turned out to be such a good and devoted daughter. Please think only of being dutiful toward your mother. I'm asking you to take my place. That's why—"

He paused.

"That's why I want you yourself to become strong. Times have changed since your mother was brought up. It's become a terrifying world. Yet on the other hand, if you're not like the women of the past, if you have a firm will of your own, you certainly won't be unhappy and you may even be happy. Mother was brought up in a time when women were less fortunate than now; then she was put into contact with an outrageous fellow like me, which made things even more miserable for her. I only loaded her with burdens. Maybe it's because she's unfortunate, but she's strong. It seems cowardly for me to say so, but that's my sole relief, really," said Kyogo.

"That's something I often thought about while wandering in foreign countries. Japanese women are the strongest of all in enduring misfortunes. They seem weak, but they're strong. It's the opposite to the Japanese men, who fancy they are strong but actually are spiritless. It seems strange. I don't know about the flashy new type of woman one sees on the streets nowadays, but a man could depend on a woman who, like your mother, belonged to the old days. She may have looked weak, but she could be relied upon. Such women were the finest of any country in the world.

"What I'm saying are the willful words of an egotist who has repeatedly caused trouble. But, Tomoko, you yourself clearly demonstrate your mother's fineness. Without flattery, I really think so."

Tomoko said nothing.

"You've grown," said Kyogo in a thick voice that showed his emotion. "You've done well. You shouldn't have come to me. Nevertheless, I'm glad you did. I'm grateful."

❋ ᘰᘰᘰ XV ᘰᘰᘰ ❋

LANDSCAPE

Kyogo now was calm. He was keeping his feelings within limits. Not that he was making a particular effort to do so. He didn't need to. Even when he reached the hotel with Tomoko he said no more than: "I've brought a guest back with me."

He didn't introduce her as his daughter. But his love for her shone strong in his eyes.

A cold wind rose suddenly, and immediately afterward the sky began to cloud. There was going to be a shower that evening. Father and daughter had gone up to the porch over the river and sat down facing each other on the rattan sofa. The hanging paper lantern swung with the wind. Gray clouds were raveled in the sky over the Eastern Mountain like a spray of black mist. Lightning flashed in the distance. The thunder was still far away, and the slanting white lines of rain had not yet crossed the mountain.

"It'll cool off if it rains." Kyogo was watching the movement of the clouds. "If they don't come this way, they'll go toward Mount Hiei. That's Hiei over there."

He pointed it out for Tomoko and then leaned on the railing and looked toward it. "Of course, you may not feel about it as I do, but for me there's something awesome in that tremendous temple being way up there at that vast height on top of Hiei. I sit here gazing at it, and never cease to wonder."

The way he was speaking sounded a bit awesome to Tomoko, but Kyogo looked as calm as ever, though he was very serious. "It's incredible that they should have conceived of building a temple on such a high mountain a thousand years ago. It shows the power of religion, of course. Look at the Japanese today. They'd be completely incapable of any such grandiose scheme. Even now the temple looks superhuman, mythically vast, like some great dream of humanity, and they calmly set to work and made it real a thousand years ago, before the country was half civilized. They had no trucks and cables in those days, and they went to the top of that mountain to build a temple larger than any you can find on the plains. Go and see it sometime. Its size will astound you."

Hiei was enclosed in gray vapor, but its contour stood out firm and strong among the vague masses round about. Of course the temple was invisible; Tomoko could see only a very high mountain a great distance away.

She was in a very receptive mood, and had been growing conscious of it. She had never imagined she could be at ease with this new-found father of hers, but she was, perfectly at ease, and enjoying herself as she watched the scenery.

"Another flash of lightning!" Kyogo pointed it out. "It's raining heavily around Yamashina. The storm looks as though it'll move out toward Hiei and Sakamoto. That means it won't rain here, and it'll be hot all night."

Tomoko remembered that she was leaving Kyoto by tonight's train. Her purpose in coming had been accomplished. But she was unsatisfied—something remained to be done, something important. Something to do with her father, right here next to her. She looked at him, and saw only a quiet gentleman, an unobjectionable, right-thinking man. He was smoking and following the rain clouds in the sky.

The thunder sounded quite near at times, but no rain

came. The river down below was obscure in the gathering darkness. A half-naked fisherman stood in the stream, casting his nets. He was going on with his work, unafraid of being soaked if the rain came this way.

Just at that moment a new idea rose in Tomoko's mind and shocked her. Her father had abruptly broken off what he was saying, his words lapsing into silence and cigarette smoke. And the thoughts that came into Tomoko's head then were unwomanly, bold and forceful. She had been feeling dissatisfied at having to leave her father this way when night fell, but now she wondered: "What if father were not so correct, what if he overstepped the bounds a little?"—and was shocked to realize that something in her rather wanted him to. What if he should say "Stay here with me" instead of "Go back to your mother"? And if he did, she would have to obey. The very idea made her heart flutter. She seemed to be wishing for this compulsion from her father.

Of course, she couldn't really do any such thing. It was impossible, for her mother's sake. That was what she had come here to say. But an even more frightening and fantastic idea was beginning to rise from the secret depths of Tomoko's heart, as storm clouds seethe into the sky.

What if her mother should come to join her here? Tomoko thought of this and her heart was like the clouds in the sky before her, wild and wind-swept, thinning here and massing there but looking somehow static as they moved over the mountains, rumbling occasionally with rainless thunder. Tomoko stared at them and said nothing.

The rain did not come.

The clouds broke near the Western Mountain and the last rays of sunset shot one strong beam through them into a ravine on the Eastern Mountain, outlining the pines and temple roofs there in a single stretch of mellow clarity amid the clouded, foggy scene. There were more and more people on the road across the river as evening came on, apparently office workers going home. Some of them rode by on bicycles. The willows along the river were beautiful, but Tomoko realized that this was an ordinary evening street scene. These people were not tourists in Kyoto. This was part of their daily routine, and they were performing it as mechanically as Tomoko did in Tokyo. Oki's house, from parlor to narrow kitchen, passed through her mind, and, more sadly, all the work her mother had to do in those rooms. Would life never change?

The landlady turned on the switch in the hall and the light came on in the room.

Kyogo turned around toward her with a smile. "Well, the rain's passed us by after all."

She had changed into a beautiful evening costume. "So it has!" she answered in her soft, humorous, high-pitched voice, as she sat on her heels and looked across the eaves at the sky.

Tomoko looked out also, across the river at the houses on the opposite shore. The lights were going on, shining brightly in the growing darkness. The pedestrians on the road had become invisible except for splashes of white in their clothes.

"Why don't you go to the station straight from here, instead of going back to your hotel first?" Kyogo suggested. "I'll see you off."

Tomoko thought of Saeko waiting for her at the hotel and inclined her head thoughtfully.

"You can call your friend and let her know. Just go downstairs and ask them to let you use the phone."

Tomoko didn't feel like leaving her father. She nodded without thinking, and went downstairs. She was at the bottom before she remembered that Saeko's being here was a secret.

"I've been waiting for you. Did you meet him?" Saeko's voice came over the phone.

Tomoko told her reluctantly: "He wants to see me off. He says I should go to the station with him, and not go back to the hotel."

"Your father's going to take you to the station?"

"That's right."

Saeko was silent for a while. "I understand. . . . It turned out well, Tomoko; you're happy, aren't you? You haven't said anything about me, have you?"

"No, I haven't."

"No? Good. . . . You *are* happy, Tomoko? He's a wonderful person, isn't he?"

Tomoko had been uneasy, but Saeko didn't seem very upset.

"I want to see him too, but I really can't. I *am* afraid of him. But maybe I'll meet him at the station."

Tomoko didn't answer.

"No, it would be safer to watch him from a distance. Anyway, don't bother about me at the station, Tomoko."

This little secret had begun to weigh on Tomoko. How true was the story Saeko had been telling her? She still had her doubts. It would be in Saeko's nature to show herself to Father at the station. That's what would probably happen. Saeko was stronger than she said. She was sure of herself, not easily surprised. And she seemed to have some definite purpose in coming to Kyoto. She seemed to be moving according to plan. She bemoaned her loneliness, but she didn't look so lonely. She said she was afraid of Father, but she didn't look so terrified as all that.

Kyogo was having his after-dinner whisky in his room. The paper lantern on the porch outside looked cool.

"What did she say? All right? Fine, that's fine. Have some wine. We still have plenty of time."

They really hadn't told each other anything, Kyogo realized. They were in a cramped little taxi on their way to the station.

They were about to separate, and Kyogo could not bring himself to make any promises for the future. The sidewalk trees and bright city lights flowed past the windows like water.

"I really don't know anything about this daughter of mine," Kyogo thought almost desperately.

Tomoko was sitting very stiffly and correctly on the edge of her seat, staring ahead as the taxi raced on. There was nothing to expect. She was conscious of only one thing. Every second of the rapid drive was shortening the time she could be with her father.

He put out his hand suddenly. "Show me."

She didn't know what he meant. It was the pocketbook on her lap he wanted.

"I can't imagine what a young lady like yourself carries around with her. Let me see, if you don't mind."

His warm voice tempted a smile onto Tomoko's face.

"I shall make an examination," and he looked mock-serious. "One's personal possessions are the best clue to one's character. You've been too mean to tell me anything about yourself, so I'll find out what I can from your pocketbook at least."

"I'd be embarrassed."

"No need. I won't breathe a word. Just let me see. . . . They say you can tell what sort of person a man is if you see the room he lives in. It's the same with the things one carries around with him."

Tomoko handed her pocketbook to him without further argument.

"It's very heavy. I thought so when I saw you with it at the Golden Tower Temple today."

"I have books inside."

"You like to read, then. Good. There's one thing I've discovered about Tomoko."

He looked cheerful, but there was a sadness eating into Kyogo's heart. "Next—I can tell this much without opening it—you have some make-up inside."

"Yes," she laughed. "You're right."

"Then, some money."

She nodded agreement.

"A handkerchief, still dirty from your train ride. There must be one inside."

Tomoko started to laugh, and suddenly remembered that the diamond Saeko had given her was inside too.

Kyogo smiled as his big hands released the clasp and opened the handbag. "You're not likely to prove a very bad girl, I think." His voice was affectionate and near. "You like to keep things in order. Handkerchief, compact, notebook. I'll respect your privacy enough not to look at what you've got written in here. Is this little cat your mascot? Two books. . . . You keep a ring in this case?"

It was wrapped in the same thin Japanese paper she had received it in. Kyogo unwrapped it, sprang open the lid of the little jewel box, and saw the diamond glittering on its purple satin bed.

"Quite a gem!"

"Someone gave it to me."

"A present? As valuable as this?"

His practiced eye judged it to be a two-carat stone. Even in the dim light of the taxi, its well-cut surface had magnificent luster and sparkle.

"I dislike things like that," Tomoko spoke up.

Kyogo looked up at her, surprised.

"Someone gave it to me, but I'm going to give it back. That's why I have it with me."

The simplicity with which she spoke proved that she meant what she said.

"Who gave it to you?"

"I think I'd better not say."

"Why not?"

"Well, it wouldn't be fair to the person, since I'm giving it back anyway."

Kyogo was too interested in the side of Tomoko's personality she was showing him to pursue the question.

"You dislike diamonds, you say. Why?"

Tomoko smiled. "Well, it doesn't do you any good to have ornaments like that."

"That's true, but they have other uses. In our troubled world it sometimes stands you in good stead to own things like this."

Tomoko shook her head.

"There's nothing evil in luxuries."

"No, I think they're unnecessary. So—"

Was Tomoko being completely honest? Kyogo wanted to find out. She sounded perfectly innocent and straightforward.

"Everybody's badly off nowadays. It can't be right for me alone to be lucky. I have a job and can support myself. I don't need gifts like that from other people. Especially diamonds—it wouldn't make any difference if there were none in existence, would it? And if I start collecting diamonds, pretty soon I'll be wanting other things I don't need."

"You don't want it because it may rouse other desires. Is that what you're saying?"

"Yes. It's beautiful, I admit, but I don't feel I should have it."

"Who taught you all this?" Kyogo snapped the box shut. "Your mother again?" Tomoko laughed. "No. I think of things myself sometimes."

"I'm pleased with you. If you had asked my opinion, I'd probably have said very much what you just did. If you're sure of yourself, you can do better without superfluities!" He paused for a minute. "So, a girl like you is mature enough to think that way. Everything I've seen since my return has been a horrid mess. The picture seemed all black. But you've just made it a little brighter.

"And I'm happy that it's my daughter I heard this from. For the world you live in is a mass of ruins. I've been looking at people's faces and wondering how much confidence was left in the Japanese. I was always alone through all those years abroad, so I had to learn to depend on myself. But the Japanese have always lived in reliance on something outside themselves. Now that that authority has crumbled, they're desperate, naturally. I have no master but myself. I want you to live that way too, Tomoko. I want you to be strong. Your mother's brought you up to have a job. I'm grateful to her, infinitely grateful. You understand me, Tomoko? I'm going to go on ignoring you and Mother. But that doesn't mean I won't be thinking of you, not at all. You understand me, Tomoko? That isn't what it meant in the past either. I could never forget you. You were never absent from my life. Wherever I was, you were always here, deep in my heart, every minute of the time."

Kyogo turned away and stared out the window.

"You're certainly capable of strange things when you're young. Some friends and I took government money from our office. I was having an extraordinary run of luck in gambling and insisted I could win it all back in a night if I had a stake to begin with. So we took more

office money, and I played the game of a lifetime for myself and the others. I lost every cent. It was pure foolishness, but I had to take the responsibility. I left the Navy.

"All the fellows who were in it with me became high-
ranking officers, and today every one of them is at the
bottom of the Pacific. I'm the only one left alive. That's
the whole story. I'm not bitter at anyone, I have no
reason to be. It was just youthful rashness. I've never
talked about it to anyone. Especially now that the others
are dead and can never speak again, I should keep silence.
You're the only one I've told, and it's for your ears
alone."

When he turned back to Tomoko she was looking at
him gently. There was a brightness about her, as though
her skin was glowing. His hand went out to hers. He
took it and grasped it firmly.

"Forgive me. I was a fool—but young, absurdly young.
That's all it amounted to, really. I can't repent what
happened, even now. Sometimes I laugh about it. But
for you and your mother, what it's meant to you—to you
and your mother—what can I say?"

The driver adjusted his rear-view mirror. Something
told him that the conversation was getting interesting.

"Driver!" Kyogo was unexcited. "You shouldn't listen
in on what your customers are saying." But his mood
was cheerful. He went on, oblivious of the driver. "That
trivial little incident has determined all the rest of my
life." He was smiling peacefully.

"It was youth, I said, but also it was a certain kind of
foolishness that all of us had in common in those days.
Maybe it's become incomprehensible already. Being cau-
tious and careful was the worst of crimes. You could
drink yourself sick and get rough with your friends or
superiors, and when you met next morning, neither the
brawler nor his victim would say a word about it. No

apologies and no complaints. Night was night, and day was day. We'd just snap to attention, put the official glare on our faces, and exchange salutes. There would be no ill feelings left over."

Kyogo was remembering, and his recollections were bringing smile after smile to his face.

"In that atmosphere, this was a terrible business. I had to take responsibility for the whole affair. That way, it would be over with the least mess. No clouds would be left hanging over everybody's head. Foolish? H'm? Was I foolish?"

Tomoko shook her head. She was inexplicably happy.

"You understand? You?"

She nodded deeply.

"Thank you," her father said. "Well then, if my daughter can see her way to pardon me a little, I'm happy. That's all that troubled me. I feared what I had done might be clouding your lives."

Tomoko spoke quickly. "I knew you had to be a good man. I was right."

"No." Kyogo sighed, and glanced out the window. "We're here."

They were drawing in to the vast structure of the station at an angle. They saw the glaring night lights, and the black shadows of the people milling in and out.

"I won't get out," Kyogo said. He looked at his daughter. His eyes were intense. "I won't go with you to the platform. I don't want your traveling companion to see me. Let's shake hands."

With her hand in his, he spoke again. "Thanks again. I'm glad you came. Take care of your mother for me. I know now that I don't have to worry about you two, even though I can't be with you. Nothing means more to me. Take care of yourself too."

Tomoko got out. He nodded and smiled good-by, and ordered the cabby to drive on.

Kyogo left the cab halfway back to his hotel. He had to walk to relieve his feelings. Automatically, he chose a back street, so dark and quiet that almost no one used it at night. He could hear nothing but the sound of his shoes as he walked.

He looked at his wrist watch when he reached a street lamp. Tomoko's train had left Kyoto already. The rows of houses on either side seemed to press toward each other, leaving a narrow street between. In the sky overhead shone summer evening stars. The large avenues were probably still hot, and their starlight fogged.

"That's the end of it"—the words pushed themselves out in an audible whisper.

But he remembered the feel of Tomoko's hand when he had grasped it, and its delicate warmth, and emotions too deep to shake off settled on him. The bond of blood. That's all it was, he told himself. But why were all these various and uncontrollable feelings seething within him at the same time?

"I'm Tomoko."

He remembered how she had looked when she told him who she was—that worried, earnest, somewhat frightened face. She had been beside him all the rest of the day, she herself, in her living body, and he felt that if he turned his head she would still be there next to him, walking alongside, real and tangible. This was a new feeling for him. He had never had it when he thought about Tomoko before. He had been thinking about an unsubstantial shadow then, but now this shadow had a real body, it had warmth, it breathed, it could chatter gaily. The music of its voice still played in his ears.

He was happy she had come, and he had confessed it to her honestly. But this unshakable loneliness—where did it spring from? He was confident that in his long life abroad he had made himself too strong for any human being to weaken him. He loathed sentimentality. He had shouldered his destiny, chosen his road, and he did not intend to change it now. But the irresistible yearning in his heart, where did it come from?

"I've become weak since I came back to Japan," Kyogo thought.

And that seemed to be the truth. The intense consciousness of solitude that had given him his strength while living abroad had been growing thinner and thinner here in Japan. He seemed to be fusing somehow with the people he came into contact with, indeed even with the scenery he saw. Now, when he took his walks along unfamiliar streets, he could look into the tiny houses from the sidewalk and see people still sitting or standing in the electric light. And those strangers' lives would mingle with his somehow, so that he seemed to know the sufferings and joys of their daily lives and understand the minutest motions of their hearts. He had never felt like that in his walks over the stone-paved streets of Europe. But he was on the soil of Japan now, really, he could not help but know it. He meant to stand alone, but something was moving in the blood with which he had been born, something compelling stirred in the unknowable recesses of his soul.

Kyogo tried to cast off these feelings, but his heart was strangely heavy.

Europeans lived behind thick walls, and could be indifferent to their neighbors, but in Japan only thin paper panels and bamboo fences separated one from the street outside. There were no barriers. A man could not be alone in his daily life. People had too much to do with one another, they rubbed against one another constantly in their crowded living. And then life was so poor here. There were endless conflicts and compromises, but it was impossible to find a harmony within oneself alone. There were just too many people. This was a narrow land.

The odor of incense came to him through the darkness. He looked about and saw an old, solid structure, in ancient style, on the corner of the block. It was the Pigeon Rest, the famous incense store. He had wandered onto Temple Street. Many of the shops were still open, and their lamps illuminated the street. Just ahead there was a more glaring mass of light. He walked up to it and found a tennis court in a cleared space in front of the city hall. Some foreigners were playing under the powerful lights, which glared straight onto the court so that even the white lines stood out brightly, as did the men in shirts and shorts hitting the ball back and forth. An intensely vivid scene. Kyogo's eyes had become used to the dark in his back-street ramble, and the tennis court was almost hallucinating in its dazzling suddenness. It was all the more startling because everything around it was blacked out with night, and because this was in the very center of Kyoto. They were turning night into day in one of the oldest cities in the world.

Kyogo could not help admiring the strength of will that had accomplished this wonder, but he couldn't help smiling a little too. What a vast distance yawned between this game of tennis and the life that had gone on for a thousand years in the old houses of Kyoto, where no one had ever dreamed that night could be anything but a noiseless, tranquil time of rest. Even in Europe Kyogo had never seen anything like this at night. The European countries were old too. They had long his-

tories behind them, like Japan. No European would ever
be wild enough to think of turning night into day.

Watching the hare-like movements of the muscular
men in the strong light, and listening to the twang of
the ball against the strings of the rackets, Kyogo was able
to forget about Tomoko at last. He even felt cheerful,
consoled by the sight of the strength that youth confers.

He walked away finally, and the road was soon dark
and silent again. He had walked an awfully long way, he
felt, and he went back to his hotel. In his room he found
a letter, left for him on the table.

He had hardly corresponded with anyone since his
return. He turned the envelope over, puzzled, and read
the name Tatsuzo Oki. That was even more surprising.
Oki would have no business with him. It must be about
the daughter he had just seen to the station. He felt it
at once. It was about Tomoko. He tore the envelope open
immediately.

Tomoko went across the station bridge and walked
down onto the platform for the Tokyo line. It was early
yet, but people were forming lines here and there to wait
for the train. The loudspeaker was announcing where
the second-class cars would stop. Tomoko walked straight
ahead, looking for the post with that number. It was a
long platform and rather attractive, perhaps because it
was prewar. Where was Saeko? Tomoko looked for her
as she walked. A young man smiled and shouted hello to
her from one of the queues. Tomoko was sure he was talking to somebody else, and walked past without paying any
attention to him. He dropped his Boston bag in his
place on the line and raced after her.

"Where have you been?"

Tomoko turned around. It was Yukichi Okabe. He was
sunburned.

"You!"

"I was amazed myself." Yukichi had his usual quiet smile. "Are you alone?"

"No, there's someone with me." And Tomoko looked around again for Saeko. "Have you been sightseeing in Kyoto, Mr. Okabe?"

"Not by a long shot. The office sent me. I had to pick up a manuscript from a professor at the university here. I left last night, arrived this morning, and have to return by this train. An express errand. Now, if the manuscript hadn't been ready, I could have stayed two or three days to make sure he finished in time. But he had it all done, worse luck."

"Oh, too bad! You haven't seen anything, then."

"Just walked around a little. . . . You're going second-class, I suppose?"

"Yes."

"Well then, go on, don't let me keep you. I'll come and talk to you after the train starts. It's awful not to get a seat—you have to stand all night."

"Is it going to be that crowded?"

He had started back to his line, but turned back. "They say it won't be too bad. I tell you what. I'll get onto the car next to the second-class carriages. They're all the same."

He went to get his bag and came back. They walked ahead together rapidly.

"I haven't seen you since that day we toured Yokohama with Mr. Onozaki."

"That's right." It made Tomoko happy to recall that day early in summer.

"Is Mr. Onozaki well?"

"Same as ever, I imagine." He lifted his head. "He's probably still painting people in trouble. I understand he's been haunting the railroad stations lately to sketch the repatriated P.W.'s from Russia. He takes his work seriously, doesn't he?"

"The lady traveling with me is an acquaintance of Mr. Onozaki's." Tomoko was taking this chance to introduce Saeko to Yukichi. He should be seeing her soon, anyway. "She should be here already. I wonder what's become of her."

It was almost departure time. Tomoko was getting worried. Maybe Saeko wasn't going to take this train at all. Maybe she was going back to Tokyo alone.

Tomoko was unhappy. She gave no outward sign of the grief she was feeling at her parting from her father, but she knew that if she were alone for any time she would brood about it, feel worse and worse, and finally lose her self-control. Yukichi's sudden appearance had been a real deliverance. He would keep her mind away from the sorrow that might become unbearable if she thought about it. Tomoko had always liked this student veteran with his solid manliness and attractive personality.

"Here's where the second-class cars stop. I go right over there." He left Tomoko on one line and went to leave his bag at the end of another. He was back beside her in a moment. "They say it's dangerous to leave things around, but I can watch from here, so I don't think it'll be stolen." He laughed. "Of course I really didn't need a bag. It would have been better to travel without anything. But now the manuscript I picked up is inside, and I'll be in trouble if it's taken."

"Nine minutes more?"

"Yes. It'll be in soon."

"She hasn't come yet."

Tomoko was worrying about Saeko. The stairway entrance was concealed by a freight elevator, and she couldn't see it from where they were standing. Everyone was in line by this time. No one was walking around on the platform any more.

"She'll probably get here just before departure. There's a five-minute stopover here, you know, so your friend can make it even if she comes after the train pulls in. . . . What were you doing in Kyoto?"

"Oh, I had a little business."

"It's as lovely as they say, isn't it? And absolutely untouched." There was wonder in his voice. "I toured the secondhand-book stores. It was amazing—they have everything. The prices were amazingly high too, but in Tokyo, you know, you still can't find half the books you need. And not only the book shops—the city itself is wonderful. I had a good time just walking around. They should preserve the old cities like this that are still standing, not allow any bold modern architecture—they should turn them into public parks in their entirety, as they stand. Anything like cheap cabarets, for example, would ruin them. Kyoto should be kept as it is forever, so that people can come from all over the country to get a glimpse of the old Japan. They shouldn't change it too much."

The loudspeaker started suddenly and announced the arrival of their train. And there it was in the distance, nearing slowly through the darkness, its headlight gleaming like an eyeball. It grew larger gradually, and Tomoko turned around again to look for Saeko. The platform was vibrating under the weight of the approaching train.

The second-class car was empty. Tomoko had no trouble getting a seat. Neither would Saeko, even if she came aboard late. The window was open and Tomoko put her head out as she waited. The departure bell rang. The platform was empty except for a few people waving good-by to others on the train.

Yukichi came in from the third-class car. "Hasn't she come yet?"

The train started, and in a minute had entered the tunnel through the Eastern Mountain. Tomoko hurriedly leaned over to the window to shut it and Yukichi helped her. But the smoke got into the car anyway. Tomoko took out her handkerchief and covered her nose and mouth. Yukichi didn't, but the noise was too deafening for him to talk. He looked up at the ceiling.

Windows rattled open as they came out of the tunnel and the fresh air blew in.

"So she missed the train. She had her own ticket, I suppose?"

Tomoko was puzzled. It was incomprehensible, unnatural, that Saeko should go to such lengths to avoid her father. Yukichi seemed to be worrying about it, so she told him something had probably come up to make Saeko change her plans, and explained no further.

The house lights near Yamashina flowed past coolly in the vast darkness outside. And a series of black shadowy masses almost scraped against the window. They seemed to be bamboo thickets.

"It's been raining here," Yukichi said.

She looked out and could see that the soil and trees were wet, and the surface of the road glistened moistly in the lights of passing automobiles. She recalled the storm that hadn't come in Kyoto earlier this evening. Her father had been sitting face to face with her then. She remembered exactly how he had looked. It seemed incredible that this should be her only meeting with her father, that she should see him once and never again in all her life. She felt sad, but, even more, angry about it. She looked out the window. "Anger is good, but no tears!" her father had said in the Golden Tower Temple. His words came back now, heavy with significance.

The train entered another tunnel. It was a long one, and the smoke came into their car even worse than before. Yukichi couldn't stand it this time either. He had to get out his handkerchief too. It seemed that the tunnel would never end. They rode on and on in darkness, and the smoke filled their car with its black suffocating vapors. The passengers were coughing.

They were out of it finally, and pulled with relief into Otsu station. Everyone rushed to open the doors and windows, and a cool breeze flowed in. Tomoko revived and looked up to see Saeko coming in through the open car-door. Her clothes surprised Tomoko even more than the fact that she was there. Saeko was wearing a summer kimono, cool and elegant and excitingly gay in the night lighting.

"Pardon me, my dear, I must have worried you. But I couldn't go looking for you with all those tunnels."

"Then you made the train?"

"Yes. I got on the first third-class car—just as the train was pulling out." She laughed and the light flickered over the hard, smooth surface of her painted face. "A slide-in."

Tomoko hadn't known that Saeko had Japanese clothes with her. She stared wide-eyed at the unlined josette kimono in dark blue with vertical stripes. The sash was tied tightly around it.

"That suits you wonderfully. You really look beautiful tonight." Even more beautiful than usual, she wanted to say. Saeko's hair was different too, she noticed. She had done it over since this morning.

"A dress would have been better for the train, but I just felt like wearing a kimono. And this way, I don't have to worry about mosquitoes, if there are any on the train. By the way—"

Saeko was going to speak about her father. Tomoko hastened to introduce Yukichi.

"Oh—you're a friend of Mr. Onozaki's, are you!" Saeko

turned to him with a bright smile. "I haven't seen him for a while now. We became great friends when we were in the South together. He's a very interesting person, and so cheerful."

Yukichi was standing up.

"Please sit down."

"No, thanks. I'm traveling third-class. Now that Tomoko isn't alone any longer, I'll be going back."

Saeko turned quickly and looked into Tomoko's face. "Did he go with you to the platform?"

Tomoko shook her head. "Just to the front of the station."

"Uh!" Saeko looked surprised. She went on, indifferent to Yukichi's presence. "Wasn't he a nice gentle man, your father? . . . I wanted to see him too. Should I or shouldn't I? I tortured myself trying to decide—and, finally, I just couldn't do it. I shouldn't have come for this. . . . You really didn't speak about me at all?"

Tomoko shook her head again. And then she thought she saw something like disappointment pass fleetingly over Saeko's face, and wondered whether what Saeko wanted of her wasn't just the opposite of what she had been asking for up to now. Another, vaguer anxiety began to trouble her at the same time. Saeko looked down, took out a little fan from her obi, and put it on her lap without opening it, in what seemed to be an unconscious gesture. And her mood changed instantaneously to one of utter gaiety.

"But if you're happy, Tomoko, it was worth while coming here anyway."

Was she happy? Tomoko asked herself. "I have you to thank, Saeko."

Saeko opened the fan, which had a pattern of bedewed autumn grasses, and held it just below her bosom as she fanned herself. The gesture was as beautiful as a work of art. Tomoko was troubled by it. For there was something in it she could not understand. Falsehood or technique? The more beautiful Saeko's motions were, the more unreal they seemed; she was like an elaborate artificial flower. Wasn't it to impress her father that Saeko had dressed this way? Tomoko caught herself suspecting it, and felt ashamed.

Saeko was speaking to Yukichi with her practiced charm. Had he been sightseeing in Kyoto? A nice quiet place, wasn't it? How wonderful that it went undamaged in the war! All the usual platitudes on the subject.

Tomoko was outside the conversation. She watched Saeko's lovely posturing, and the odor of falseness it gave off became unmistakably strong. Perhaps falseness wasn't the right word; artificiality might be better. And what Saeko had said about her father seemed to cover some secret that Tomoko did not yet know. The diamond in her pocketbook occurred to her suddenly. The time to give it back was now. The nonchalance with which Saeko had handed her this little treasure seemed artificial too, suspiciously so. The problem was what excuse to make when she gave it back, so as not to wound that terrific pride.

"Well, I may feel differently about it when I'm old, but right now a man my age wouldn't want to live in Kyoto."

Yukichi's usual calm tone attracted Tomoko's attention.

"It's too quiet, too pretty." Yukichi leaned his head back in a young, wryish smile. "You wonder whether there really was a war, when you're in Kyoto. Of course that's part of the charm of the place, but I was a soldier, and I feel I shouldn't forget the war. It would be unhealthy to forget it so soon. That's why living in bombed-out Tokyo gives me so much more of a feeling of being in my own time. Life seems more worth while there, even if I do have a miserable job. And that attitude of starting from absolute zero is better for Japan. Our country's become desperately poor."

"My!" Saeko's reaction showed neither agreement nor rejection. She looked a trifle vague and smiled toward Tomoko as if for assistance. "It's certainly true that Japan's impoverished."

"We young men feel overwhelmed too," Yukichi said, "but the past has weighed on us too much in Japan. Now we've been relieved of the burden of history. If we can make up our minds to march forward completely empty-handed, unhindered by anything from the past, something really new will come to life here in Japan. That's the joy of living in Tokyo. Everything's gone, all the lovely ancient things Japanese get sentimental about have been destroyed. That's the strength of Tokyo today. There's not the slightest chance of rebuilding the dead past. It would be impossible. Sooner or later we'll realize we have to build something different, something new. And building it will make our lives happy. Kyoto is a consolation, but nothing new is being born there. It's in Tokyo that there are dreams and courage, just because it was burned down."

Honesty was written all over him. Tomoko realized that Yukichi was saying exactly what he felt, utterly unaware of Saeko's dislike for this troublesome sort of conversation.

He went back to his own car in a little while.

"What does that young man do?"

"He's still going to college. But he also helps out on the staff of a magazine."

"A very serious fellow, isn't he?" Saeko laughed and shrugged her shoulders. "But it's not his philosophy I'm interested in. Tell me what you talked about with your father. I've been dying to hear."

Tomoko looked troubled. "We didn't talk about anything."

"What do you mean?" Saeko asked softly, and looked at her.

Tomoko's expression changed. She seemed to be in pain. "He said I shouldn't have come."

"You? He said you shouldn't have come?"

Tomoko nodded. There was a vehemence in her nod, for she had suddenly decided she wasn't going to let herself cry. She couldn't talk about this, she shouldn't, and the reason wasn't in herself so much as in Saeko. She was beginning to feel stronger.

"That's strange, after you'd gone to so much trouble to visit him."

"After he said that to me, I realized he was right. I shouldn't have gone."

"But why?"

Saeko's voice was low. There was something different about Tomoko now as she sat there quietly, her eyes wide open and staring fixedly ahead of her, warning Saeko that she could not sway her.

"Wasn't he happy to see you?"

"I got a scolding."

Tomoko swallowed her voice. Her excitement showed only in her hands on her lap. In the pitch-black night outside, the lights of some village slid slowly backward as they passed.

"I went there for my mother's sake. And he scolded me because my visit wouldn't help my mother, it would hurt her."

"How strong he is!" Saeko whispered, drawing in her breath. "But, Tomoko, that proves that your father still loves your mother and you."

Tomoko was silent.

"He certainly hadn't forgotten about you. He's been thinking about you always."

Tomoko turned and looked Saeko straight in the face, boldly. She nodded vigorously before she spoke. "I know," was all she said; then she lowered her eyes and remained silent.

Saeko watched her for a moment, then asked softly: "You really didn't speak about me at all?"

Tomoko nodded again. Moving as if half asleep, she opened her pocketbook and said: "My father said I shouldn't have accepted the diamond."

Saeko couldn't speak. Her face turned white and hard like a piece of sculpture. Finally, staring at Tomoko severely, she said: "Then you did speak about me, didn't you?"

"No." Tomoko looked as innocent as she was, and felt quite easy. "I didn't mention you. Father just happened to feel like rummaging through my pocketbook. He found the diamond and said I shouldn't take such things as presents. That's all that happened."

Plainly Saeko didn't believe her. "Very strange," she muttered. "Surely he knew it was I who had given it to you."

"He couldn't have. I didn't tell him."

"Really? No, your father knew it was I." Her voice was heavy, incisive. "He does hate me, then."

"No, no. He asked me who gave it to me, but I told him I couldn't say."

"He knew it was I."

There was no way of convincing her. Tomoko was bewildered. Saeko had decided the matter by herself, and sat there worrying about it.

"You don't have to tell him. He sees everything at a glance. I remember. A frightening man!" Saeko seemed deeply anxious. "And especially since it was a diamond. When he saw that, he knew immediately who it was. He didn't say anything to you, Tomoko, really?"

"Nothing. . . . But, Saeko, it's very bad of me, I know, but since Father told me to—"

Saeko didn't answer. But her exquisite profile showed terrible anguish. She was trying to bear something she found unbearable.

Tomoko drew in her breath. "Really, Saeko, I didn't say a word about you to Father."

"All right." A smile thawed out her frozen face. "What's done is done. That's what I always tell myself when anything terrible happens, and it gets me by. But your father did know who it was. Even if he didn't realize it at the moment, it came to him later. Maybe he'll be angry enough to come to my house and tell me to behave myself. But I don't mind. I'll see him if he does. Don't worry about it, Tomoko."

Her voice was gay, her eyes sparkled. At that moment Saeko felt new life flaming up within her, as a dying ember flares when blown upon. In her face was a savage strength that Tomoko had never seen before.

❀ ᔐᔐᔐ XVI ᔐᔐᔐ ❀

FOGGY NIGHT

Kyogo didn't reach Tokyo until well into autumn. He walked out of the Yaesu exit of Tokyo station and stood waiting for the streetcar on the municipal line. The old outer moat of the Palace ran alongside the block. It was half filled with dirt and bricks from the fires, and trash was moving sluggishly in the little water still left there, altogether desolate and sordid in the bright autumn sunlight.

Kyogo gazed at the moat and remembered a story he had once read by Henri de Régnier. A very ordinary man, after a very ordinary barren life as an office clerk or bank teller, grew old enough to retire. He was pensioned off, and the pension, together with the little he had been able to save, made it possible for him to buy a little house in the suburbs, where he could live as he wished, however modestly, for the first time since he had been born. He settled down to a happy old age, for he was a good, simple man with few desires and, like the typical Frenchman he was, satisfied with small joys, content to live quietly, troubling no one if no one troubled him. From the living-room of his new house he found he could see an old acacia on the sidewalk. It was a vast old tree, and its branches spread wide and beautiful. He saw it for the first time the day he moved in, and from then on the tree became the companion of his threadbare little life. He loved the shape and sweep of its branches. Looking at it gave him a sense of richness. It was a perfect friend. There were no complications in its friendship, as there might be with a human being; it just filled his quiet days with satisfaction. When he got up in the morning and went to raise the blinds, he was thinking of his acacia tree, and when he actually saw it out there, branching and glowing in the morning sunshine, he couldn't help congratulating himself on the happy life he was leading. His daily occupation was to take a chair out into the garden and sit in the shade of his acacia, reading, or having his meals. He had no talent or ambition, and so he was convinced that no man could ever have had a happier old age. Life was sweet to him for the first time. Not till now, in his last years, had it ever seemed worth living. In a little while the acacia, old like himself, had become his dearest friend, and he had begun to feel that their lives were bound up together somehow, his and his tree's. A very natural feeling for a lonely old man to have.

One morning, while he was still in bed he heard an unusual sound outside. He jumped up and rushed to the window. Some laborers had been sent from the city hall. They were at his acacia. They had lopped off the branches already, and were starting to fell the naked trunk. The acacia was a hindrance to traffic, standing where it did, and it had to be removed.

The pathetic sight of the moat in the process of being filled in had reminded Kyogo of the story. It was useless, so they were filling it in. God knows what they would build here afterward. Water made a wonderful difference in a city. It softened its atmosphere, gave it a certain charm. But no one thought about that. They were just rushing the job in good Japanese fashion. Nobody cared that this was the famous Yaesu quay, named after Jan Josten, the foreigner who had come to Japan when it was still sealed off from the rest of the world, or that the moat itself belonged to Chiyoda Castle, famous in history long before it became the Imperial Palace. The moat was useless in modern Tokyo, so no one regretted the truckloads of rubble that were gradually filling it up. It wouldn't be that way in Paris, Kyogo was sure. Paris was full of communists, to be sure, but let anyone start changing a historical ditch or street and the whole citizenry would be roused to noisy, stubborn protest. They would acknowledge the inconvenience of the old landmarks they lived among, but not stop loving them for that.

Kyogo looked away from the shrunken stream in the moat. The trolley had arrived. And it did no good, his thinking about all this. He was being a little silly, he told himself wryly. After all, Tokyo was a vast boarding-house for all sorts of people from all parts of the country. Hardly anyone thought of it as home or cared a whit what changes were made here. Least of all, the officials in charge of these public works; they symbolized the general indifference.

Kyogo got off at Singlebridge and walked to Kyoritsu Auditorium. The poster out front bore in large black letters the subjects and speakers for today's lectures. Tatsuzo Oki's name was there, and his theme was "Ethics in the New Culture." A lecture was under way already; there was no one to be seen in the silent entrance.

They told him at the ticket office that the lecturers' waiting-room was around the corner and through the side entrance. Kyogo walked down the block. The autumn afternoon sunlight shone straight in his face, around the side, and onto the pavement, gilding the leafy sidewalk trees in the blinding luster of its reflected light.

He opened the door and went in. A metallic microphone-filtered voice sounded down the corridor from the lecture hall. The waiting-room was down the hall on the left. From the doorway Kyogo looked into the wide empty room and saw three or four men around a table, smoking and deep in conversation. None of them paid any attention to him. But a middle-aged woman was making tea in the corner nearest him. He made his inquiry of her: "Is Mr. Oki here?"

"Oki? I don't really know. . . . Is he a lecturer?"

A young man straddling a chair inside the room looked around and gave Kyogo his answer. "Professor Oki is lecturing now." He looked at his watch. "He should be through in around ten minutes."

"I'd like to see him. May I wait here?"

"Okay. Come right in."

A tattered sofa stood near the window. Even there, Kyogo could hear the voice from the auditorium, traveling down the long, narrow hall. Tatsuzo Oki's voice was rather shrill, and young-sounding for his age. Kyogo wondered what he was talking about. He even felt like walking down toward the auditorium and listening. He remembered having seen a picture of Oki in some magazine, but had never seen him in the flesh. Nor did he have any desire to do so. Oki's unexpected letter had asked him to call when in Tokyo because there was something the professor wanted to discuss with him. But Kyogo had been unable to work himself into the mood for the trip and hadn't even sent an answer.

Oki's letter hadn't said why he wanted to see Kyogo, but it most certainly had to do with Tomoko, so that, however uninterested Kyogo felt, he couldn't ignore it. The letter had kept coming back to his mind and gradually become a sort of burden, weighing down his spirits, painfully. He had realized he would have to go and see Oki eventually.

Applause started in the auditorium, and a group of six or seven men emerged into the hall. The man in front was wearing Japanese costume and wiping the sweat from his face with a handkerchief. One look at his high bald forehead and big eyeglasses and Kyogo recognized the Tatsuzo Oki he had seen in the magazine. A man in morning coat, the chairman or manager perhaps, followed in his wake with a number of students. They came in and their talk sounded thunderous in the silent waiting-room.

"The weather's still a bit too warm for lecturing, isn't it?" Oki was in a good mood. He wasn't speaking to anyone in particular. "But we had a very good audience today—it was serious."

The men who had been chatting at the table got up and came over to them. Someone pulled a chair over for Oki, and he sat down in it. The man in the morning coat took a formal posture and delivered his official thanks.

"We are sincerely grateful for your profitable lecture. On behalf of the entire management I wish to express profound gratitude for your presence here today. The audience was also delighted. Your lecture was a magnificent success. Thank you."

"Oh, that's all right." Oki nodded with arrogant simplicity, then inquired of someone in the entourage: "You've got in touch with the newspaper people, I take it?"

"Yes. The round-table starts at six, they say. There's still lots of time. Your car's come, incidentally. Will you be going now?"

"What a crowded schedule!" one of the others said, evidently awe-struck.

"Oh, nothing important, really!" And to demonstrate that no schedule could be crowded enough to make him lose his nonchalance, Oki took a cup of tea from the waitress and drank it down. One of the students asked him to autograph one of his books, and the fountain pen moved over the paper with mechanical efficiency. Kyogo saw no chance of talking to the professor, so he just sat on the sofa and watched. A busy man, he thought.

"Professor Oki, I've been hearing rumors that you're going to run for the House of Councilors."

"Just a journalist's fantasy. Many of my friends and pupils have been urging me to run—that's how the story started, probably—but I have no such intention at the present time."

"I'm sorry to hear that, sir. We share the conviction that the candidacy of a man of character like yourself would be an invaluable aid to the purification of politics."

"If I should run, it would have to be on a very idealistic platform. I'd not campaign at all, sit absolutely still and leave everything to my friends. I'd rather lose than engage in one of those futile, dirty rumpuses that have passed for election campaigns up to now."

"Your name is known all over the country. You'd certainly be elected. By all means, sir, you must stand. We beg it of you."

"Well, we'll see," Oki deprecated, and was suddenly in a great hurry. "If the car's here, I think I'll leave right away. I have a business appointment tonight, as well as the round-table."

They helped him on with his Inverness, he donned his hat, and, accompanied by his retinue, he started for the door. Kyogo walked over and addressed him.

"My name is Moriya. You wrote to me in Kyoto."

"Moriya?" He stared at him through his glasses, amazement quickly covering his face. "You?"

"I should have come sooner, but was unable to."

"You should have let me know you were coming. This is rather inconvenient." Oki was irritated, his voice curt. But he realized that he was encircled by his admirers and that they were watching the scene. "All right, then. Please come along. We'll talk in the car."

He marched straight out into the corridor, pouting

and pompous. His manner indicated that Kyogo would naturally follow behind. The rigid shoulder line of his Inverness shrugged up a bit off his body. He was a meager little man, who had plainly passed his life in his library.

When they got to the car, Oki got in first, without apology. A young man in a Western suit, who was going to ride with them apparently—Oki's secretary, was it, or an escort of some kind?—stood back politely to let Kyogo enter first.

"Please," he said.

"Pardon me." Kyogo sat down beside Oki, and the man closed the door and went to sit beside the chauffeur. The car slid away from the curb, past the faces of Oki's entourage.

"Ono," Oki called to the young man up front, "the round-table starts at six, you say?"

"That's right, sir."

"I have something to talk over with this gentleman between now and then. Could you get us a room in your company offices where we won't be disturbed?"

Ono must be a newspaper reporter sent to see Oki to the round-table, Kyogo thought.

"Would the reception room be all right?"

"Excellent," Oki answered stiffly, and set his face toward the window, dead silent. Evening had come on already, and the shadows of the trees and passers-by were long on the sidewalk. A canal ran beyond it.

Kyogo tried to begin the conversation. "I apologize for not letting you know I was coming, but I saw an announcement of your lecture in the paper and realized I could see you at the auditorium, so I didn't wait to ask for an interview."

"I see." Kyogo wasn't sure what the answer meant, but plainly it was designed to cut him off.

"We'll talk when we get to the newspaper. I'll be free until the round-table starts, I think."

"I'm sorry to come upon you at such a busy time."

Kyogo was still unable to believe that the man sitting next to him was his wife's second husband. He couldn't think of them together. It was too improbable. But he had set out to see Oki determined to accept the realities of the situation. Tatsuzo Oki gave him the impression of being a man of importance in the world of scholarship and thought. He gave it quite clearly, from the moment you saw him. But Kyogo was alien to that world, and he was chiefly impressed by Oki's overweening assurance that he had a right to assert his authority even outside the very limited sphere in which it obtained. His arrogant silence was not for Kyogo's benefit in particular, probably. Oki merely had become unable to abandon his sense of the importance he had acquired in his own special field even when he was with people entirely outside it.

Kyogo wasn't too offended. There was nothing very remarkable about Oki's behavior. When there were still soldiers in Japan, he remembered, they had carried their soldierliness everywhere. And monks were ubiquitously monastic. To Kyogo's mind, this was just another effect of Japan's poverty. If Tatsuzo Oki had to exert his professorial authority when dealing with strangers to the academic world, one could only doff one's hat and give him right of way. If anything, he deserved sympathy. How uncomfortable he must be! A flexible human being, with all the variability of life, had been molded into this rigid pose.

The reception room at the newspaper was bare of ornament. There was only the china ashtray on the table across which they faced each other. The hum of the presses vibrated through the walls and floor. They introduced themselves to each other formally.

Tatsuzo Oki's style of conversation varied, it seemed, depending on whether or not a third person was within earshot. He was at his ease now and smiled at Kyogo rather genially. "It was Tomoko I wanted to talk to you about."

Kyogo hung his head. "I can only say that my conduct has been inexcusable."

"What do you intend to do? What are your opinions on this matter?" Oki paused to light a cigarette before he continued. "You mean to see the girl, of course?"

To see the girl? Then Oki didn't know that Tomoko had been to Kyoto. This was perplexing. Kyogo's sole concern now was to keep Tomoko's secret.

"I feel that I have no right to voice an opinion about Tomoko. I'm no longer a parent to her."

"You don't intend to see her?" Oki peered at him through his glasses. "I'd reached the decision that the time had come to give her back to you, if you and she should so desire."

Kyogo was astounded. It was a while before he could answer. "The idea's never occurred to me."

"Her father, and the idea's never occurred to you? To a man like me that's utterly incomprehensible."

"I don't think of her as my child. And I doubt that Tomoko thinks of me as her father. I don't know whether you know the circumstances, but my status has become so questionable I'm not sure I'm legally alive. It may be cowardice on my part, but I'm sure Tomoko would be happiest staying on with her mother."

"Indeed!" Oki inflected the word rather oddly, then looked out the window in a steady stare. "I've come to love her over the years, of course, but now, surely, the right thing to do is to give her back to you."

Kyogo said nothing.

"I don't know what Tomoko's feelings on the matter

are. But now that you're here, it would be irregular, to say the least, for her to go on living in my house."

"Irregular? Surely you have no reason to fear any criticism of that sort."

"And why not?" Oki inquired in a cold, grating voice. "I am an instructor of the young, Mr. Moriya, and want no taint of scandal in my house. Of course, if you weren't in Japan, things would be different. I would simply be taking an unfortunate off the streets, in that case, and caring for her. But you are here now. That puts a different face on the matter. Don't you see that?"

Nothing changed in Kyogo's features. Oki's implication was perfectly clear. Kyogo felt the invisible slap. But his mask did not slip. Insult strengthened him. He held his feelings and his words in powerful constraint.

Oki now laughed with controlled geniality. "That's the point, Mr. Moriya. Don't you think you're being irresponsible?"

Should he plead for himself? Kyogo rejected the idea with scorn. But he bowed his head again, in apparent dejection. "It is as you say, sir. I can say nothing to excuse myself."

"That's just running away again, Moriya. You just keep on running away. That's what's wrong with you. If you really loved your daughter, you'd have realized it was wrong to come back to Japan. Can't you see that? If I had been in your position, I would have understood that much. However much I wanted to come back, I should have stayed away."

Oki was warming to his argument. Fervor crept insensibly into his authoritative voice as he moved in to overwhelm Kyogo. This was his usual way with adversaries; he carried on scholastic debates in the same contemptuous tone.

"Of course as things actually are, Japan is helpless to

keep any sort of fugitive from coming back, and coming back fearless and triumphant. We are a defeated nation. I don't object to the communists and pacifists—they have their ideals, at least. They suffered for their doctrines. But you, sir! You've called yourself a dead man, but that doesn't entitle you to any special privileges, even in postwar Japan."

"Mr. Oki." Kyogo opened his mouth for the first time in many minutes. He was pale but calm. "You are quite right."

"Then the question is, what are you going to do? Was it to make some priceless contribution to the reconstruction of our devasted country that you returned to Japan, Mr. Moriya?" His voice was heavy with ridicule.

"I am not such a fool as to say that, Mr. Oki. I have never had the fantastic self-infatuation that might lead me to imagine anything of the kind. I am a useless man, a completely useless man. Not only to my country—there is no one in the whole world who would miss me if I were gone. Yes, that's the truth, the whole truth, sir. I am just such a ne'er-do-well, as you have perspicaciously described me. But that I was doing injury to the character of Professor Oki—that I hadn't realized. I'm not only a useless but a harmful man, it seems. One thing I'm always ready to do, however, and that is to avoid harming or hindering others. I shun daylight, Mr. Oki, and don't show myself in public. Especially not to people who would know me as Kyogo Moriya. On that point you can trust me without fear."

"But, still—"

"No." Kyogo's tone was now stronger than Oki's. "I am a corpse, that's true. A corpse can infect those who come too near. Knowing that, Mr. Oki, how can you think of sending Tomoko back to me? Wouldn't you pity her plight?"

"She's your daughter, isn't she?" Oki was curt, cold, and cruel.

Kyogo's eyes were steady, unwinking. Oki had thrown off his mask, shown himself as he was. Oki did not love Tomoko. What he had just said showed it. Perhaps one shouldn't expect him to; she wasn't his own daughter. But Kyogo wouldn't have felt that way about it. His lonely life had made the difference between his own children and other people's less distinct for him. Kyogo mused on this, and his musing, strangely, roused a passion of parental love for Tomoko. Outwardly he retained his composure, but there was a chaos inside him.

"Her mother wouldn't let her go," he said as calmly as he could. "Have you consulted her mother about what you're saying now?"

Irritation flashed across Oki's face. "No!" And he explained no further.

"Then this is all your own—"

"Of course. It is my individual opinion. But I doubt that anyone at home will disagree."

"But—"

"No buts. It is my decision. I have been called to the high position of educator. I no longer teach in school, it's true, but the work to which my old age must be dedicated is the instruction of society."

"I see!" Kyogo was sharp. "But Tomoko has had nothing to do with all this. She's innocent. Certainly—"

"Moriya, are you sure there haven't been any strange people around where you live? You spoke of corpses and infection. Don't you know that there are ghouls about, ready and waiting to dig up corpses!"

"What in the world!"

"This would all make a wonderful newspaper story, I mean. Ex-Navy officer who stole government money and disappeared overseas comes back to defeated Japan after more than ten years. It would get top place on the social-problems page. Any reporter would consider it a scoop. There was one at my house recently. He'd heard you were back and wanted to know where you were. I have a friend on the staff of his newspaper and managed to quash the story. But if any of those second- or third-class scandal sheets gets hold of it, even I won't be able to do anything. You can't tell when or how the story may leak out. If I should make a slip later on tonight and the people here find out it was you I was talking to in their reception room, they're not likely to neglect you, even they. To a journalist you would look like perfect material for a latter-day hero. It isn't only your extraordinary past that would interest them. They'd discuss your views on the Pacific War, and what doctrines, God save the mark, you might hold on war and peace in general. The public loves that sort of thing. It's a stupid, disgusting, contemptible business, but the Japanese people love it. This would be perfect. You'd become the spectacle of the hour. Runaway Kyogo Moriya would be the hero of our times."

Oki's excitement had grown with each imaginary detail. He looked aside now, and exclaimed: "You've brought terrible trouble upon me. I'm desperate."

"I humbly apologize." Kyogo said it like an obedient schoolboy, but his eyes belied his words. Set firmly on Oki, they were growing steadily bolder and more confident. Kyogo had almost smiled at Oki's last, undeliberate words—*I'm in trouble, I'm desperate.* He could only talk about himself. It was this egoist who found Kyogo's presence in Japan most troublesome and inconvenient. Tomoko and Setsuko had nothing to do with it.

"Am I really that well known?"

"You're laughing!" Oki seemed ready to leap on him. "Do you think I'm making this up?"

Oki was in a passion. The flight from concept to concept which enlivened his writings was happening in him now. He had created the danger of newspaper publicity in the heat of argument and was now compelled to push it to its logical extremes. The purely imaginary menace was real to him now, and imminent.

"The fellow's been to my house a number of times. It's strange he hasn't been to yours."

"And if he should come, he wouldn't get anything out of me. Not the things you're worrying about, anyway." Kyogo said it quietly, then burst out laughing. "Would they really ask my opinions on the Pacific War and pacifism? Seriously? I find that funny. It's so absurd."

"They put that stuff in when they write the articles. They would think it kindness to you. Writing you up that way might help you out."

"Indeed? Kindness, is it? Well, I won't dance to that tune."

"Nevertheless—"

"Now, now, Mr. Oki, I don't think you have anything to worry about. I'm absolutely sure you don't, as a matter of fact. I can promise you you don't, on my honor. I've kept myself close-mouthed up to now. Nobody knows about me."

"You underestimate reporters."

"You mean I can't keep hidden forever? But—" a smile bubbled up from the depths of his heart—"I don't care if they do find me."

He had nothing to fear. It was Tatsuzo Oki who was trembling and appalled. The crowded society of Japan did that to people. Tatsuzo Oki could never have achieved his reputation in this society except by seeking the approval of others, and justifying himself before the public. Kyogo looked up. Exile had tempered him so that there was no one he had to fear or placate except himself. But he was in a deep amazement now. His position of solitude had been imperiled. There was Tomoko. There was Setsuko. He meant to stand alone, but he could not help considering the way he was affecting others' lives. His eagle pinions had lost their strength, and just because he had come home to Japan.

He looked at Tatsuzo Oki, who was trying to maintain his dignity in his fretful panic, an emaciated little dried-up man. It was Kyogo who had been forced to surrender, but it was he who pitied his adversary.

"I shall do as you suggest," he said softly. "But first I must ask her mother's opinion. She is really Tomoko's only parent. Neither you nor I deserve that title. Her mother's feelings must not be slighted. Do you consent, Mr. Oki?"

Oki didn't answer. But the superiority he had maintained up to now crumbled beneath Kyogo's gaze and his face became shockingly weak, and cowardly, and vague. He hadn't been prepared for this. He had only planned to attack Kyogo where he knew he was vulnerable, mercilessly enough to drive him off. For him this whole affair was a matter of face, Kyogo could see that. All of Oki's fear was for his miserable reputation.

It was quite dark outside. Night had painted in the streets. A mist had descended, obscuring the sidewalk trees like rain. The unlighted areas loomed shadowy.

Kyogo walked away from the back-street section and toward the Ginza. The only sound was the noise of his own shoes on the broken pavement, but he felt persistently, as he had that night in Kyoto after seeing Tomoko to the station, that she was walking with him, right there beside him, soft and warm. And not only Tomoko. Setsuko had come along tonight. Of course, the young Setsuko who had been his wife so many years ago.

Kyogo was irked in his unhappiness. When he looked for them, naturally they both disappeared. But Tomoko's familiar figure, her shoulders and breast, had been so real —and there was nothing there but shadow. A trolley rattled over a crossing far ahead, its lights shining strangely red out its windows and through the mist. It had appeared suddenly and vanished just as quickly, suggesting somehow the loneliness of Kyogo's present life.

"What a person!"

Kyogo tried to hate Tatsuzo Oki, but failed. A pathetic little creature! And just the type the Japanese would glorify in their bright new age.

More and more people were walking on the block, he noticed. It had become impossible to walk in a straight line on the narrow sidewalk. People, people, people! Countless, multitudinous people! He turned onto a side street to avoid them and sighted a bar sign at the entrance to the underground floor of a big building. He went in and down the stairs without a moment's hesitation. There was no one there yet, except a young waitress standing behind the bar. She was looking at him as he came down.

"Whisky," he ordered, and then noticed the telephone. "Ah! Have you got a telephone book?" They were scarce in Tokyo.

"Yes, we do." She took it out from behind the bar and put it before him.

He riffled the pages and found Tatsuzo Oki's number. Oki was still at the newspaper for that round-table. If Tomoko was home, he could ask for her. The waitress told him how to dial the number.

"Hello!" A woman's voice came faintly through the receiver. It was Setsuko's voice. His face tautened.

"Is Miss Tomoko there? I'm from her office—Ono is my name. I'd like to talk to her, if I may."

The receiver was silent again. Kyogo felt himself sweating. She sounded just the same! There was a pressure in his chest.

Tomoko sounded far away. There was some static on the phone as she began.

"Hello. This is Tomoko. . . . Who is it?"

"It's me. You know who I am?" Kyogo said coolly. "It's me."

There was no answer, but her shock came clearly over the wires. She was congealed, silent.

"There was something I had to ask you right away. Mr. Oki doesn't know about your trip to Kyoto, is that right?"

Tomoko seemed to be forcing herself to speak. "That's right."

Plainly, her mother was near by.

"Everything's the same, h'm? Nothing's happened at home? Everything's going on as usual?"

"Pretty much, yes."

"All right, then." Kyogo's voice deepened. "I was afraid you might have got into trouble or something. I was worried, so I called. That was all. If nothing's happened, I'm satisfied. I just happened to be in Tokyo for a few hours, you see. I'm going right back."

Tomoko was silent.

"Remember what we talked about in Kyoto. I'm all right and well. . . . Good night."

Kyogo hung up. The waitress was looking at him. Her face was still very young. Her eyes were laughing.

"What's the joke?" he challenged.

"Doesn't come cheap, does it?" She leaned across the bar. Her voice was gay, disgustingly so. "You were calling her just now, weren't you?"

"Uh-huh. I was."

"You've got to pay."

"Uh-huh."

"You took her all the way to Kyoto with you. That sort of thing doesn't come cheap, you know." It seemed to be the only idea in her head. She kept repeating it. "Take me next time. I'll give you service."

"How old are you?"

"Twenty-one." She laughed. "Eighteen, really. Twenty-one's my Japanese age."

Kyogo gulped down his whisky straight, and went up the stairs and out onto the street. He was still dry. He wanted to get drunk, dead drunk. He was in a turmoil. He pitied everyone alive, including that girl in the bar. He pitied them so much he couldn't bear it. He had set a value on human beings while he was abroad, and set it very low, so that nothing he saw would ever shock him. "That's just what human beings are," he could tell himself, and never have to hate or pity. He had been an indifferent spectator and guarded that position with all his strength. But those defeated soldiers he had seen in Malacca after the war—they seemed to be here in the Ginza with him, in the flesh. Why should such a feeling overwhelm him now? And the soldier's knapsack left hanging on the branches of the tree in that rubber plantation, that was here too. That filthy knapsack with the scrap of paper pinned to it: "Salt—not dirty." "Salt—not dirty." He said it out loud, without meaning to.

Someone was brushing past, and must have overheard him. Kyogo stared at him. Then he grasped the fellow's arm, with the unsurpassable joy of the intoxicated. "It's you!"

"Uh-huh." The other's eyes flashed with recognition too. "Are you all right?"

"Am *I* all right! Are *you* all right, that's the question. How have you been?" His tone was moist with affection. He took Toshisada Ushigi's hand. Whom else in Japan had he been able to talk to openly except this defeated officer? "And how's the wife?"

"Complaining, but still alive." Ushigi sounded like old times. "I should tell you, by the way: I've taken your advice. I've got myself a job of sorts."

"Wonderful!" Kyogo roared and shook Ushigi's hand, still in his grasp. "I'm glad. That was the right thing to do."

"I don't know whether it was or not, but—"

"Where?"

"A soap factory." A smile crept slowly into Ushigi's face. "Head of the delivery department, they call me. The 'head' is pure charity. Every day I watch them load soap onto the trucks and drive away. I'm ashamed to take the salary they pay me. It's unpardonable—a fellow like me!"

"Why in the world?"

"Why, you ask. Haven't you seen these repatriates, shipped home stripped of everything, jobless, shut out of everything, no place to go? While I—you know!"

"Don't talk like that!" Kyogo shut him up. "You have a right to live too. Let's drink. Let's go some place and get drunk. You commute from Kamakura?"

"Yes. The company's over there."

Kyogo's heart was soft, melting. "A soap company! Really?"

"They took me out of mercy. Like taking a corpse up from the street."

"No, that's not true either. They took you because they knew whatever job they gave you, you'd do it honestly. A frank, open, serious man, that's what you are. Your character's a rare and precious commodity these days. There's nothing wrong with Toshisada Ushigi's handling soap."

The wrinkles had deepened on Ushigi's face and softened his severity. In his worn suit and felt hat, he had none of his old dignity. Only his posture, straight as ever, reminded one of the past.

"I'm a stranger in Tokyo. Where should we go?"

"Don't ask me. I'm a stranger here myself. Never did know the place—and know it less and less as time passes." Ushigi smiled wryly. "I might be in a foreign city, for all I know."

"I'd feel more at home in a foreign city." There was real feeling in Kyogo's voice, feeling too strong to disguise. "There's always someone in my way here, wherever I go."

"I feel the same way. I've been dreaming of being on a ship again. I want to try the ocean once more."

"Come down in the world, haven't you?"

"I certainly have." Ushigi laughed. But there was resignation in his voice. He looked like a perfectly ordinary old fellow now. Even *his* stubborn pride had been deflated. "Soap. You don't know what soap means. You see one cake in the bathroom, and think nothing of it. But when you have to sit looking at a whole warehouse full of it, it gets on your nerves, until you wish the horrid stuff didn't exist." He burst out laughing. "I suppose too much of anything all together would have the same effect. You forget it's what gives you a living."

"So you see visions of the sea in soap bubbles. Well, nothing wrong with that. The important thing is that your infatuation with death is over. You're finally cured of the war. That's what you needed."

"Yes. I want to live now, as long as I can, and see what's going on in the world. . . . The worst thing was seeing fellows I used to know brought up for trial. But I've changed. I saw the outcome of the trials, and didn't care. I was shocked at my own indifference. Why, I even wanted to attend some of the sessions. There are things in me also that need the knife, I felt. I shouldn't evade it. All I pray for is that Japan be cured by this surgery. Japan should have been able to solve her own problems without going to war in the first place—but no use moaning about that now. We've come to this. All we can do is lie down on the operating-table and not make things more difficult by struggling. I'm no expert on Chinese poetry, but I remember reading a phrase in Tao Yuan Ming: 'The sun sets and the myriad aimless movements cease!' 'Aimless movements'—that's the right expression. That's exactly what Japan was like. It could never find itself."

Kyogo was glad that his stubborn old friend had freed himself enough to criticize. But he had to argue the point. "But Ushigi, it's still aimless movement. The state is dead, but the aimless movement hasn't ceased. Is there anyone in Japan who lives in accordance with his own definite opinions? That's what I wonder about." He remembered Tatsuzo Oki's bespectacled face. "It's a narrow land. And the people—they're so poor, so terribly poor! There's no room to dream, no leeway. The Japanese can only work up enough courage to grab somebody's legs and beg for food. A pathetic people!"

"I don't think that's the whole story."

"No sympathy! For a while at least, we've got to be absolutely merciless—do nothing but criticize the botch Japan has made of itself. That's another kind of surgery. Relent before the job is done, and the aimless movement will never cease, but drag itself on forever. There are exceptions, I know. It was a Japanese who discovered the meson, the discovery that made the atom bomb possible. We have that kind of human potential among us. But the average Japanese is nothing like that. Most of us have no solid roots in the ground. That's the basic problem.

Aimless movement, yes indeed, everything here is just that. The rootless plant blows as the wind lists."

A shadow of loneliness flickered across Kyogo's face.

"People are saying now that it was Army pressure that made them co-operate in the war. The excuse is true, so far as it goes. But how contemptible of a human being to have to make it! They were put into motion, that's all. The wind of insanity blew, irresistibly, and they were swept along by it. But what a tragic thing it is—if they could only see themselves well enough to recognize it— that they had been made that movable. But it's still aimless movement, even now just as it always was. The roots still haven't grown down into the soil.

"Quite a jeremiad I'm giving you tonight, I'm afraid." Kyogo laughed at himself. "Maybe it's my Japanese sentimentality coming back in this Japanese climate. That's one sign of it, isn't it?—deploring the state of the nation. I'm beginning to yearn for the drier climate abroad. It's lonely being by yourself there, that's true enough, but you *can* be by yourself, wherever you go. Life was less troublesome that way, the line between oneself and others was so clearly drawn."

They wandered about for a while and went into a bar they happened to come across. They sat at a corner table and drank beer. The place was crowded. The customers were nondescript but included a lot of young people who kept on ordering drinks without limit, consumed them enthusiastically, and whooped it up accordingly. A band played on a little dais and then went around the tables, entertaining the guests to order. A group of waitresses joined in the fun with a rendition of the "Tokyo Boogie." It was the first time either Kyogo or Ushigi had seen anything like it.

Kyogo was watching Ushigi. For all his Western suit, he looked like a monk and turned a surprised and innocent face to the provocative "Hey! Hey!" of the singing waitresses. Ushigi was an old man, a wasted man already, his face grown gentle. He had changed so much that if you put him in uniform now it wouldn't seem to suit him.

And as he watched, Kyogo ruminated on the feeling rather like pain he had had since his meeting with Oki. Tomoko and her mother had pushed themselves into his life, once and for all. He could not keep himself from pitying them—and yearning for them.

When they went outside, the fog was even thicker than it had been.

"What are you doing now?" Ushigi asked him.

"What am I doing? That's what I was just thinking about. I don't mind especially, but I'm living like a ghost. My life's just as unreal. For I have no home. I've come back to Japan, but I have no place to go."

His face was dark in the mist as he looked up and went on. "Men don't live for themselves alone. They have to have someone to live for and work for. Their wives or children, or parents. But I have no one."

There was no answer.

"I've just realized it—I've lived only for myself all my life. I really am a ghost. What reason do I have to do anything?"

His voice was hoarse. A car drove by from behind, and Kyogo saw his own shadow moving on the mist before his eyes as the headlights caught him. It was very late, and this part of town was deserted. He pulled himself together and delivered a formal invitation. He had taken lodgings in Hakone. It was early for the autumn leaves, but wouldn't Ushigi visit him? He gave him the name of his hotel.

❀ ൜൜൜ XVII ൜൜൜ ❀

THE VISITOR

Kyogo's inn was in the Gora section of Hakone, a former private villa, fallen on evil days and remodeled, but with no modern efficiency, into a lodging-house for travelers. The rooms were laid out haphazardly, and there was waste space enough for comfort, but only one bathing-room in the establishment. In a dressing-room next to it Kyogo was shaving in front of the mirror. There was no partition between the two rooms and he could hear every word the bathers were saying. They seemed to be soaking in the tub—no splashing of water obscured their voices.

"It's autumn already," one of them said.

A much younger man answered: "But it's still beautiful. Yes, indeed, it's lovely here. All these trees and leaves! No matter what anybody says, it's wonderful. Not like those barren, rocky mountains. You know, I must have been left lying on that stretcher a good five hours, until the train came. I was wrapped in a blanket, and in a weak semi-conscious state anyway, so I didn't feel the cold. But I'd sort of wake up every now and then and look around me, and see that clear, cold blue sky overhead with a few thin flakes of snow fluttering down, and beside me that barren ground and those stony mountains. I'd realize I was still on the continent, for a moment, and that I might pass out for good and die right there. I'd worry like that as I slipped off again, but then scenes I'd known in Japan would start floating through my head, hazily, like a dream, and I'd be happy. I can't tell you how happy. Not that it was such magnificent scenery I was seeing—when I think of them now, they were ordinary, uninteresting scenes."

They grunted as they stood up, splashing the water a little.

"Just places in Japan, with grass and trees growing. It would be some place in springtime for a minute, and then I'd be seeing a mountain cliff in autumn covered with red and yellow leaves, and then it would be summer —inside some temple enclave where I must have gone catching cicadas once. My mind came perfectly clear a few times, and even then I tried my hardest to go on seeing country scenes in Japan, and not think of anything else. Otherwise I couldn't have borne the waiting— it felt like that train would never come, when I was conscious of where I was. But the strange thing is, my father and sister never came into my head. Not that it was too painful to remember the people I knew—I just didn't think about human beings at all. Only about places in Japan—scenery—and with all the strength and feeling I had. It seems funny now that I think of it, but that's how it was when I was lying there. Could that be how it is when a man is dying?"

"That's it, maybe."

"People vanish first, and only scenery, nature, is left in your mind, is that it? You'd think it would be your family you'd think of most at a time like that. But with me it was just the opposite."

One of them put down the wooden water-bucket, and the hollow sound re-echoed roundly from the ceiling of the bath.

"The warm water's tired me out. Let's go, h'm?"

Kyogo spent the time between supper and bed every night over a glass of cognac, savoring it and musing alone. It had always consoled him in his solitude, this amber liquor.

There was a spring in the garden, and its water purled over pebbles, so clear and melodious that Kyogo felt immersed in its rippling as he sat inside on the matted floor under the electric light. He had grown used to water sounds in Kyoto. The Kamo River flowed outside his hotel, of course, and in the gardens all over the city he had heard the subtle music of water deepening the silence around it. Sometimes only the dripping of water from an old bamboo pipe. There was nothing like it in the life of other peoples. How much the ancient Japanese must have loved the sound of water, to make it thus the unbroken accompaniment of their sleeping and waking hours.

An extraordinary taste, when you thought of it. And of course it was not the sound of water in itself that they liked—no one could tolerate a running faucet. It was water as it sounded in nature, or as close to it as possible, that the Japanese wanted to hear, and they built their houses accordingly. Even if the water had to be brought in artificially, it was done so as to give the most natural effect. The sound they wanted was nothing like the cascades that fell into a Western fountain amid bronze and marble statuary. If the Japanese brought the water deliberately, they were discreet enough to try to hide the fact. A peculiarly Japanese custom.

Didn't all Japanese find the fountains in the modern parks distasteful? All the artificial fountains in Japan were badly designed and executed, to be sure, but that wasn't the reason. Show them the most beautiful fountain in Paris, and they might be impressed by its magnificence, but that's all; it would have no more depth and meaning for them than just that. But many a Japanese would stand listening to the bubbling whisper of water in an artesian well. It was the obviousness of human intention that they disliked. Their lives were bound in the living, and they were trained to find pleasure in meager little things. But this was more—a special sense bred in the blood over the generations, and inherited from their forebears. No foreigner had it. It would be a shame to let this tradition die. Could anyone deny its loveliness?

Kyogo sat alone thinking about it as he listened to the water. He could hear its purling everywhere, over the lamplit ceiling, and in the dark-colored walls. What the young veteran had been saying in the bath, earlier that evening, as Kyogo shaved, came back to him quietly now. It made him happy somehow that a young soldier, seriously wounded, and waiting for the train that would carry him to surgery, too sick to think of his family at home, should have seen only nature, and banal nature, in the hallucinations of high fever.

He had almost cried as he stood there facing the mirror. It was a pathetic, touching story. And as he remembered it now, cupping the glass in his two hands, he nodded. Yes, blood meant something; the meagerly, sadly nurtured blood of the Japanese.

The same blood flowed in his views. Thinking of people meant sorrow. It was only nature he could rely on to give him peace. After traveling all over the world, was this the conclusion he had drawn on human life?

Someone had entered the outer room of his suite, but it could only be the maid come to make up his bed. Kyogo didn't even turn round to look.

Saeko sat down in a formal posture and looked at Kyogo, but said nothing in the rain-like rippling of the water.

Kyogo's eyes turned back into the room from the moss-covered rocks and leafy trees in the night of the garden. He saw her sitting there. Astonishment reworked his features. Under the lamplight she was as beautiful in her kimono as a peony in bloom.

She met his eyes without flinching, holding his strong gaze in her own. She spoke distinctly. "I've come at last."

It was not until she had said it that she became aware of the shiver running up and down her body. It wasn't cold that she felt, rather a tingling warmth over her skin. As though Kyogo's strong steady stare had sent an electric current through her. Unable to maintain her formal pose, she dropped her hands to the floor and leaned forward to support herself.

"This is a surprise," Kyogo said softly, almost to himself. "Are you staying in Hakone?"

"Yes," she answered meekly, "since yesterday. To-night, finally—I came."

"In this hotel?"

"No. I didn't dare. At a little inn a bit above here."

"I thought you were a ghost," Kyogo laughed. "I was feeling so lonely that even a ghost would have been welcome. But, instead, I find your charming self. How does it happen that you're here? But of course, you must have heard from Ushigi. . . . Let me offer you some cognac. I'll have the maid bring a glass."

He clapped his hands and waited for an answer, pensive, motionless, his hands on the table. He meant to say nothing, but a smile came of itself, and he could not hold it back. "Are you really here? Or am I dreaming? Japan must be as small as they say. You know, I'm leaving tomorrow. You came just in time."

"You're leaving already? You'll be going to Kobe, I suppose?"

He looked up at her. "You keep yourself well informed, I see." Then, smiling politely again: "Yes, I'm going back to Kobe for a while, but from there I'll be moving on to more distant places—I don't know where exactly. I'm going traveling again. Probably Hong Kong or Shanghai to begin with. One day later and you'd have missed me."

"Abroad again?"

"That's right. It seems to be my destiny."

"After finally coming back to Japan?"

"It's a narrow country, Mrs. Takano." There was a deliberate distinctness in his tone. "And then, as I think I told you once in Singapore, I seem to be adapted by temperament to living abroad. I can avoid emotional complications that way, and accept my own loneliness without deceiving myself. I came back to Japan homesick for my birthplace and my fatherland. As it's turned out, I might as well have been a tourist here for the first time. A lonely thing, but that doesn't matter to a man like me."

He looked aside and his face grew taut as though he were struggling with that loneliness. He won his battle, and his composure was not disturbed again.

But Kyogo seemed completely oblivious of the past. Saeko had been so frightened that his unexpected indifference threw her off balance. Her feelings fluctuated uneasily in her confusion. He was looking at her calmly and there was no hostility in his deep stare. After what she had done? Could he have forgotten it already, or was it possible that he still didn't know it was Saeko who had done it?

He spoke, suddenly, about something else entirely. "I've seen my daughter, Mrs. Takano."

He sighed and didn't try to conceal it. He looked calm, but a sparkle was creeping into his eyes.

"It's the only thing I've gained by coming back to Japan. But it was a great deal to gain. It's given me the courage to go on living. How can I describe it, though—really, how can one put into words what one's child means to one? I can be surprisingly unconcerned about my wife, but not my daughter. It amazed me, how much I loved her."

There was something awesome in the intensity of feeling his words conveyed. They held Saeko motionless and speechless. She wanted to say something, but no merely proper remark would do.

His voice deepened as he went on. "Now I can leave without regret. To be sure, wherever I go, I shall be alone again, living among people who have no interest in me. When I open my eyes in the morning, I shall be alone. When I go walking outside, I shall be alone. And at night I shall go back to my room alone, to sleep in my cold bed. That will be my life. But this time, Mrs. Takano, I shall never be able to forget that I have a daughter. A daughter brought up to live bravely. And I shall know she is alive, and think of it again and again. And some day, I'll tell myself, some wonderful day I'll be able to feast my eyes on her again. I shall have that hope now, as I drag out my wandering life abroad. My homecoming's been brief enough—I've barely seen the country—but it's given me this, this vast gift, and I'm satisfied. So—I'm leaving. Again."

He had drunk a good deal. When the glass came, he poured one for Saeko and another for himself, swallowing it straight down. He went on, as heavy a drinker as he had been in Singapore. "Thinking about your child purifies your heart. That's the meaning of parenthood, isn't it, Mrs. Takano?"

His voice was soft, but bespoke deep feeling. He stopped, and seemed to lose himself in the sound of the water outside, his palms around the cognac glass. But he looked up smiling after a minute, and spoke almost in a whisper: "But the country's swarming with people, all sorts of people! What is it you want?" His eyes opened wide as if he were just waking from sleep, and his large pupils settled on Saeko in the strong stare she knew so well. "You are a very strange woman indeed."

His words brought a smile to her face as the wind shakes a flower into fragrance. She had made herself up with great care tonight after bathing. Her face shone with a luster that seemed to come from beneath the skin. She spoke out boldly. "I've come ready for the worst. Do what you will to punish me."

"Oh, let's leave the bygones till later. Who knows, I may reward you instead. But you are beautiful, as beautiful as ever."

"You're joking."

"You mean you don't think you're beautiful? Come now, this Japanese modesty is not for you. You may live in Japan, but you're not Japanese."

Saeko put on the same look she had used in Singapore when he asked her about the diamonds and she deliberately failed to understand. It was a beautiful look. Even her falsehoods showed her to advantage.

"It's tremendous, really. You live by your wits. How many other women in Japan could do as much? And that sort of life doesn't seem to make you feel lonely."

"But it does, Mr. Moriya!"

"No, it doesn't. You haven't a drop of sentiment. A very unusual type of woman for Japan. You're even stronger than I am, perhaps. I was shut up in that Malacca prison for many months. In solitary, walls on three sides of me and a blind steel door on the other. I knew the war would end soon, but couldn't imagine what would happen after that, so I spent my time going over the past. I tried to reconstruct every detail. It kept me busy. I hated you so much then that just killing you wouldn't have satisfied me. But at the same time I came to admire you terrifically. If I got out alive, I'd certainly pay you back. And I had more than enough time to think about it. All I could see from my cell was the tips of some palm fronds, through an opening way up near the ceiling. Only the fronds, and the concrete walls, and the cot —that's all I had to look at day after day. In such a situation, you can't help getting ideas. The only occupation I had was chasing the shadows of my thoughts over those monotonous walls. At times I thought I'd go mad. And do you know what saves you at such times? Thinking of the person you hate from the bottom of your heart. It's healthy to hate someone. You think of what you'll do to him when you get out, you make plan after plan about how you're going to torture him, and then you feel better. That's how the demons of revenge do their work. Shut a man up inside concrete walls, and there's no cruelty he won't become capable of."

Saeko was pale when she spoke. "I shan't run away. Here I am."

"Yes, here you are. You came by yourself."

"I couldn't help coming. I'd think of you at night, and be unable to sleep for the pain. . . . I'd walk outside, and think: 'When will I see him?'—it was unendurable. Now, I'm relieved. I'm not afraid of anything any more."

Kyogo laughed. "But you haven't come till now, the day before I leave."

Saeko had been looking down at the floor. She lifted her face and covered it with both hands. She spoke, and her voice was hoarse with passion, almost a groan. "You asked me once in Singapore to sleep with you. Please, ask me again."

Kyogo's stare was unshaken, brutal. Saeko lowered her face again, still covered. He watched the flush creep excitingly up the nape of her white neck. "You're frightened, h'm?" There was laughter in his voice.

Saeko shook her head, denying it. Her body was ready even now for him to take her in his arms.

"The question is, which of us is the more cold-blooded." Kyogo stood up. "Pardon me. I'm going to take a bath. They've been warming the water for me. I seem to be the more cold-blooded one, don't I? I should warn you, though, Mrs. Takano, the revenge I decided on also consisted of making you denude yourself."

She heard his footsteps over the mats, out into the corridor, and vanishing toward the bath. Then she took a compact out of her obi and retouched her face. Her heart was beating wildly, and she was still flushed. The rippling of the spring was more noticeable now that she was alone. She strained her ears to hear it, and as she grew intent on the pleasing sound, happy fantasies built themselves up in her mind of the power she had to keep Kyogo from going abroad again. She could do it. She was sure of victory.

When Kyogo came back, she was embarrassed, but greeted him with her eyes. She believed her weapons were invincible, and that belief, naturally, made her even more beautiful. A radiance welled up from the depths of her body and sparkled out through her pores. It was a delicate shading of light, playing over her skin. Her glossy black hair glittered too, and the strong desire burning within her had set her lips and eyes aflame.

Kyogo was combing his hair in front of his mirror. The muscles tautened in his powerful shoulders, masculine and beautiful. His irritating composure suggested, not crudeness, but great secret strength. "Have you ever done any gambling?"

Saeko shook her head from side to side.

"I bet you'd be lucky, though. The god of chance is fonder of women than of men. And you are the most adventurous woman I know. Your star's always been in the ascendant."

"You're the only one I ever lost to."

"Nonsense. Not that I'm unlucky at gambling. As a matter of fact, it was gambling that got me thrown out of the Navy. I was bitter about that, and had to find some way to make a living, so I decided to wrestle with the probabilities in real gambling. I made it my profession, as it were. Fighting with luck's no good—you get excited. You've got to stay cool and calculating. Keep your wits about you and wait for a favorable tide. The god of luck is always fair, in my experience. If you wait patiently, he's sure to smile on you sooner or later. But tonight, Mrs. Takano, we'll not do any waiting. We'll play one game, and no more. You may win or I may win—let's leave it to the gods of chance to decide."

Kyogo picked up a deck of cards from the dressing-table and walked over to her.

Saeko smiled when she saw them, and moved to sit beside him. "What shall we play for?"

Kyogo was looking through the deck. "For everything we own. Our whole property."

"Penny ante, aren't we!"

Kyogo looked up at her. "Understand me. The loser is stripped of everything he has, every single cent." He was speaking in his ordinary quiet voice. "It's a simple game—red or black. I give you diamonds, Mrs. Takano, the queen of diamonds. If that turns up first, you win. My card is queen of spades. You cut and turn the cards yourself. I'm a professional, as I just told you, and you'd have no chance in a longer, more complicated game. That's why I've picked this childishly simple one. It's to your advantage."

"Are you serious?"

Uneasiness showed in Saeko's eyes. Kyogo wasn't joking. His manner was too calm, too normal.

"If you lose, I get everything you have, Mr. Moriya?"

"That's right. This was what I finally decided on in Malacca Penitentiary—to take away from you what you cared for most and relied on most. But as you're a woman, I've chosen the fairest, simplest game I could think of. I shan't touch the cards."

Saeko had paled. She was silent for a while, then laughed loudly. "I was thinking of marrying our two fortunes and making them one."

"Just our fortunes, h'm? . . . The point is that a person's body suffers no harm by being used. It's still there. But if you lose money or property, it's gone, and there's nothing left. It's the loss of the irrecoverable that everyone finds most painful."

Saeko said nothing.

"Well, are you willing? Or do you want to run now?"

"You've chosen the cruelest revenge."

"By no means. The chances are absolutely even. I may be the loser."

"No, you won't." And she laughed beautifully, with the fervor of dying embers blown by the wind into one last burst of flame. "I was in love with you, Mr. Moriya. I loved you more than anyone in the world. I loved you so much, it hurt. That's why I came."

"Please don't try to browbeat me." Kyogo was as calm and even-toned as ever. "Mine was a small offense, and it's followed me all my life and will till I die. Indeed, it's made my life what it is. I want you to know what that means. What you did reminds me of the Queen of Navarre in medieval France. When she liked a man, she'd order him to sleep with her, and the next morning command her attendants to put him in a bag and throw him living into the Seine. You're a lovely flower, Mrs. Takano, but you have thorns, I've learned. Don't prick me, I beg of you. Instead, try to turn up the queen of diamonds and turn my revenge against me. Strip me, why don't you? You have the courage. Try!"

"Won't you forgive me? You don't know how I've regretted what I did."

"I'm no longer interested in forgiving or condemning. To tell you the truth, I was almost delighted by the resoluteness with which you acted. It was so un-Japanese. And that's why I've sacrificed my natural advantage and given you these equal terms. What makes you so sure you'll lose?"

"I don't care if I do lose."

"That's the spirit! When you feel that way, you're certain to be lucky. Go on, try! If we don't decide it now, we'll regret it forever. Not only I; you'll feel the same way. You're not such a weakling as all that. That's why you fascinated me when I first met you. Make me remember you the same way. Try to be more like yourself, tonight at least. I leave tomorrow. This is our last evening together."

"Ah, then you *are* going? All right. Will you cut this deck?"

Saeko hated Kyogo suddenly. She knew she hated him passionately. And she was going to win this simpleminded game. She felt it. And that made her want to win. The blood rushed to her head. She cut the deck herself and put the cards down on the table.

"If the queen of diamonds comes out first, I win. Is that right?"

"That's it, Mrs. Takano."

"Pure luck, h'm?"

"That's right, a game of pure chance."

Saeko sat up. She was afraid her hand might tremble,

but it didn't. She stretched it out to the deck, and it moved with the tranquil elegance of a white flower. She started picking up the cards and throwing them face-up on the table. "Where is it?"

"It will come, Mrs. Takano. You're going to win."

When the queen of spades turned up instead, black as hell, Saeko gasped with surprise.

"Have I won?" Kyogo asked. "Luck wasn't with you, I'm afraid." He started turning over the cards left in the deck. The queen of diamonds was second from the top. Kyogo wasn't even surprised. He knew how frequently that sort of thing happened. Nor did he console Saeko.

"I'm leaving early tomorrow. Permit me to say goodnight now."

When Saeko reached his hotel next morning he had already driven off down the mountain to catch the first express at Odawara. The branches of the garden trees stood out distinctly in the morning sunlight on the mountaintop against the cold bright autumn sky. He had left a letter for her at the hotel. It contained a draft on the Hong Kong-Shanghai Bank, and a note asking her to donate it, together with an equal amount of her own money, as she had promised, to some charitable work for vagrant children or other victims of the war. He had signed it "Ahasuerus."